Praise for Toni Bergins and *Embody*

"*Embody* is a profound guide to rediscovering the joy and authentic power within your body. As a creative, powerful, and deeply insightful leader, Toni masterfully brings the power of dance to life through these pages, making her life-changing JourneyDance method accessible to all. Her words, music, and movements guide you every step of the way, helping you feel, heal, and love your body from the inside out. Absolutely brilliant, Toni is a powerhouse who has done the deep work, enabling her to share her powerful methods in such a beautiful way. Proud to call her not only a peer but also one of my teachers."

—**Cristi Christensen,** author of *Chakra Rituals*

"I've witnessed the depth and meaningful impact of Toni's work at the Kripalu Center for Yoga and Health. *Embody* is a true reflection of her in-person teaching, guiding you through an innovative and transformative practice, wherever you are."

—**Coby Koslowski, MA,** author of *One Degree Revolution*

"At a time when so many of us have become estranged from our hearts, Toni offers a sacred path to help us come home. In Embody, she has distilled decades of personal development, study, and teaching into a treasure chest of transformational tools. Through wisdom, story, and therapeutic practices, she invites us to embrace the full spectrum of our humanity, and write a new story for our life. I've experienced the power of her work many times. Every time I've danced, dreamed, or collaborated with her, I've come away inspired, moved, and more alive."

—**Carrie Grossman,** devotional singer

"Toni Bergins invites us into a transformative journey where she masterfully guides readers to reconnect with their bodies, rediscover their innate joy, and embrace their full range of emotions. Toni's profound understanding of embodiment shines through every page, offering practical insights and heartfelt encouragement. Toni's words are a beacon of light, and *Embody* is a powerful tool for anyone seeking to enhance their resilien ... onal well-being."

—**Rochelle Schieck,** founder ... of *Qoya: A Compass for Navigating an ... ree*

"As a dear friend, soul sister, and colleague of Toni Bergins, I have had the honor of dancing alongside her, witnessing firsthand the transformative power she infuses into each movement through her profound embodiment practices. Toni emerges as a genuine healer using movement as medicine. *Embody* serves as a sacred testament to her divine fusion of embodiment and dance, inviting readers to embark on a journey of self-discovery, initiation, and healing."

—**Parashakti Skye,** founder of Dance of Liberation®

"Toni is one of those rare spirits who bravely makes a stand for those ready to lean back into their wilderness and creative expression. She creates a safe space for the daring work to begin, calling us home to ourselves. In the most simple yet profound ways, she guides people back to the body, where true healing always begins."

—**Brothers Koren,** founders of Your Big Voice and Webby TV series *The Journey*

"Toni is a powerhouse teacher, facilitator, and visionary leader that has blessed us with her profound wisdom, healing work, and life experience in her new book Embody! This is a must-read for anyone on the (r)evolutionary journey, and I'm so grateful she's brought this medicine to the world. Through movement, dance, ritual, music, and channeling your emotions, you truly can return home to yourself and transform your life. This book will show you the path. Get ready for a journey of a lifetime."

—**Lainie Love Dalby,** founder of Sparkle SHAMELESSLY, author of *The Sacred (R)evolution Oracle Deck,* and coauthor of *Sacred Body Wisdom*

EMBODY

Feel, Heal, and Transform Your Life Through Movement

Toni Bergins, M.Ed.

Creator & Founder of JourneyDance®

Foreword by **Jim Curtis,** world-renowned wellness pioneer

Health Communications, Inc.
Boca Raton, Florida
www.hcibooks.com

Embody is intended as a reference volume only. It is not intended as a substitute for the advice and/or medical care of the reader's physician and/or mental health provider, nor is it meant to discourage or dissuade the reader from the advice of his or her physician and/or mental health provider. Before beginning any exercise program, please consult with a physician.

Library of Congress Cataloging-in-Publication Data
is available through the Library of Congress

ISBN-13: 978-07573-2500-7 (Paperback)
ISBN-10: 07573-2500-9 (Paperback)
ISBN-13: 978-07573-2501-4 (ePub)
ISBN-10: 07573-2501-7 (ePub)

Publisher: Health Communications, Inc.
301 Crawford Boulevard, Suite 200
Boca Raton, FL 33432-3762

Cover, interior design, and formatting by Larissa Hise Henoch
Illustrations by Sam Laiz

I want to dedicate this book
to the wounded little one in each of us,
so we can reclaim our bodies and our power,
learn to feel and heal, do what is right,
and create a future of belonging
for our children and communities.
And to all my students, participants,
and dancers who make my work worthwhile.
To all the ancestors who danced into altered
states and brought us their medicine,
and to all the music makers of the world who
inspire us to dance, sing, and feel.

Dance, when you're broken open.
Dance, if you've torn the bandage off.
Dance in the middle of the fighting.
Dance in your blood.
Dance when you're perfectly free.

—RUMI

Toni's Students Share

"Toni Bergins' program has been the most extraordinary experience for me. I don't think I would be where I am on my healing journey today without it.

"The wisdom of my body was taken from me at the tender age of five, and I was dissociated from my body for decades. I had to keep myself safe, constantly watched over my shoulder, protecting myself from everyone and everything. I played small. I didn't use my voice, never wanting to call at-ten-tion to myself. When people would look at me, I felt fear and retreated.

"I was thirty when I had my first memory of the event, and spent the next thirty years searching for myself, who I was, what I was, opening myself up to what could be. Ten years ago, I danced with Toni and finally felt free. Although I've done many different healing modalities, this is the experience that reconnected me and brought me most deeply back into my body. I could move my body in a really safe space. I remember feeling a lot of joy and feeling connected to myself, really in my body for the first time. The deeper I get into my body, the more I understand, and the more I trust myself.

"Now, at sixty-two, I'm finally sensual. I've had two momentous healings in the last year through JourneyDance. I've made room for beauty to come back into my life—this empowerment, this strength, this confidence, this self-love, this self-compassion. I am now seeing myself, healing myself, my light, my beauty, my wonderfulness, my awesomeness. No more searching, yet always still growing."

—Logan M.

"I had such self-loathing about my body, a lot of which was passed down generationally. Toni taught me that the journey back to the body is always evolving. I've learned how to release pain and trauma through movement, which has given me a whole new confidence. My soul lights up and shines when I am able to move and dance. This program keeps revealing new op-portunities for self-discovery. I am breaking out of the hiding place that was my addiction. I have moved away from isolation, fear, and regret and now embrace a profound sense of self-love.

"The first time I told my story of addiction and recovery to Toni, my hands were shaking. Now, three years later, I've completed my teacher training, and I am ready to bring her embodied healing practice to the world."

—Thomas E.

CONTENTS

Foreword • xi

Introduction • 1

Part One
The Embodiment Experience: An Emotional Workout • 17

Chapter 1: Welcome to *Embody* • 19

Chapter 2: Weaving a Physical, Mental, Emotional, and Spiritual Journey • 41

Part Two
The Qualities of Transformation • 69

Chapter 3: Embodiment • 71

Chapter 4: Awakening • 93

Chapter 5: Immersion and Expansion • 111

Chapter 6: Funky Connection • 133

Chapter 7: Evocative Emotion • 151

Chapter 8: Alchemy Transformation • 177

Chapter 9: Empowered Celebration • 201

Chapter 10: Sensual Freedom • 219

Chapter 11: Open Heart • 237

Chapter 12: Prayer and Bliss • 255

Part Three

Move into a New Story • 277

Chapter 13: Dancing into Self-Mastery • 279

Acknowledgments • 301

About the Author • 307

FOREWORD

I've explored hundreds of healing modalities in both my personal and professional life, and I have found that there are many effective ways to start to release pain and trauma and return to wholeness. Healing modalities are like utensils; it doesn't matter if you use a fork, spoon, chopsticks or your fingers as long as you get the food in. The one aspect the best modalities have in common is they help you transcend the conscious and critical mind and begin to reframe the subconscious mind—which I believe is part of our physical and energetic body. These healing modalities let go of the machinations of the mind to release stuck emotions and stored trauma while reframing beliefs.

What I've come to learn is that "the work" that "works" for anyone has to deeply resonate with them. Even though we know that it's beneficial, not everyone enjoys meditating. Not everyone wants to do yoga, or introspective journaling. So, if you are looking to make a change in your life, no matter how big or small, and have tried practices or programs that weren't quite hitting the mark for you, take a look here.

Toni Bergins is offering a fresh way to tap into your transformative energy and let you get to the self you truly want to be.

Toni is a vibrant, thriving light focused on helping people heal. Her practice is about embodiment—getting out of your head and back into a true connection with your body. In this book, she takes you on an energetic journey that uses movement, dance, music, and transformative rituals to change the powerfully limiting thoughts and beliefs that may keep you from thriving. Her practice has the potential to put you back in coherence with emotions that you may have been consciously or subconsciously suppressing. She offers the opportunity to build a relationship with your deepest core self and explore subconscious terrain. You'll learn how to tell your authentic story in a whole new way, dancing your way to freedom.

If you're like me and don't really dance all that often, I don't want you to be dissuaded. You don't have to be a trained dancer to move your body to the music and find your hypnogogic state—you can even do it from your desk chair. There are so many layers to this book, so many ways to tap into and engage your neural programming, that you can, as Toni says, feel, heal, and transform your life without stepping out (onto the dance floor), but the playlists she's created are so evocative that you may surprise yourself.

—**Jim Curtis,** world-renowned wellness pioneer

INTRODUCTION

Welcome! I'm so excited that you are here!

I created this book to provide you with an opportunity to experience *embodiment*: an authentic sense of presence that comes from reuniting the *mind* and *body*, so you can experience an integrated connection with yourself and the love that you deeply desire.

Every day I teach my students how to get out of their minds and back into their bodies so that they can process and digest their experiences (both the wonderful and difficult), so they can live full lives with a wide emotional bandwidth, courage, and real resilience. The change is dramatic: they shift from dissociation to presence, and from a place of stagnation to one of flow and limitless possibilities. If you are feeling stuck, numb, or overwhelmed, you too can safely expand the confines of your comfort zone so that you can finally feel, heal, and transform your life.

I know from my own personal experience, and what I've seen on the dance floor with thousands of my students, that healing is not for the faint of heart. In fact, I believe it's for the brave and the courageous.

I also know that with the right tools, the rewards and possibilities for doing this work are endless. Think about it: What if you could change your beliefs and thought patterns, and open yourself to new experiences that inspire, ignite, and allow you to authentically express passion and pleasure? What if you could process your story mindfully and fully love yourself just as you are? What if you could access your divine spark—your truest, wisest self, your energetic essence?

You are about to embark on an active, experiential, therapeutic journey in which expressive movement, guided imagery, ritual, music, and creative expression work together. While my program is not dance therapy, it is therapeutic. While there aren't specific dance steps or choreography, there is a deliberate, essential flow to the practice. It will take you on an emotional journey, where you will get in touch with all your feelings and let go of your "messy" mind (the one that's comparative, judgmental, negative, and runs old limiting beliefs and criticisms on a loop). And it will take you on a *spiritual* journey, where you can be completely in the present moment and experience a mystical state. It's about revealing, recovering, and rediscovering your innate, intuitive self. It is a dynamic, conscious practice that can help you release what no longer serves you. Stop stuffing/numbing and start feeling; stop negative thinking/limiting, and literally get moving!

My Story

Ironically, I spent much of my early adult life trying to get *out* of my own body. I was raised in a family that emphasized the importance of education and knowledge (that forced us to prioritize the mind over the body), expected success, and had high expectations that we would "choose" careers that would create financial security. Suffice it to say, I was raised to become a lawyer—like my father—and can argue like one! Meanwhile, the family was emotionally dysfunctional with a pervasive pattern that alternated between explosive anger and deeply victimized sadness. Now we know that this was generational trauma, but at the time no one spoke about it. My grandparents immigrated to the United States in 1905 from Europe, seeking physical safety and financial opportunity—their number one and two priorities for survival. Their experience deeply affected the way they raised their own children, my parents: they were super overprotective and influenced by their pervasive deep worry and fear of persecution.

During adolescence, I picked up all the external messaging about what a girl, and then a woman, should look like. I started down the pathway of trying to be perfect in my teens, even though I was a very awkward, insecure girl. I was what they used to call "a late bloomer" in terms of my physical development, and then when I bloomed, it was way too much. I was suddenly very, *very* female, and I remember getting a lot of male attention that I was not prepared for. I felt sexualized, stressed, and afraid. In fact, I was attacked when I was twelve, going on thirteen (#metoo), and have experienced other traumatic events that caused me to repress, or misuse, my sexuality and sensuality for years in order to protect myself.

I didn't have any idea about how to process these feelings, so my mom sent me to therapy. Yes, I started early. In therapy, I was asked to recount my attack in graphic detail, which doubly traumatized me. Instead of learning how to express my grief and my sadness, I pushed through and stuffed under my emotions and became an exercise junkie. By the time I was sixteen I was going into the gym every day, trying to be powerful, strong, and have some sense of self-esteem. I enjoyed the endorphin rush of working out. I was very protective of my sensuality and my sexuality: I always wore layers of clothes in an effort to cover, hide, and contain my body.

After experiencing my very first love, and then total heartbreak and betrayal at seventeen, I discovered that I could add a further layer of emotional control with food and fad dieting. My mom and I tried the LA Diet, South Beach, Scarsdale, Pritikin, juicing (I gained weight and turned my hands orange), low carb, and the craziest of all: eat all your carbs in a sixty-minute window when you could eat *whatever you wanted*. I tried it all. When my feelings came up, especially if there was grief, discomfort, or sadness, I went on a binge-and-purge cycle of numbing out, which was somehow soothing. (Little did I know that I was beginning an addictive cycle that has since been scientifically studied.) I kept this part of my life hidden for years and years and years, telling no one.

By the time I was twenty-three, I had been suffering for years, yet if you met me, you would never have known. So many of us are living this duality, where our inside thoughts and feelings and the way we show up to the outside world do not match!

My strategy was to project happiness: I had a wonderful friend group and was active and high-energy, but inside I was battling with self-hatred, self-abuse, and perfectionism. I was a mess, struggling with an eating disorder, always feeling emotionally overwhelmed. I worked out excessively; I was literally going to the gym ten times a week. Every day I'd go twice to step class or aerobics, and then layer on weightlifting and ab crunches. My daily routine centered around work, bingeing, napping, and going out partying. I knew that the life I created wasn't sustainable, and I wasn't finding any answers to really help me.

So, I left New York City for the summer. I went to visit my sister who lived in the Berkshires, and I camped out in her backyard and enrolled at the Kripalu Center in Stockbridge, Massachusetts. It's now the Kripalu Center for Yoga & Health, but at the time, Kripalu was a fully operational ashram. The guru was still in place, and all day we did yoga, listened to his teachings, and ate little vegetarian meatballs. Every day, there would be a break between talks where we could fill our time with either meditation or a high-energy movement class that in the ashram days was called "Dancekinetics." Some of the guru's disciples came from professional dance backgrounds; others were gymnasts, actors, and many were creatives. The story goes that a few disciples would go down to a barn and just let loose with wild dancing, and more and more people were interested in joining. When the guru heard about this, he was at first skeptical. Then he saw that from the energetic release from dance, people were able to get deeper into their yoga, and it became a daily offering.

I was looking for answers to address what I thought was a hopeless negative and self-abusive mind. I tried a multitude of therapists, meditation, creative visualization, affirmations, yoga—literally anything and everything I could find. I had struggled with meditation because of my difficulty sitting still. I was already doing tons of yoga, so I chose to do something different: the movement class. It was the best choice I ever made. It changed my life forever and put me on a completely different path that I had no idea was possible!

I walked into the studio and there was Yuri, with his long blond hair and purple leotard, standing in the center of the room. He told us that he wasn't a professional dance teacher, but he had suffered severe trauma as a child, and he said that dancing was the only thing that brought him joy. Instantly, I loved him because he told the truth. I thought his revealing honesty was something profound that we don't see in the everyday world.

His dance class was nothing like any of the ones I had ever been in before. There were no mirrors. We were all barefoot. And it was ecstatic and playful. I loved moving my body to the music, I loved feeling free and wild, I loved expressing myself without worrying what I looked like in the mirrors, and I felt something I had never felt before. I was present and not overwhelmed. I was in my body and my mind was QUIET!

At one point he looked at us and said, “You’re all so beautiful.” I felt his words penetrate my mind and my heart, and I remember thinking, *Oh my God, he sees my soul.* For the first time I was able to hear and embrace that I was a beautiful being, not in the physical sense, but as a whole person.

At the end of the class, he had us come into child’s pose with our hands forming a triangle on our foreheads and told us to bring our heads to the floor. I broke down in a puddle of tears. I cried and released for the full five minutes of our deep relaxation. I call that spot at Kripalu Center “the Toni puddle.” It was full-on catharsis. At that moment, I knew I had just connected my body, my soul, and my divine spark because I felt a sense of love I had never felt before. For the first time, I realized I was beautiful just the way I was. And at that exact moment I thought, the only way I could heal was by reuniting with my body. *I’m never going back to the gym. I’m never going on a diet again. I’m done abusing myself. I’m going to love myself now!*

My divine spark was speaking to me, and my body was shouting, telling me to dance. I knew that the way that I was exercising before wasn’t the answer; I needed to find out for myself why Yuri’s class was so cathartic. I realized that the disassociated way we live our lives—in our heads, separated from our bodies and our hearts—is not healthy. In this state, we inadvertently cut off our ability to feel our feelings and be empathetic and compassionate with ourselves and others, and therefore perpetuate disempowerment, stay stuck in self-destructive patterns, and make bad decisions.

I realized that the only way I could heal was by facing my feelings instead of staying numb, and I could only do that by reuniting fully with my body. Really letting the feelings come, being with them, and expressing and integrating myself was liberating. Without expressing my feelings, I could now see that I was not truly living.

As my still perfectionistic self, I returned to New York City and began voraciously studying all forms of yoga, dance, and body practices, including contact improvisation, body-mind-centering, jazz, African dance, Afro-Haitian dance, hip-hop, breakdance, modern dance, and modern release technique—everything I could find. I found my love for expression!

I had such a love/hate relationship with NYC and finally got the courage to leave. I took a job teaching English and drama in Northampton, Massachusetts. Once I relocated, I continued my studies. I was thrilled to discover that there were fusions of psychology and drama, called *psychodrama,* which has been practiced in various forms for years. I dove in deeply, studying Gestalt psychology, psychodrama, and theater, and jumped into Dancekinetics teacher trainings at my beloved Kripalu Center with Dan Levin, who taught movement based on the fluid systems of the body, Megha Nancy Buttenheim, who leads from the chakra system, and Ken Scott Nateshvar, who inspired free experimentation. I was also part of a psychodrama theater company for the next seven years.

By combining all that I learned, I created my own healing elixir that worked for me and now thousands of others. I call this JourneyDance. It's a weaving of movement, dance, music, creative visualization, hypnotic suggestion, shadow work, psychodrama, voice work, and psychology. Twenty-seven years later, there are more than 1,500 people teaching my JourneyDance method internationally. More importantly, this work has taught me how to be an independent and empowered being. I am living proof that anyone can overcome their fears, be resilient, and move forward.

Welcome to JourneyDance®

I created JourneyDance for people just like you and me; it's the best way I know to achieve emotional intelligence in a physical, fun way. My purpose is to help you become embodied so that you can overcome the "I'm not good enough" crisis, leave perfectionism behind, own your value and your worth, end self-abuse, embrace your heart, and expand your emotional bandwidth.

This is not to say that the journey is going to be easy. Stepping onto a dance floor, even in your own bedroom, can be unsettling. You may be timid, inhibited, or feel uncomfortable in your own skin. You may be feeling like you're not the right size or the right shape or the right image, or that you are bumping up against society's perfectionist mindset about who you're supposed to be. You may be terrified of being connected to your body because of past trauma. These are all valid concerns. When you get more deeply engaged with your body, all of you will start to open up, and the emotions and feelings that you've been hiding from might surface. Whether you feel sensual, emotional, or angry, will depend on your life experiences, how much you've processed and digested, how much that is repressed needs to be expressed, or just plainly how comfortable you are expressing and moving your body. Yet I can promise that once you get the hang of the practice and can recognize and express your emotions safely, you will feel your physical, empowered, beautiful body and fall in love with it!

Move into a New Story

What if you could move into a new story, where you see yourself in a new light, not just mentally, but emotionally and physically? Moving into a new story means that you can rewrite your "old story"—your destructive or dysfunctional patterns, inhibitions, avoidances—and truly become that person you long to be. This transformational process has just four steps; while it may seem simple, it takes commitment, practice, and courage.

Step One is to embrace the idea of getting back into your body. When I say *get into your body*, I don't mean that you're not physically in your body. Obviously, you are *here*, and you have a body. Yet I'm guessing that there's some part of you that is not quite *here*, meaning *fully present*. Sometimes, as we go through difficult experiences, whether they are small "t" traumas or big "T" traumas, we automatically protect ourselves with brilliant defense mechanisms, and some of them can literally separate our minds from our bodies. While these strategies may have been absolutely essential in the moment, as we want to live more fully and have real connections and relationships, we need to fully *reinhabit* our bodies.

You can read all the books in the world about creating change, but reading about change is not going to change you. Literally, you have to have a *somatic*, or bodily, experience. You have to be in touch with your body, feel, and understand your sensations. You have to move, and the best way I discovered to do this is through dance.

The origins of dance can be traced back over 9,000 years to ancient artifacts found in Africa, India, and China. Of course, artifacts simply mean representations of dance, as dance leaves no trace for historians to find. All over the world dances have been passed down for thousands of years through traditional ceremony and expression. Across cultures, people have used dance to enter into altered states.

When I move and dance, I have the experience that there's more to me than what's going through my head, and I can actually change the narrative as I become aware of the present moment. I have a new sense of inner power, and I can make different, better choices that are right for me. I feel more available, and with that, I can be more compassionate.

Step Two is to feel your feelings. You may have heard the phrase, "Feel it to heal it," which is an idea that I live by. This concept illuminates the connection between emotion, thought patterns, and physical ailments or symptoms, and showed how feelings, repressed or explosive, impact the body and your life. Our collective challenge is to learn how to navigate our emotional system so that we can process our lives and experiences, and courageously feel all our feelings. The goal is not to suppress your feelings but to express them in a self-respecting way.

It can be difficult or uncomfortable to be with your feelings. As hard as you may try to stop yourself or numb yourself to them, they don't just go away. Instead, your energy becomes stagnant and your heart a little bit hardened. I will show how you can turn your angst into art so that you can process and digest your feelings. Then, you can open your heart and let yourself feel safely so that you can move through the emotions and see that the emotions don't actually last that long.

In this program, you'll express your feelings and tell your story to the dance floor. When I move, I can access my sadness, anger, grief, or joy just by using my body and making shapes, instead of projecting it onto someone in my life. It is probably the most powerful part of the journey, and I promise that you will get to the point where you can feel that self-love and self-forgiveness is a possibility, regardless of whatever has happened in your past.

Step Three is to break down your negative thoughts with my MindBusting technique. The first person who taught me that "you can choose your own thoughts" was my spiritual teacher, Ariana Shelton. The idea that I could choose a preferred thought was brand-new to me, and I have been teaching this concept ever since. Just like *Ghostbusters*, we need all the tools we can get to edit, change, and sometimes obliterate our repetitive negative thoughts! When we go into a thought loop, we create a story about ourselves that further reinforces negativity. Instead, I will show you how to switch a thought by identifying your feelings without judgment. Through this process, you will feel empowered to be curious enough to discover a new awareness of yourself. Being human is a layered process; it requires learning as much as you can about yourself so you can navigate your inner world. We're all on a path, and it's our destiny to evolve.

Step Four is to repeat the cycle whenever you need to. When you do this process often—getting into your body, feeling your feelings, and using the MindBusting technique—you will change. You will grow. You will feel more resilient. You will honor yourself, including the parts that have been hurt, the parts that have been wounded, and even the parts that have hurt others. And you will have the potential to heal.

DANCE WITH ME!

If you need a little motivation and inspiration, you can join me in person, in the online community, or continue to practice at home. A JourneyDance, guided by me or my team, takes place every week. Or find a JourneyDance in your area on JourneyDance.com. And, you might not have noticed yet, but this is a flip-book. Enjoy!

How This Book Works

You'll be creating the embodied experience of JourneyDance right in your own space. The beauty of this program is that whether you are dancing in a group or doing it privately, you are not alone in your process. You are now part of a community of people who want to heal through movement. Enter the practice however you feel most comfortable. If you are currently limited in your ability to freely move, you can still follow the practice by focusing on the music and doing creative visualizations, journaling work, and meditation. The mind-body connection is so strong that you can experience the work by feeling, imagining, writing, contemplating, and creating a stronger love for yourself.

In many ways, the material in this book can take you even deeper than my classes because you're going to have a full understanding of why an embodiment practice is so effective. The main goal of my program is to create an efficient practice to move through any hurt and pain, feel the feelings, process your life, and finally, move forward and experience joy. I want you to get closer to your heart so that you can have amazing relationships, feel your own power, and stand up for yourself. I want you to love yourself, even when you are sad. And I want you to love your body so much that you can treat it with a new level of kindness and respect.

Full disclosure: I am not a research scientist. I am an experiential explorer, combining ideas from psychology, movement, music, and ritual to create a holistic program. You can move at your own pace, and you can feel your own truth. And you can read up on and study more about everything I bring into the program.

In Part I, you will learn how emotions are stored in the body, and how you can move with and through them, be with them, embrace them, and learn from them. When you can be with your emotions, you can heal. That doesn't mean that you'll never feel pain or sadness again, or that every single incident that ever happened to you will be processed; healing is a state of *wholeness* where you no longer feel broken, you no longer feel empty. It's a state of wellness where you can live your life moving forward with passion, energy, and enthusiasm. You can live your life with courage and resilience, and have a method to practice for when life gets hard. To me, healing is not always the removal of all past pain, but it might be. Healing is the ability to reframe your past so you can find strength in your vulnerability and expand your capacity for love and joy. When you heal, you can be inspired to help others in their own healing journey.

The chapters in Part II introduce the qualities of Transformation: Embodiment, Awakening, Immersion and Expansion, Funky Connection, Evocative Emotion, Alchemy Transformation, Empowered Celebration, Sensual Freedom, Open Heart, Prayer, and Bliss. The qualities mirror the hero's journey of spiritual growth and self-mastery. Each quality builds on the next as you become more present, embodied, and empowered.

Each of the qualities has the same basic structure, beginning with an explanation of the theme. Inside each chapter you will find a playlist, and you can access these songs, and more, on tonibergins.com. Expect to spend thirty to forty minutes exploring each quality. Then, once you've experienced the whole practice one quality at a time, you can follow the complete playlists that will run through all the qualities together to re-create the JourneyDance transformational flow.

MY IDEAL PRACTICE PLAN

We are programed to look for the quick fix, the life hack, but like any practice that can take time to deeply change, though you will feel the effects rapidly.

I recommend moving and dancing indoors to avoid weather and structural concerns. Dress comfortably, and dance whenever you feel inspired. If you have any physical limitations, please modify my suggestions to meet your needs. Read the whole book through, and then explore the movement practices. You're going to have fun!

I would recommend practicing twice a week to titrate your growth and exploration. Practice little by little, layer by layer, peeling the onion, at your pace, slowly increasing your exposure to each quality. You can always play the upbeat music anytime you need a pick-me-up, or the more melancholic music if you need a good cry.

The movement suggestions are the heart of the experience, but they are not the only experience. My prescription for a comprehensive healing journey is comprised of six core elements:

- **Movement:** You will move your body in many ways: stretch, roll, shape, pulse, create, feel, express, energize, and flow. When you connect with your body through creative expression, you enhance your ability to be present and be in the world with profound confidence. Telling your story to the dance floor is a powerful method for gaining clarity, releasing old patterns, and opening yourself to new ways of being and feeling.
- **Music:** Music cracks the shell of emotion. My playlists are specifically curated for each part of the journey, featuring songs to match each quality and what emotions or experiences you want to work on. Music opens the doorways of impulse,

imagination, creativity, and healing, and has the power to change your state, mood, and awareness. Weaving wide selections of world and popular music together with my original compositions, the music of Embody is meant to profoundly influence both body and soul.

- **Mystical Inquiry:** My unique guided visualizations provide a deep and mystical inquiry into an altered state, where you can investigate past hurts, seek guidance from within, learn to trust your instincts, and find your inner voice. By doing so, you can create new energetic pathways and overwrite old patterns and conditioning. You will learn to trust your intuition, your feelings, and your inner voice. You will awaken your connection to the mystery itself, being in conversation with your body, energy, and divine spark.
- **Prayers and Invocations:** Prayers and invocations are meant to offer another way into embodiment. I've found that when we read out loud, we are actually grounding new, positive intentions into the body as well as the mind. Your thoughts influence your reality, affecting your emotional well-being, and can even change your health. The prayers and invocations I've created can raise your energetic vibrations, soothe your emotions, and help you amplify your desires and intention.
- **Journaling:** My journaling exercises integrate the feelings we're experiencing in the body. They allow you to process what you've learned about yourself on the dance floor and express yourself in new ways, channel your insights, and discover your true inner wisdom as you see your perspective shift right on the page.

Part III contains lessons for you to weave your mind into your practice so that you can move toward a sense of self-mastery and move into your new story. You'll learn to inhabit all of you, maybe even fall in love with yourself. You can walk through the world with confidence, self-esteem, and self-love, and with a greater sense of gratitude and an appreciation for what you have. And when life gets challenging, like it does for all of us, you'll know exactly where you have to go in order to be fully aligned with who you are and who you want to be.

You came to this Earth to BE, incorporated into a body. You came here to be YOU. How do you uncover your true soul essence, that divine spark, and be your authentic expression? Embodiment is your ACT of being. Your intention. Your physically manifested existence.

And so we begin . . .

PART ONE

The Embodiment Experience: *An Emotional Workout*

CHAPTER ONE

Welcome to *Embody*

So many people come to JourneyDance knowing that they're looking for something, but they don't know what that *something* is. Yet once they experience the somatic benefits of being *embodied*, or being fully present in their body, they find that they can tap into their deepest selves, bringing in confidence to allow their emotions to surface, and face the story (or stories) holding them back. It's only then that they are able to address the past, face the present, and become empowered.

Embodiment is an action as well as a state of being. When we get into our body, when we decide to be present in our own skin, a whole set of experiences opens up. You can gain a new perspective on yourself, your life, and the stories that you are telling yourself. You can delight in the world, experiencing a whole range of feelings that have been repressed or suppressed, that need to be felt.

Did you know that you can trust your body as a guide? Most of us make decisions using our minds, based on the available facts, "thinking through" our dilemmas to come up with the right reason.

Yet when we live in our minds, we rarely pay attention to our bodily sensations or physical reactions that are also providing useful information. Your body's wisdom is speaking to you all the time. And if you listen, you can call it *self-trust* or *intuition*.

What does intuition feel like? Have you ever broken out in a sudden sweat, had the sensation of getting the "chills," or a gut-tightening feeling? Can you sense the energy of a room? When you can recognize your body's primal response to a challenge or a new situation, you can learn to *feel* when you are making the "right decision." Being embodied means that you can rediscover your true "yes" and "no," and move more effortlessly in the world.

Cultures across the world have long recognized the idea that our bodies and spirit are completely connected and interwoven and must be considered in a holistic way. Think about Chinese medicine, the Hindu chakra system of yoga, the Jewish Kabbalah, the medicine wheels of the indigenous peoples of North and South America, and the African dance traditions of storytelling through movement. All these systems share the idea that we are more than just physical—we are vibrational beings.

Recent scientific research into these energy systems validates these beliefs. For instance, Candace B. Pert, PhD, the author of *Molecules of Emotion*, explains that "the chemicals in the body, the neuropeptides, move in vibration. They wiggle, they shimmy, and they even hum." I love this phrase because our entire body moves just like these chemicals: We are vibrational beings that wiggle, shimmy, and hum. We are a living dance. Dr. Masaru Emoto, scientist and author of *The Hidden Messages in Water*, compares how people are like molecules of water, interacting on a vibrational level. He writes, "Human beings are also vibrating, and each individual vibrates at a unique frequency.

Each one of us has the sensory skills necessary to feel the vibrations of others."

I transformed my life when I connected with my vibrational energy. I first explored the mental and spiritual realms, learning about astral projection and soul travel. It was all very interesting, and everything I tried taught me something new, but in retrospect, I can see that I was trying to learn how to "leave" the body. All my searching eventually led me toward embodiment, and I was finally able to get present and into my body through movement and dance. I found the most meditative experience occurred after all my emotions were released on the dance floor. For me, there's a lingering energy, and when I feel it, I can come into the fullest expression of my being. I can sense my own energy, literally like particles, like bubbles, or a streaming liquid light; what you might know as *chi, qi, prana,* or *life force*. That's when I know that I'm no longer living in my head, in the thinking mind. I can literally rub my hands together and feel the energy between my hands. I can move the energy, see it, and know that I am a spiritual being. I am a soul. I am energy, not just a person with a mind struggling for control.

When you're fully embodied, other people can sense your energy, and you can tune into the energy around you. When you're with someone who is not embodied, you can feel that too. You may feel a sense of longing for the person to be present with you. Have you ever felt lonely in a relationship? We innately seek deep communion, connection, and belonging, which you can't have without your full presence. The antidote to loneliness and dislocation, as physician Gabor Maté speaks about in his book *The Myth of Normal*, is connection and deep presence, which nourishes the mind, body, and soul.

INTO ME SEE—A COMMUNION WITH MYSELF

I feel freedom in my bones, in my skin, and my energy.

I feel the freedom to move and to feel. Joy comes easily to me in the dance.

Joy comes into me in the doing, in the loving.

But in the stillness, there is a sadness, like a tiny drifting breeze, like a candle flame wavering in the dark, like a bee buzzing alone in the garden bush, like a cat sleeping in the corner, like a guitar waiting to be played, lying there and waiting for me to pick it up and hold it for a while.

Not for a little while but for long enough to feel uncomfortable and want to leave.

But I stay and I stay, and I hang on, I hold on until she says, the tear, it's okay, I can let go now, and fall down your cheek.

She doesn't hold back now, she lets go and streams down, down, down into an ocean of salty sea, her favorite place to be.

Maybe the sad ones love the sea more than anyone, because like attracts like, and I am salty. I am salty with power and love and life! I am fervent and vivid and vigorous and passionate! I am full of flavor, and I will not hide my teary salty self.

I will be true, and honest; that is all there is. I will reveal myself.

And as I do right now with this intimacy.

Into me see.

I long for that, I long for that merging of souls, into me see, in the salty, sticky wild waves of the vast realness.

Into me I see.

Are You "In Your Body"?

Many of us don't realize that we're not *in* our bodies, so let me ask you a question that might sound strange. Can you feel your butt on the chair as you're reading right now? Can you feel your body against the bed? Or if you're listening to this audiobook, can you feel your hands on the steering wheel of your car or your feet as you're walking on the ground?

These questions were asked by one of my favorite therapists. At the time I was working in New York City. I was obsessed with yoga and had created this very extreme practice, where every single day I was going to different studios all over the city. I was still in my perfectionistic mindset. I wanted to be an amazing *yogini*. I had also found a Gestalt therapist, and her very first and most pivotal question to me was: "Can you feel your butt on the chair?"

I was like "What?!" I knew I *was* sitting in a chair. But I really couldn't *feel* my butt in the chair. When I thought about it, I realized that I was like a bolt of energy. I had no sense of stillness, no anchoring. I was not located. I started bumping around in my seat to awaken my sensations. I was so numb and I didn't even realize it. I thought I was so "in touch with my body" because I could put myself in a hundred different yoga postures. Stuck in my perfectionistic mindset, I practiced daily, but I was dissociated and emotionally numb. So when she asked me again, "Can you feel your butt on the chair?" I realized that I couldn't. I had been masking my feelings by partying, bingeing and purging, working out excessively, and smoking cigarettes, all of which are numbing devices. I was so focused on not feeling what was going on in my mind that I also became numb to my body.

Take this quick test:

- Shake your hands, wiggle your body.
- Bounce up and down on your feet.
- Put your hands on your chest and breathe deeply.
- If you want to make a noise, do so.

I hope you felt something, because we are calling attention to your bodily awareness. We often operate on autopilot and forget about our bodies completely. Being embodied requires a gentle reminder, like this exercise, to stay in a state of grounded presence. You can learn how to move through, reset, and clear your emotions through movement. That's what the body is for. It's an expression of you.

If emotions come up, or if you feel any sense of discomfort, don't panic. Coming back into the body can be an intense reunion. It can also be a cathartic and joyfully ecstatic moment when you recognize that you haven't been in your body and suddenly, you feel *alive* again! Note: if you have experienced physical or sexual trauma, becoming embodied can stir suppressed emotions (feelings that need to be released and processed) and potentially the joy of returning home.

Let's call ourselves a *system* instead of separate entities of the mind, the body, the emotions, and energy. We are a system because all aspects of us are operating simultaneously and together.

Take a moment to assess where you are on these three scales:

The EMBODIMENT Scale

Feeling weighed down, lead balloon, no activity, no motion, no flow

Grounded, can feel the body against the chair, present in your own skin

Spacey, disembodied, lack of feeling, constant thinking, daydreaming, functions automatically, lost in thought, constant activity, no rest

The EMOTIONAL FLEXIBILITY Scale

Numbed out, flat energy, closed off, shut down

Centered, open, joyful, resilient, empathetic

Activated, reactive, extreme sensitivity, stressed

The ENERGY FLOW Scale

Boundaries, locked, no flow, stuck

Connected, flowing, inspired, motivated

Vast open vortex, permeable, absorbent, without boundaries

Embodying Emotions

Every emotion affects the body. When you experience an emotion, a brain chemical cascade begins, connecting the mind and body, and we have a physical sensation. When we feel anger, we may feel it in our guts: you might get a stomachache or tighten so much so that you can't breathe. When we feel sadness, our chest might cave and we hunch over and feel sunken. And when we feel joy, we may experience an elevated state. Our whole body could feel light and we can fill our lungs freely. And for some of us, our emotions were crossed and confused during the formative years. We may cry when we feel angry—or become angry when we feel sad—and never recognize the difference or be able to verbalize what we are feeling.

Sometimes, we block, compartmentalize, or ignore difficult or upsetting messages we're receiving from either the mind or the body. We put our body's messages and our emotions on the back burner, become numb to them, or worse, interpret these messages as bad or wrong. If we don't have the capacity for *feeling* anger, sadness, frustration, embarrassment, excitement, inspiration, or the full range of emotions, we will energetically suppress these emotions into the body and create patterns of tension.

Myofascial release, a hands-on technique used to manage physical pain, can help illustrate this concept. Practitioners of this treatment focus on the *fascia*, or connective tissue, that runs through the body, which tightens as a result of feeling unsafe or experiencing trauma. Relaxing the tension through manual manipulation often releases the emotion and memory held in the body at the same time.

The Embodiment of Trauma

So many people are overwhelmed, either by the traumas they personally experienced or those that are constantly occurring in the world. The sad truth is that there's always been trauma, yet the recent increased focus and study of trauma has brought forth many new methodologies, and we have a greater chance to heal than ever before. Embodiment is a key component in the new trauma healing modalities.

Trauma is a response to a particular event or incident that takes away your power and feelings of safety. As Gabor Maté writes in *The Myth of Normal*, "The meaning of the word 'trauma,' in its Greek origin is 'wound.' Whether we realize it or not, it is our woundedness, or how we cope with it, that dictates much of our behavior, shapes our social habits, and informs our ways of thinking about the world. It can even determine whether or not we are capable of rational thought at all in matters of the greatest importance to our lives."

One could be traumatized by living through an event as a child or as an adult, or by carrying the stories of their ancestors, known as generational trauma. Some people are haunted by their trauma and cannot move forward in life. Others compartmentalize their trauma and are able to move forward in certain aspects of their life while others are continually processing their trauma in hopes of finding a sense of wholeness.

Regardless of the cause, our response to trauma changes the brain and the body in an effort to reframe the way we can feel safe going forward. You might sense danger where no real danger exists and avoid new situations, or you might be attracted to people who match your wound, re-creating the subconscious pattern set in place from the trauma. You might create the safest possible environment so that you don't have to experience those feelings again, writing new rules to create a new life. These strategies are important defense mechanisms. Defense mechanisms are there to protect us, so we can say thank you for having them. Yet when these old patterns no longer serve us but keep running the show, we need to begin a self-exploration journey, become embodied, and learn to feel so that we have another way to process our experiences, using the body and spirit.

One of the most common trauma responses is *disassociation*, a process of disconnecting specific thoughts, feelings, memories, or sense of identity from the body. You may feel like you've checked out of parts of your life. Or, you might feel like you are not fully present in your body. I refer to this defense mechanism as entering the *escape hatch*. Think of it as a small space that exists above your head, slightly to the left or right, where you "go" when you've reached your threshold for feeling. In the escape hatch, you are literally existing "out of body" in a state of comfortable avoidance, cutting off your emotions and intuition, and making decisions only with the rational mind. Most people stay in the escape hatch because it's safe: you can function in the world, but you won't deeply connect with others.

Fear puts us in the escape hatch, and self-love can get you out. When faced with uncomfortable challenges, we tend to blame the external world for our withdrawal, but I believe that each of us is truly able to change how we show up in life, how deep we are willing to go, how honest we are willing to be, and how much we are willing to feel.

When we live in our head, in the escape hatch, our only response to our own trauma and upset is to process information logically. The problem is, not everything is logical. If we become activated by the external world and don't have the capacity or bandwidth to feel our emotional response, we're going to repress our emotions. Our patterns become solidified, creating a neural network of reactions that keep us trapped using personal defense-mechanism patterns like numbing, shutting down, and avoidance, or exploding in anger, self-blaming, guilt, and shame—or however you unconsciously react. For instance, if you're in a relationship that you recognize isn't working, you may choose to avoid feeling anything because, if you felt your emotions, you know you would have to leave. Instead, you stay in the escape hatch and muscle through. This is why so many of us stay in our escape hatches, as it is often easier than feeling, processing, and changing.

To be fully present and leave the escape hatch, you have to be in your body and be willing and able to experience the full range of emotions. Feeling is living; living is a sensorial experience. As Gabor Maté says, "No emotional vulnerability, no growth."

When we go into the escape hatch, our emotions are still in the body, but they haven't been expressed or processed. You may have heard the expression from the title of the groundbreaking book *The Body Keeps the Score*. Psychiatrist and author Bessel van der Kolk's research shows that even if we can compartmentalize the traumas that have happened to us, they are still living within us, changing the nervous system to suit the traumatic experience, and keeping us stuck in a protective pattern that may not actually serve us.

When we repress our feelings, we get stuck in patterns created by our defense mechanisms. One of the goals of *Embody* is to create a path toward release. Rather than staying stuck, we can teach the body a new way to feel safer so that trauma can be processed. In many cases, when the body learns how to relax, feel joy and exuberance, and regain sensuality, we can overlay the body's system with new, supportive experiences. We invite our stories to be told with our bodies, without words and through the language of movement. And then we bring empowerment, joy, and celebration to the body so that we can connect deeply with others.

As renowned therapist Peter A. Levine, PhD, practices in his body of work, Somatic Experiencing, when a person is given the opportunity to restore the sensation of safety in the body, they can remember how strong, resilient, and capable they truly are. His method aims to reframe traumatic memories by completing the organic physical response of protection, fight, flight, and freeze. This act of completion regulates the nervous system. The body feels safer, with more resources, and can experience other emotions, not just the trauma response. Being able to experience different types of emotions fosters integration: the body can feel again.

Since we store emotions in the body, we have a real opportunity: we can continue to look away, *or* we can start the embodied healing process, where we choose to look at our pain in a new way and turn our vulnerability into our strength. Van der Kolk says, "In order to change, people need to become aware of their sensations and the way that their bodies interact with the world around them. Physical self-awareness is the first step in releasing the tyranny of the past."

That's what we'll do on this journey. We gain sensory awareness and create new, positive, *embodied* emotional experiences to overlay past patterns of hurt and get ourselves unstuck.

ISSUES IN YOUR TISSUES

The phrase "issue in your tissues" is often used metaphorically to describe the idea that unresolved emotional or psychological issues can manifest as physical tension, discomfort, or pain in the body. Issues in your tissues implies that there are intricate connections between emotional experiences, the nervous system, the immune system, and the body as a whole. As Denise LaBarre explains in her book, *Issues in Your Tissues*, "Our bodies continue to experience physical symptoms as long as we carry the emotional 'charge' or vibration associated with them. If you have not also released the sadness or anger or fear in those tissues, your body will continue to let you know there are still issues to work on."

I became interested in the body and its stories when I got my very first massage at twenty-one. The practitioner was working on my lower back and all of a sudden, I burst into tears. Maybe you've had an experience like this. I was quite surprised by my reaction. I cried for a while, and the therapist asked me if I wanted to share what was coming up for me, what images I was seeing. I had a memory that played like a movie in full color and full emotional content. I was a young woman running through a field with a baby in my arms that I had to give up. I had no idea what it meant until much later in life when I studied past lives, "Akashic records," and shamanic journeying. I was tapping into a generational wound from my lineage where women were forced to give up their children.

I cried through it, and she told me that this happens often when people are open to receiving her energy work.

The Effects of Conditioning

Conditioning is the absorption of negative cultural messages. These "not good enough" messages are everywhere: on the news, on social media, and in your family of origin. They can range from ideas like your body isn't the right skin color, your gender is less valuable, your age is a detriment, or your size isn't healthy or acceptable. Sonya Renee Taylor, in her radical self-love book, *The Body Is Not an Apology*, explains, "Living in a society structured to profit from our self-hate creates a dynamic in which we are so terrified of being ourselves that we adopt terror-based ways of being in our bodies. All this is fueled by a system that makes large quantities of money off our shame and bias."

Brené Brown writes in her book, *The Gifts of Imperfection*, "Perfectionism is a self-destructive and addictive belief system that fuels this primary thought: If I look perfect, and do everything perfectly, I can avoid or minimize the painful feelings of shame, judgment, and blame." I was exposed to these perpetual messages and perfectionism conditioning about my body during my formative years, as are so many tweens and young adults of all genders. Weight, size, and food became so interconnected with my emotional life that I had disordered eating and became addicted to exercising, all because I felt "wrong" compared to the images of "perfect" women that I would see all around me. I would barrage myself with negative thinking and self-criticism, and if any emotions surfaced even remotely, I would numb them out with an addictive binge/purge cycle. I didn't know it then, but this cycle activates the parasympathetic nervous system—the body's relaxation response—which quiets the intensity of feeling, bringing the calm, relaxed state I was desperate for. All I knew was if I could master my emotions and my body, I could keep my true feelings under control.

If your emotions are living in your body, why are you living in your mind? It's not your fault, it's the misdirection of "progress," the way we are valued and measured by "smartness" and "success." We no longer live with imminent threats while hunting and gathering, but we have lost parts of our body intelligence. Our body wisdom is not honored like mental wisdom.

It takes a lot of deprogramming to release perfectionism, systemic racism, and internalized patriarchy. This is why you can't just rely on your mind, your thoughts, or your judgments in order to break free from the conditioning. You have to feel your emotions, even if it's uncomfortable. You have to listen deeply to, and get comfortable with, your body—just the way it is. Whatever body you have, we will all have different layers to uncover based on our size, race, and gender, and the expectations, subjugations, and history we have lived.

Now, when I hear one of my old *you're not good enough* trigger phrases playing in my head, I have a choice. I could get upset with myself and believe the thought and go down a rabbit hole of torment. I could get mad at myself for still carrying this old tape, which would jump-start habitual patterns of self-abuse. Yet I am embodied, I am aware, so I take a different route. I choose not to believe that old thought because I know that it is totally untrue. Instead, it is a signal to me that I need to cry and feel the emotions that I am hiding from. The negative thought tape is just a reaction to what's happening in the moment and is trying to take me out of my body and put me back into the escape hatch. But I'm going to say *no*. I'm going to stay in my body, take care of myself, let my feelings surface, and have the cry or the emotional release that is needed.

Can you identify a thought that totally takes you out of your body and down the rabbit hole of self-abuse? Have you heard yourself saying, "You're too fat, you're too thin, you're too old, too young, you're ugly, you're gross, you're not good enough, you're never going to make it, you're stupid . . ."? The list goes on and on. We can change this experience by remembering that we have the power to choose our thoughts. It takes awareness, embodiment, courage, and commitment to listen to these harmful words and then choose to say, "I love myself. I love me, right now." I know it's not simple, but I know it's possible.

Ten Questions to Investigate

Throughout this book you'll find lots of questions to contemplate. You can start your journaling with these questions that will point to how you are currently feeling in and about your body, energy, and emotions. Just addressing these in your own heart may give you some needed information. As you learn how to better *be* in your body, feel your feelings, and clear your energy, you will gain a new sense of presence, capacity, resilience, and even inspiration.

1. **Do you feel numb, or are you "too busy" to explore your feelings?** Numbness can provide an excellent distraction so that you don't have to feel what's really going on. The problem is, if you make a commitment to never feel one thing, you can't really feel anything. If you never want to feel your anger, you are shutting down a natural life force within you. Anger, an emotion most people feel bad about, is actually energy that needs to move, and repression shuts down more than you intend to, leaving you stuck without the potential for experiencing joy or other emotions. What's more, if you never want to experience hurt again, or feel grief or loss, what are the chances that you will risk loving again?
2. **Are you constantly retelling your story?** If you're stuck in a pattern of retelling the story of your last breakup, bad divorce, work crisis, or past trauma to everyone you run across, it means you haven't yet finished processing the emotions surrounding it. If you are constantly reliving sad or difficult past events, please reach out to a mental health professional so you can retell your story until it is fully processed. We should never beat ourselves up for not being "over it" because it takes time to process the big stuff. I know that bringing your story to the dance floor will allow you to release stuck energy and emotions in a nonverbal way. I have repeatedly told many stories to the dance floor until they no longer have a hold on me. On the dance floor, I get to express myself to myself, and you will too. This gives me a deep

sense of relief when I feel that the story has been told by my body enough times so I can move forward.

3. **Who is running the show of your mind?** We all have "voices in our head" as I call them, and it greatly matters "who" is the narrator; who is the voice "running the show." Are you optimistic, or severely critical of yourself and others? Do you wake up in the morning and think life is good, or are you convinced that life is terrible? If you're living in a negative mindset, or if there is a negative voice that is gnawing at and judging you, life will be harder because your subconscious is always trying to prove itself to you, replaying your core beliefs. If the worrying or critical part of your mind is running the show, you'll live in a state of fear and anxiety instead of joy. Luckily, you can take your power back and unplug the critical voices, so that you can more effectively run the show of your mind.
4. **Do you find yourself frustrated or easily triggered by your beloveds?** Do you have a stress response to someone in particular, feeling frightened or out of control when you are around them? When we're activated, we're actually leaving the present moment and reliving an echo of the past. The trigger that activates you is a way of protecting you; it's not that anything is wrong with you. Think of it as a source of information. The limbic system in your brain is setting off a stress response that is connected to a time of not feeling safe. You might fight, flee, freeze, fawn (appeasing to avoid threat), or even feed. Your response might be keeping you from your feelings or causing you to erupt with a lot of feeling; either way, if it's not serving you, it needs to change. Hardwired patterns can shift with work and attention. Maybe there's anger that needs to be released, or a

conversation needs to be had. Dance and movement will facilitate a deeper conversation with yourself.

5. **Have you noticed addictive tendencies to food, alcohol, drugs, sex, shopping, scrolling, etc.**? Are you avoiding the present moment because you don't want to sit with yourself? Are you blocking the pain of your past or avoiding a current life situation? When we don't want to feel the feelings that we think will overwhelm our system, or we believe we don't have the capacity to deal with them, we may fill the moment with distractions. I've told you about some of my addictive behaviors; I've also lived with people active in their addictions and have been harmed, enabled, abandoned, and tried to save. What if we could fill these painful voids another way, by expanding our bandwidth—becoming more comfortable with emotions, increasing our capacity to be in life, even when it gets challenging—through the expressive arts, like music and movement, or the creative process of writing? What if over time, layer by layer, you could uncover what really wants to be expressed from you and only you? You can: I've seen it and I've done it myself.
6. **Do you have negative messages from your family of origin?** Some of us have been subjected to disempowering or degrading messaging from our upbringing, and we find ourselves repeating them internally or passing them forward because we've been conditioned. What if you could become the Game Changer, becoming courageous enough to step forward and say: *My generational trauma stops here. It ends with me.* This is a very powerful and brave act that requires a level of awareness and exploration. What is mine? What am I carrying for others? What are the gifts I can keep? And what is ready for release?

7. **What is your relationship with crying?** Some people rarely or never cry, and they may very well need to cry to release repressed emotions. They will not allow themselves to cry and show their vulnerability because it's too terrifying to do so. Other people cry very easily, feeling very sensitive to the world around them, or carrying a sadness for which they can't pinpoint the cause. Those of you who are considered highly sensitive may have been told you are "over emotional" or "too much." You might be very empathetic, where you take on the energies of others as a way to bring soothing to the world. Crying is a natural and necessary physical response, not to be repressed or criticized; it is as pure an expression of emotion as laughter. We have been trained to be in control of our emotions so as not to overwhelm others, and in many cases, we cry when angry instead of expressing our anger. I have come to know that there is a balance of expression that we need to cultivate to feel empowered and present in the moment. What if your tears are worthy? What if they are the clearing and releasing you need?
8. **Do you feel that you have a voice?** Do you find it hard to express yourself, be heard, and share your authentic truth? When our voice is shut down, we can feel powerless and unseen. In the embodiment process, you will be merging the physical body, the emotional body, the energy body, the mental body, and the soul into one unified field. When we feel this unification, we step back in our power. Our voice is there in that power and presence, and there's no need to "find it," only to claim it.
9. **Do you feel a sacred rebel inside you, waiting to come out?** When I say rebel, I don't mean a bad person. I mean someone who wants to break out of their box, take risks, and live their

dreams. If you want to make a change, it must come from an inner place of spiritual rebellion and deep self-trust. With your fully embodied presence, you can begin to feel safe enough to step off the suggested path and set your *own* course forward. My intention as a sacred rebel is to change the culture for women and create the evolution that is needed.

10. **Do you love your body?** We are all so conditioned to define loving our body based on how we look instead of how we feel. There are so many reasons for us to say "no" to this question because of the way society has idealized only certain bodies. Because of the body positivity and anti-racism movements, these limitations are being discarded, and there's much more opportunity for you to say "yes" to this question, to find love for your miraculous, amazing, beautiful body. Through movement and expression without "right/wrong" or "good/bad," we can say, *Yes, I do love my body, even though it doesn't look like anyone else's. I love* me. Welcome to my anti-perfectionist movement!

Overriding Limiting Beliefs Through Embodiment

The embodiment practices in this book can change the score. It can help you end the pain, integrate, understand, and digest your experiences of life. Whether you have been through big T to small t trauma, you can feel, heal, and transform your life. You can, little by little, layer by layer, come home to a new sense of well-being. As we re-inhabit the body and reengage with sensation, we are healing.

Throughout this program, you will see how embodiment can help you reclaim your inner wisdom. But the real work is using that information for growth, strength, and resilience. You will learn how to honor all the disparate parts of you, and let go of what is no longer serving you, so you can thrive. Once you realize where trauma or conditioning is coming from, you can work with it and shift its hold on you. The goal is to identify its effect on your psyche, your body, the way you feel and think about yourself, and then be able to subtly and slowly, or quickly and easily (depending on how intense it is), say, "With this awareness, I choose to heal." Then you can reprogram, replacing negative thoughts with other ones that serve you better. Just doing the work of giving a voice to our desires, where we dance with our dreams, we're opening ourselves for positive results to happen. Positive results beget more positive results. That is the journey: every day we can build self-trust, listen to our hearts, and expand our bandwidth so that we can experience more inner freedom, more potential.

A Life-Changing Embodiment Experience

During one of my weeklong retreats there was a woman participating who appeared to be totally together. You would never have known anything about her life's path from looking at her. She looked very powerful, with a cool, stylish haircut, physically fit. She was very much a part of the group, dancing and moving and exploring the work. Just a couple of days into the program she started shaking during a dance, so much so that she went to lay on the floor. Everyone in the class noticed and was concerned: Was she depleted? Did she need a banana or electrolytes? Should I call 911?

I too was concerned and asked, "Are you okay, do you need help?"

She said, "I'm okay, please let me shake. Please let me shake. I have never ever done this before. I need to shake this out. I know exactly where it's coming from. I'm completely with you. Just let me shake."

I double-checked to make sure she knew where she was, who she was, and where we were. She was totally able to communicate with me, so I told the group, "Don't worry, we're going to let her shake. We're going to let her body do what it needs to do and go through this process." I stayed with her, and my team continued moving with the group.

I sat by her side for the next ten minutes and she shook, dripping with sweat. When she was done, she rose slowly and took a seat. She was so grateful that we were able to let this happen instead of stuffing that shake back down into her body, as she had done for more than thirty years. She shared with me privately that she went through the most unspeakable sexual trauma as a child, and this was the first time she had ever shaken in her life.

The next day she came back and was literally a shining, vibrant being. Without needing to tell her story to anyone but me, she released this pent-up energy. She later shared that even though she was able to put the rest of her life together in an amazing way, she had stored so much fear and rage that shaking brought her more release and, ultimately, joy than she had ever experienced.

Many animals have to shake off trauma to stop the limbic system from producing the stress response. When an animal is attacked and runs from danger, it must stop and shake for a long time until its limbic system stress response is over. In this woman's case, she was able to release some of the physical trauma by being present in her body, and repatterning her ability to feel.

I'm grateful I experienced and studied so many different forms of process work so I could hold the space for her. Sometimes, even if we look like we "have it all together," we may still be afraid to feel. If we allow ourselves to feel anything, we fear feeling everything. I know that we are all capable of going deeper, processing our past, if it means our freedom.

CHAPTER 2

Weaving a Physical, Mental, Emotional, and Spiritual Journey

Even if I gave you the best advice in all the world, and you took it to heart, you still need to engage in new experiences to overwrite the old. A full-on physical, embodied shift can put your energy in motion and help you on your path to change. The most powerful resource I can offer weaves together a wide variety of healing modalities into a single practice. Each of the following tools is a necessary element of transformation that touches on the physical, mental, emotional, and spiritual level in combination. Together, we will take a journey to remember who we are, claim and reclaim our bodies, and bring ourselves back into a unified whole.

The seven elements you will explore include movement, sacred drama, music, creative visualization, affirmation, mystical inquiry, and emotional intelligence. The combination of these elements is the unique signature of JourneyDance and my embodiment practice.

Movement Is the Secret Missing Ingredient

The late choreographer, artist, and dancer Anna Halprin once said, "Through dance, we gain new insights into the mystery of our lives. When brought forth from the inside and forged by the desire to create personal change, dance has the profound power to heal the body, psyche, and soul."

I couldn't agree more. When you become fully embodied through dance, you connect the body and the emotions, your energy and spirit, and the healing process can begin. Through this movement practice, we are going to reconnect the mind and the body so that we can feel safer in our bodies and step into our power. We're not exiting the mind or leaving the mind behind; instead, movement helps us to invite the mind into the present rather than letting our thoughts drift back to where we might be stuck in the past. When you can process and digest the past and learn how to use this knowledge to move forward, you discover your authentic self.

When you feel safer in your body, your defense mechanisms can quiet and settle so you can start processing what is needed in the psyche. You might release old negative thoughts, embrace them, or transmute them, so that you can be more of yourself, a wholly integrated being. You might release the toxic conditioning we talked about in the last chapter that has dampened your personal energy, and reawaken your self-esteem, find your authenticity, and feel your energetic vitality. You might process old stories and embrace wounded parts of you to regain your sense of power and agency. All your inner parts can become respected, loved, seen, and expressed.

Though it may seem that you are coming here to dance, move, and become more flexible and freer, this embodied movement practice is also for emotional and energetic clearing. For those who already love dance, you may have experienced dance to be both active and mood-altering; movement practices can restore your sense of joy and wholeness. And if you didn't already know this, Kelly McGonigal, PhD, did the research. In her book, *The Joy of Movement,* the psychologist shows that movement practices can alter nerve chemistry to reduce anxiety and depression and modify the nervous system to make us less susceptible to the fight/flight/freeze response. The ability to modify the nervous system creates the capacity to be emotionally resilient.

The mystery of dance is its beautiful effect on the heart and the spirit. When you dance, you can connect to an energy beyond words, find your intuitive movement, your emotional expression, your connection to self, and your self-love. You can even heal your heart. Renowned dancer and choreographer Judith Jamison explains in her book, *Dancing Spirit,* "We're dancing from here, from inside, not from outside . . . Dancing is bigger than the physical body. Think bigger than that. When you extend your arm, it doesn't stop at the end of your fingers because you're dancing bigger than that. You're dancing spirit."

At nine years old, I felt the dancing spirit for the first time, and it was a joyful surprise. I was raised in a secular household, which followed some religious traditions, but we were pretty much agnostic. I was the only one of my sisters who had to go to religious school, which I never really loved (and even got kicked out in eighth grade for bad behavior). But there was one part of that experience that I loved, and I bet you could guess what it was—when the "Dance Lady" came in. On that day we cleared all the chairs out of the room, and we learned all the traditional folk dances, holding hands and making circles, dancing the grapevine, and coming into the center and back, which has stayed with me for all my life.

It wasn't until I was in my early twenties, just after my initial embodiment experience at Kripalu, that I began to voraciously study different dance forms. I loved improvisational dance because we were given a motif, or a dance theme, which we could then take in different directions. I stopped trying to imitate other people's movements and went deeply into my own. That's when I realized the difference between movement and *dance*. Movement is part of life; we all move to make shapes, walk, be physical, work out, and do normal activities. But once we get going into a constant flow of motion and there's music playing, a feeling comes over us. That feeling is hard to put words to, but many, including the late movement pioneer Gabrielle Roth, refer to it as *ecstasy* or *total presence*.

DANCE AS SACRED CELEBRATION

Humans have been dancing throughout history and pass down dances through generations: ceremonial dances, movement rituals, celebrational dances, prayer dances, power dances, and more. Dance as storytelling originates in Africa. Ceremonial dances of West Africa, India, the Middle East, North and South America, and Asia continue to be practiced in their original and modernized forms, and have strongly influenced contemporary dance. Shaking and trance-inducing emotional-release dances are ancient practices found in indigenous cultures all over the world.

In 1996, I went to Africa to continue my study of dance and immerse myself in my spiritual path. My friends and I were driving to a lake outside Accra, Ghana, when we stumbled upon a dance ceremony. Everyone was clapping and dancing and beckoned us to join them. So, we pulled up and walked into the small village that was reverberating with drumming.

A woman ran up to me, embraced me, and walked me through a line of dancing people at the far side of the gathering. There was a young man lying on a large wooden table, dressed in special ceremonial clothes, motionless. I knew this must have been her son. The woman hugged me and led me into the line of dancers and gestured that I join them. I danced with all the energy I had, and it was emotionally moving. This was the first funeral I had ever seen that felt like a celebratory experience. To be included in that honoring of a loss, to be part of a dancing memorial of a life, I felt even more deeply the power of connection and dance.

Healing Dance Wounds

My practice is not like any other dance or movement class you may have taken. I'm never going to tell you that there is a "right" way to move. However, there will be movement suggestions that you'll be able to follow.

If you've had failed experiences dancing, feel uncoordinated, confused, or body shamed, you will not have that here! I recognize the wounded dancer—the one who didn't have the "right" body type, or didn't make it into the dance class or company, or started a little too late—because that was me. Maybe you were told, "You have the wrong feet, you're top heavy, you need to lose weight, you can't count, you didn't have the proper training, you're too old." Oh yes, I've heard these comments and so many more. So many men were told, "Boys don't dance," and how sad and dispiriting that must have been to hear.

My initial dance wound came at a very young age. I was three or four when I was enrolled in ballet classes. I'm sure my mother thought it was a wonderful idea. I remember going with my best friend with her long, red hair. The two of us were a little uncoordinated, and I was labeled "chunky." For our first recital, all the girls were supposed to be dancing in our first pink tutus. I was over the moon excited until the teacher handed my friend and me little fuzzy bear costumes. My mom, trying to soothe me, said that I got the "special" part: I was going to be first onstage, sprinkling confetti all over the dance floor for the pretty little ballerinas to dance on. For the next recital, I was graced with green stockings and a leotard because this time, I would be a wood nymph and cover the stage with leaves for the fairies. It wasn't until years later that I realized that I wasn't allowed to be a ballerina in a pink tutu because my body didn't fit the part.

I took this experience, damaging as it was, and years later created my own "no shame" dancing zone! In order to create a healing, accepting, and supportive environment for myself and all my dancers, I created the JourneyDance method where there are literally no mistakes possible and only two rules to follow:

1. **Don't hurt yourself.** I'm not just referring to the physical body. Of course, I don't want you to pull a hamstring or twist an ankle. I also mean don't be cruel to yourself—don't allow negative thoughts to permeate your mind, like *I can't do this* or *I don't know how to dance* or *I'm not good enough.* It's okay to feel all your feelings, but it's equally important to recognize when you are beating yourself up. I extend this "don't hurt yourself" rule to the addictive behaviors that can be destroying your relationships, your body, or your mind. When you decide to stop hurting yourself, love will grow within you. When you can increase your self-love and compassion for others, you'll start to see all the beauty that surrounds you.
2. **There are no mistakes—only learning.** When people first come to my class, they might worry they're awkward or uncoordinated, or that they don't look as good or move as well as someone else. That can lead to more inner criticism and negative self-talk; remember the famous quote, "Comparison is the killer of joy!"? The way you move is your body's way of telling

its story. Your shapes, your speed, your pulses, your expression are all a part of that process. You can't really make a mistake. So let yourself move and dance no matter what you think you look like. This program is about feeling and experiencing, not judging or trying to do it "right" because there is no "right" way to move here. Suffice it to say: dance like nobody's watching!

Dance into New Levels of Consciousness

It takes courage to come into this unknown experience, but I know you can do it! On the dance floor, you are invited to explore different ways of being in and with your body and experience yourself in these different levels of conscious awareness:

Inhabit Your Body. As you initially develop the capacity to fully inhabit your body, you gain a sense of *proprioception*, which is the understanding of how your body moves in space. You will also gain a sense of *interoception*, the sense of recognizing your inner sensations. Interoception can mean noticing that you have a tightness in your stomach, a little headache, or that your heart is beating fast, all of which are signaling information. According to occupational therapist Kelly Mahler, your brain uses information about the way your body feels as clues to your emotional state. So, if your stomach is rumbling, you may ask yourself, *Are you hungry, nervous, tired, sick, excited, or angry?* Psychotherapist and yoga scholar Stephen Cope says, "Most traditional therapies downplay or ignore the moment to moment shifts in the inner sensory world." When you get embodied, you develop this internal awareness that can help you cultivate new behavioral patterns based on your understanding of your body's messages.

Inhabit Your Emotions. The next level allows you to experience your emotional state in the moment and process emotions from the past. Your emotions have a chance to take up space in a physical way. You'll learn to express anger through vigor, effort, force, and sound. You can tell your story of sadness through shapes, posture, waves, momentum, and suspension. You can feel joyfulness through expansiveness, jumping, pulsing, and bouncing. You can get to know your emotional body and appreciate your emotional life. When we can feel, we can stop spiritual bypass, stuffing, and numbing, and we can open to life in all its waves, ups and downs.

Inhabit Your Identity. The third level is where you dance your way home to an empowered sense of self. *Who am I?* is an ever-evolving question and source of experimentation as we move through the stages of life. We can explore an inquiry in the dance, meeting different parts of ourselves. You will become more conscious of yourself, understand where you came from, and how you fit in, stand out, join in, lead, or rebel. You can expand your self-concept or even shift your identity as you embrace new parts of yourself.

Inhabit Your Humanness. The fourth level encompasses ceremonial healing-dance work, exploring beyond the boundaries of your body and expanding into community. You can choose to take the dance into a spiritual practice, becoming what I call the game changer, so that you can stop generational patterns and heal. This level of consciousness is informed by many indigenous shamanic traditions, which seek to heal seven generations forward and seven generations back. Moving beyond the personal, you will focus on healing and processing for the collective past and future.

Inhabit the Transpersonal. When you are dancing, you may experience what feels like an altered state of consciousness, totally connected to the mystical. We move into subtle energy awareness and have the capacity to touch glimpses of your "spiritual self," or "oneness," or "unity consciousness." For some, it may happen when you are dancing wildly and free; for others, it happens in a slower, more prayerful dance, or in deep relaxation. At this highest level, you can pray through your dance; you become the prayer itself. When you can momentarily let go of ego and identity, you can feel an expansive opening and connect with that which you call the Divine.

The Power of Sacred Drama

When I was twenty-one years old, I got my first cassette tape of a Tony Robbins lecture, and no surprise, it inspired a change in my life. Instead of walking a little bit hunched and a little bit scared and a little bit hidden, I followed his instructions: I started walking down the street in a new way. I flexed my hands, lifted my chin, and brought my shoulders back and down as I walked forward. I stood up taller, my attitude was brightened, and I walked down the street with more confidence and less fear. Changing my state of being by shifting my posture affected my physical and emotional experience. Was this shift real, though I was only acting "as if"? This lesson was the beginning of my deep dive into the teachings of theater and psychodrama.

Originally founded by psychiatrist Jacob Levy Moreno in the early 1900s, psychodrama is an active method of dramatizing and externalizing the internal landscape to gain insights into our lives. I have studied and experienced the power of many different forms of psychodrama, and I practice my own synthesis in what I call *sacred drama.*

Your story is yours to hold, understand, and process, and I consider that sacred. It's a courageous act to face yourself in this way. The sacred drama process allows us to assess and access deeper truths about our inner landscape, coping mechanisms, and the complex voices of the mind. Dramatizing our stories through dance helps us express held emotional energy. Telling our story to the dance floor can be a powerful method for releasing old patterns and opening to new ways of thinking.

Sacred drama is moving, dancing, visualizing, and playing out personal stories. You come to know your "higher" parts, which I call the *inner guide* or *your inner wise one*, and your "shadow" parts, your unloved and abandoned parts that need attention. The shadow parts are aspects of our personality that we can't see and unintentionally "put in shadow" because the behavior—good or bad—is too painful to own. We develop these parts through a protective instinct to keep us safe and keep us in connection with our loved ones, even if these relationships are dysfunctional or toxic. If our shadows are held with love and light, we can begin to glimpse them, learn to see them, and then learn to embrace, respect, and heal them.

The language of movement and dance can convey attitude, expression, emotion, empowerment, and inner purpose. Sacred drama teaches this language so that we can tell our story with our body, its shapes, and postures. You will learn to "tell your story to the dance floor," using a mix of movement, dance, and *tableaux*, a powerful psychodrama technique of making shapes to represent a situation or feeling. Again, it's an externalization of your internal life, which gives you new perspective and an embodied sense of being seen and known.

You can tell your story in shapes that are intentional and recognizable to others, even if you don't "dance." If I crouched down and put my hands in front of my eyes and hunched my shoulders, you might guess that I was hiding, or scared, or trying to convey smallness or surrender. Then when I lift my face and spread my hands, I've created an opening for you to notice me. If I lift one arm to the sky and point my eyes upward, you might think, *She's inspired,* or if I cast my gaze behind me, *She's looking for something in the past.* When you see someone in a posture that is angry or upset, you naturally read their body language and react to it. You can learn to respond with empathy as you learn your body language; it is inherently encoded within us.

In my study of Playback Theatre, an improvisational theater form created by Jonathan Fox in 1975, we tell our stories and see them enacted in the moment so that we can more deeply understand one another. In one introductory exercise, actors faced away from one another. Then a word was called out, and everyone used their body to convey that word simultaneously. When everyone turned in and showed one another their version of the word, their body language was almost always very similar in shape and facial expression, exemplifying our collective emotional body language.

You can try it right now: How would you use your body to create a shape that represents joy? Let's try lifting your hands up in the air and smiling. What shape do you make to show inner power? Try standing up tall, feet wider than hips, and hands open and/or on your hips. What does softness look like? Bring your hands to your opposite shoulders in a gentle hug.

THE POWER OF SELF-REGULATION

Every aspect of my movement practice is thoughtfully designed with a trauma-informed lens. You can create a sense of safety by slowly titrating this experience. Little by little you will be increasing your capacity to be with your emotions, to experience physical sensations, and to recognize your own power. You might experience yourself differently every time you come to the dance floor.

At any point in the practice, you get to decide how deeply you want to go into the work, using the tools of self-awareness (the ability to notice sensations) and self-regulation. Self-regulation is the ability to locate your body, reorganize and calm your nervous system, and assess if you need to dial back any of the feelings that may come up.

The purpose of self-regulation is so you don't get swept away into emotions that don't feel safe. You may have had a past, personal experience that you have compartmentalized in the labyrinth of your mind—for good reason. If an uncomfortable memory/feeling comes up, you have options. You can be with the memory and feel the associated emotions to their completion, letting them move through you. If you feel like expressing your emotions out loud by making sounds, go ahead. Or, you can stop what you're doing and come back to the practice later.

Or, you can take a pause by bringing one hand to your heart and one on your belly, finding your breath. Breath is your best friend for grounding and coming back to center. Consciously feel your feet on the floor and breathe into your hands. Gently pulse your knees to feel your weight and locate yourself. Once you feel grounded, you can rejoin the practice.

I have learned from personal experience, and those of many dancers, that if a memory surfaces, it means that it's ready to be handled, processed, and digested. It's not coming up to harm you, take you down, or make you miserable. It's coming up because you have reached a point where you are ready to process it. If any feeling becomes overwhelming to your system and you need support, please reach out to a mental health professional or whoever is supporting you in somatic healing.

Music Is Movement's Beloved Friend

I was raised on classical music—mostly Mozart—and told by my passionate father that other music was "junk" or "wretched drivel," so it was a rebellious act to listen to other music. My older sisters used to sneak me up to their rooms to play their records. We would lie on their beds and read the liner notes and spend hours swaying or dancing around. One sister was the Joni Mitchell, James Taylor, Carly Simon, Carole King, John Denver, Beatles type, and the other was into Stevie Wonder, Aretha Franklin, the Doobie Brothers, and the Jackson Five. While I appreciated my father's Mozartian fascination, which definitely influenced my love of music, this explosion of new possibility became my passion. I've been obsessed with music ever since and I consider myself a music geek.

Music is an intentionally organized art that combines sound and silence with core elements of melody, harmony, rhythm, and bass that touch us vibrationally. Music has the power to change our state, mood, emotions, and even level of consciousness. It can move you deeper into yourself, and I believe that music cracks the shell of emotion. When I hear music, I want to animate it. I want to feel what it is giving me. I let it soothe me, take me on a wild ride, or let me release my feelings. It helps me tap into my emotions, thoughts, and memories, connecting me to my senses.

Music is a portal to transformation, and for me, music is my medicine. It has saved me and continues to talk to the lost parts of me, touches my soul, and allows me to express myself in all possible ways. When I hear music, it's doing so much more than just hitting my tiny eardrums. It's hitting my whole body and reminds me that I am a vibrational, energetic being.

Cognitive psychologist and neuroscientist Daniel Levitin, PhD, and musician and neuroscientist Alan R. Harvey have extensively studied how the human brain processes and responds to music. Levitin says, "Your brain is a music machine" and can remember and recognize music as fast as a computer. He explains that every part of the brain is involved in the experience of hearing music, including the centers of memory, emotion, movement, and the limbic system, which is the most primitive part of the brain. Music listening and music-making elicit the release of good brain chemicals—not only dopamine, but oxytocin, serotonin, and endorphins—just like sex and chocolate! On an energetic level, your body responds to music's vibration, melody, rhythm, and sensation with moving, dancing, clapping, singing, and even releasing and feeling emotions.

Professor Harvey explains that when you are listening to music, your brain waves shift and move in and out of different frequencies, bringing you into the present moment. Music quiets the internal chatter. When you are dancing in my program, you won't have the mental space to worry about how you look because you will be *in* the music, and those thoughts will quiet. Even as I was writing this book, I chose a specific playlist to produce these waves and chemicals, so I could go into a deeper focus. Everything falls away like I'm in a hypnotic state.

Music is the key ingredient that transforms movement into dance as it supports the shapes and pulses of the movements. I believe that movement will open your mind to the possibilities of music, because in this practice, you're going to move and *feel* the music, not just hear the music. Music also opens us up to what I call the *soul space,* a state of altered consciousness that's similar to a hypnotic state. Alan Harvey showed that music activates the brain's beta state (alertness, active thinking, and concentration) and alpha state (relaxed alertness and light hypnosis).[1] In a separate 2015 study, dancers achieved a theta state (daydreaming, deep hypnosis).[2] Theta waves influence the strong internal focus that we go into when in deep meditation, prayer, and spiritual practices. It's a state between wakefulness and sleep, and relates to the subconscious mind, healing, and creativity.

The music I have paired with the movements may be completely

---

1 https://www.ted.com/talks/alan_harvey_your_brain_on_music?language=en.

2 Ermutlu N, Yücesir I, Eskikurt G, Temel T, et al. Brain electrical activities of dancers and fast ball sports athletes are different. Cogn Neurodyn. 2015 Apr; 9(2): 257–63. doi: 10.1007/s11571-014-9320-2. Epub 2014 Nov 23. PMID: 25834650; PMCID: PMC4378580.

new to you. It's there for you to create new responses and new possibilities. It is carefully curated to evoke specific emotions and physical responses, but not to associate with past memories; I want it to be fresh and new for you. There will be new rhythms and pulses and melodies to explore from all different genres. Sometimes you might think, *This music is weird.* I'm okay with that because over the years I've reclaimed the word *weird.* To me it means a wild exploration of freedom. Or **W**ild **E**xploration of **I**magination in **R**esplendent **D**ance.

You may already have a list of songs that supported you in a tough time or brought you into supremely joyful states. You may have memories that can be stimulated just by hearing a few notes of a song. My students love listening to my playlists because the music quiets their negative internal voices even when they aren't dancing. This is because music and movement create what I call *state recognition.* State recognition is when you hear music a second time, and the body knows that the journey is beginning. With each song your body remembers, "This is where we dance, this is where we express, this is where we release, this is where we touch our heart, this is where we feel good!" It's kind of amazing, honestly, how quickly the brain and body connect through music. Where Is Your Music Playing?

You'll notice that your favorite stores play music you love, which is why you gladly spend more time there. The next time you're at a restaurant, notice if there is music playing. Sometimes, you may be so tapped into the deliciousness of the food you're eating, you don't even notice music playing, but in reality, the music is enhancing your sensory experience. Other times the music can be too loud, and you may be distracted and can't concentrate on your meal. Have you ever watched a movie with no soundtrack? It's a completely different experience because the music makes the emotional body come alive, so you can experience the tension, suspense, romance, beauty, or whatever emotions the composer is trying to convey.

Creative Visualization

I remember buying one of my first spiritual books, Shakti Gawain's *Creative Visualization*, and I began meeting with parts of myself through my imagination. I even practiced meeting spiritual masters and guides. I learned that whatever I can imagine with vivid detail, I can bring into manifestation. One line of the book really stuck with me: "*Every moment of our lives can be infinitely creative.*"

Creative visualization is the art of using imagery and affirmation to inspire and effect inner and outer change. Using a variety of paradigms and images (metaphorical and symbolic), creative visualizations can transport us into the present moment, into our bodies, and into other states that allow us to discover the beauty within. Far from being just a mental process, a cadre of rich images sprinkled into the dances can increase the depth of your experience and open your imagination. Images give your mind a focal point, so you can move your body in particular ways that feel more expressive as you become aware of your senses and immerse yourself in the moment.

Through creative visualization, you can take your inner landscape of thought and emotion and externalize it into a physical reality. You can then observe, experiment, and make change.

We'll explore creative visualizations in some of the movement sections. For example, we'll use a scarf to represent our heart or our dreams. With your imagination and creative visualization, you'll be able to dance with your heart, talk to it, listen to it, and embrace it. You'll be able to dance with your dreams, choose one, and give it life.

Affirmation

Your thoughts are powerful! They create the energy of your reality and influence healing, affecting your body and your emotional well-being. We can choose which thoughts we want to hold on to and repattern our thinking through affirmations. This can lift dark moods and help make us aware of and transform negative self-talk.

Using the power of movement and vocalizing affirmations, you can amplify your desired emotions. Kelly McGonigal says, "When someone moves with grace, the brain perceives the elongation of the limbs and the fluidity of steps, and realizes, '*I am graceful.*' When one moves with power, the brain encodes the explosive contraction of muscles, senses the speed of the action, and understands, '*I am powerful.*'"

Affirmations only work if you can actually feel and own the message. When you can truly *embody* a feeling, the mental and verbal affirmation can come in and work its magic. When we recognize the shapes and the feelings that our body can make and express, we can actually see, feel, touch, and absorb our own inner beauty. This builds confidence, enhances pleasure, boosts power, and spreads joy. We can use this information as a resource for when we are off the dance floor. Movement aids in creating synaptic connections in the brain, which help us reprogram negative thought patterns with added affirmations said aloud or internally. As we make affirmations fully believable to our bodies and minds, we begin to own them in our psyche!

Mystical Inquiry

Mystical inquiry is a heightened state of awareness, a hypnotic state similar to what some people experience in shamanic journeying practices. You might not know it, but you are often in a light hypnotic state. The brain has natural wave patterns that range from high alertness to deep relaxation. Certain activities put your brain into different states, including the calmer, hypnotic states. For instance, reading quietly or playing music puts your brain into a mild hypnotic state. And as I've said earlier, dancing can put us into a lightly hypnotic state known as theta, which is the ultimate state of healing.

In this practice, we combine movement with music, sacred drama, and visualizations, and enact mini-transformative rituals so that you can enter into a hypnotic state. We work on ourselves and meet and communicate with our inner parts, clear old cords of attachment, and plug into what we choose.

Stephanie Shelburne, PhD, is an integrative medicine specialist, researcher, and educator. Dr. Steph studied my modality and found that the JourneyDance practice is closely matched with hypnotherapy. She points out that the totality of the Journey closely follows the hypnotic curve, a distinct pattern of mental awareness, deepening through the stages of induction, arousal, intervention, and sensory integration. Combining my specially curated music and movements with my guidance, you can go into that hypnotic state. Hypnotic intervention can result in transformative healing that is both immediate and long-lasting.

Emotional Intelligence and Emotional Release

Author of *You Can Heal Your Life*, my hero, Louise Hay's wise message is that your body is completely interconnected with your thoughts and buried emotions and can react to them as a physical manifestation. In this practice you are invited to feel and navigate all of your emotional states in a supportive space, where all emotions are valid and can be expressed without judgment. With music and movement as our tools, we can express what we may normally "keep a lid on" or stuff down. We can move with our emotions in a new embodied expression, without self-sabotage and abusive behavior. By tapping into these stored or stuck emotions, you can experience a flow of well-being by releasing the trapped energy.

In my embodied transformation coaching, I have learned that instead of asking my clients for their story first and digging for their emotions, I ask them to use their body to tell me their story, revealing the emotions, which we then amplify to feel through it, and release the charge. Then we can have a deeper conversation and unpack it, instead of digging in the mind.

We gain emotional intelligence—the capacity to be aware of, control, and express one's emotions—as we understand how our bodies are communicating to us. Then we can sense what needs our attention and give our body what it needs. From there, we can learn to effectively communicate our needs to ourselves and others. By learning how to identify and express our feelings, we can increase our understanding of our emotions, our relationships, and our roles within our complex lives.

A New Hero's Journey

The journey you are about to embark on—music, movement, psychodrama, creative visualization, transformative ritual, and mystical inquiry—is the map I created for my own personal healing journey. I brought what I have learned onto the dance floor, and now directly to you. My journey is not complete, as none ever is. I'm still learning, growing, and creating every day. I hope this will be a powerful and enriching step in your healing process. The main goal of my program is to create an exhilarating and efficient somatic, psycho-spiritual movement practice to move through hurt and pain, feel the feelings, process your life, move forward, and ultimately step into your power and your joy. I want you to get closer to your heart so that you can have amazing relationships, feel your own power, and stand up for yourself and thrive. I want you to love yourself, even when you are sad. And I want you to love your body—the only one you've got!—so much that you treat it with a new level of kindness and respect.

In many ways, this practice will take you on your own mythic hero's journey, much like acclaimed writer and professor Joseph Campbell shared with the world. His work in comparative mythology and comparative religion discusses his theory of the journey of the archetypal hero that is shared in various world mythologies. If you've seen movies like *Star Wars*, *Lord of the Rings*, or *The Matrix*, you know this archetype.

The Hero's Journey always begins with a *calling*: something that has brought you to a place of desire, change, growth, or need. Since you were drawn to this book, your calling may be any of the following: *I want to feel. I want to heal. I want to fully reclaim myself. I want more access to my emotions, my energy, and my presence. I want to share more of me, my wisdom, my love, my joy, and I want to inhabit my life more fully and with confidence. I want to process my past through the body and reclaim my joy.* What is your calling?

The next step is *embarking*—crossing the threshold from one place into another. You are embarking on a mission to get into your body, to tell your story to the dance floor, and be with whatever feelings need your attention.

Next you encounter your *allies* or a *spirit guide* who fortifies your sense of readiness, confidence, and safety. I'm happily going to be your guide and ally, providing mentorship and support. You also will encounter your own inner allies, the parts of you that are already wise, empowered, and love you deeply.

Now the journey truly begins. You will be traveling through what I call the *Qualities of Transformation*. The qualities are the core of my program because they provide the road map. I have found that you just can't go deep into your feelings without the proper support. Each quality builds on the next, like layers; we need each layer for the journey.

The first quality, or stage on the hero's journey, is *Embodiment*, where you will literally lay your body down on the earth and experience a series of luscious movements to find your grounded, connected presence. The next stage is *Awakening*, which beckons you to explore new movements, rousing dormant parts of yourself, leading you to a sense of invigoration and vitality. Your energy will be enlivened and your "sensationality" becomes activated. Next, you flow into *Immersion* and *Expansion*, nurturing a positive self-perception, seeing how you move, and taking up the space around you. Your joy and confidence build in *Funky Connection*. You feel fluid and have fun with the music, uncovering joyful parts of your personality. You will store this joy in every cell and keep it for when you need it most.

Now, you are ready to face your *ordeal*. Every hero encounters obstacles, conflicts that force us to face our story. This is when we confront the foe—a manifestation of your past or an aspect of yourself that is holding you captive—what I often call *the saboteur within*. It goes by many names: your inner critic, inner demon, gremlin, self-abuser, abandoned or shadow parts, or trigger. Whatever you want to call it, we all know it when it comes. You'll face your own story: *What is the story that I am holding onto? What is holding me back? What keeps me stuck? Why can't I feel? Why do I feel so much?* Each of you will have different obstacles to face. Then, you go deeper: *What is old and what is no longer mine to carry?*

In *Evocative Emotion,* we explore our emotional landscape, which challenges us to break free from old patterns and embrace our feelings, particularly the difficult emotions of sadness, grief, rage, or anger. We may face another series of challenges here, processing old stories, expressing ourselves about current situations that need to be moved, or just feeling and releasing energetic *glunk*—the fears, doubts, worries that feel bad.

In *Alchemy Transformation,* we take our story and transform it from pain into power, from angst into art, from compost to fertile soil—fostering resilience, courage, and progress. Through an act of transmutation we alchemize our challenges, turning them into our personal medicine. This is when we look back at our journey and see how we have changed, and can then use our experience to become a beacon and inspiration to others.

Having completed your ordeal, you feel *Empowered,* and a *Celebration* marks your triumphant homecoming. This homecoming signifies a profound transformation—we recognize ourselves as the heroes of our own narratives. We now give ourselves permission to revel in our accomplishments and our resilience to overcome and work through our story. On our journey home, we recognize the power of joy and give ourselves the freedom to love ourselves wholly. The *Sensual Freedom* quality allows us the space to become gentle and tender with ourselves. We take respite in our sensory bodies and enjoy the movement and feel the moment. In our creative sensual energy, we open the door of manifestation. Here we dream of what could be.

We near the end of our journey in *Open Heart,* where our reward is the ability to listen to our newfound wisdom of love and self-acceptance. We connect with the divine, solidifying a true sense of home. Finally, *Prayer* deepens our connection to the divine mystery, culminating in a profound sense of completion. We integrate all of this in *Bliss*, which is a returning to the body, whole and complete.

Creating Your Personal Container: Your Transformative Ritual Space

A ritual can be as simple as setting an intention or lighting a candle, or as complex as a sacred drama practice. I have created many transformative rituals that combine all the modalities—creative visualization and focused intention with music and movement—to bypass the mind's role of questioning, doubting, and negating. Rituals work with intentions from empowerment to forgiveness to self-love and self-worth.

In each quality you will enter your own "container" where you'll explore your practice. Your container is your home for your transformative ritual process work and creates a boundary so your mind can differentiate between regular time and space. This intentional demarcation allows us the freedom to explore and express ourselves in a metaphorical, contained sacred space. In your container you can move difficult emotions, shift your feelings about difficult situations, have inner dialogues with your parts, and play different characters.

Your container is a wholly supportive space that you create in your own home. I like to think of a container as a fish tank versus an ocean. There's no way anyone could control an entire ocean, but if you had a container of ocean water, you could look at it, play with it, and make it your own. When you do the *Embody* process work, you're going to move and create in the confines of your container; you're not being asked to jump into the ocean.

Your container can be whatever space you feel comfortable in that you can move around without obstruction and not be interrupted, even if you only have thirty minutes. I know we're very busy people. So set time aside (talk to your kids, family, etc. ahead of time so they know you'll be occupied for a bit). Once you get comfortable in the practice, your family will happily give you the time when they feel the results of your embodiment.

Have access to drinking water and a journal book. You want to feel good in the space that you've created. If you have an amazing sound system that will fill your room with music, definitely play the music out loud. If you are someone who loves using earbuds, the music I've chosen will be delicious in your ears and will block out any other ambient sound. Each method provides a very different sensation, so if you can, definitely try both. I want you to feel immersed in the sound, like the music is talking to your body.

You can dance on pretty much any surface, even outside. You do not need to install any mirrors to dance or move in front of because there's nothing to see in order to do this work correctly. In fact, the fewer mirrors the better! And if you ever need to see me, just jump on Instagram or Facebook or into the website portal that goes with this book with many tutorial videos, and I'll be there dancing. You can practice with me if you don't feel like practicing on your own.

Let's create your dedicated movement space by clearing the floor and building a small altar, or placing colorful cloths or scarves around the room, or maybe some lights that you like. Make it sacred for you. Keep it simple.

Now we can begin.

Come Get the Playlists!

Join me in the *Embody* portal on my website (www.ToniBergins.com), where you will find exclusive content for this practice:

- Videos of me moving and leading you in each quality
- Links to the complete playlists
- Here is the key to the *Embody* book portal. Scan this QR code.

Start the music as you read the following invocation. These are the songs that have been specially chosen to welcome you to this journey.

This is the beginning of the playlist:

- "Game Changer" by Toni Bergins
- "Inner Peace" by Beautiful Chorus
- "Dance Me to the End of Love" by The Civil Wars
- "Afterglow" by Phaeleh and Soundmouse
- "Follow the Sun" by Xavier Rudd

Find the full playlist in the *Embody* portal.

A Welcome Invocation

Say aloud, and feel the power of your words:

I welcome myself to this space.

I invite all of me to this practice: my body, my emotions, my thoughts, my story.

In this sacred space, I give myself permission to explore and create.

I give myself permission to be exactly where I am in this moment.

I am grateful to have this time to get to know myself better.

I wish myself my highest healing now.

And so it is.

The Welcome Dance: A Movement Practice

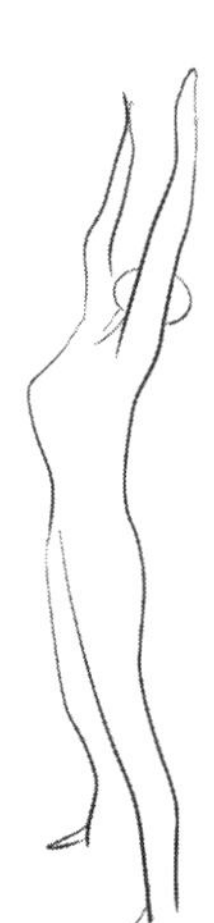

Once you enter your container, please choose a piece of music from the list of Welcome songs and begin the journey with the Welcome Dance, using the following instructions:

Stand up, raise your arms to the sky, and invite the cosmic flow of energy to move through your body. Reach and sway side to side, like you were saying hello to the sun, moon, and stars. Gently touch your hands together and chose one to glide up your arms from your fingers to your shoulders and welcome your body into the space. Allow your hand to cascade down the sides of your body to your legs. Now allow your body to roll down with your hand facing the ground and welcome the earth energy into your space. Imagine you have roots going down into the earth and feel them beneath you, almost like a reflection of yourself underground. Now as you roll back up, imagine you have wide gorgeous branches reaching up to the sky. Here you are, present between earth and sky. Take your right arm and open the space to the right, then the left arm to the left, like you were opening a light gauzy curtain, gently pushing clouds away, opening your body to the space. You can do this motion in all directions, up over your head, down toward the ground, into the space, welcoming yourself and your body. Move through your space, blessing it with your arms and gestures, as if offering something beautiful to the room, the windows, the space.

Dance this opening "welcome to yourself" until you feel ready to continue on your journey.

A Song I Wrote for You

To deepen your practice, listen to my song from the playlist, or read the following out loud:

GAME CHANGER

All I wanted is to take you here
Show you the way my dear
All you need is some mending time
There's no need to pretend

I'm changing the game
I'm lighting the flame
My life rearranged
I'm taking the stage
To be dancing free

Now I know you are a restless soul
Now I know you have so much to
give
A life unlived

Trapped like a deer in those
headlights
Frozen in fear, you defend
Once we face our fragile side
with this embrace we ascend

I'm changing the game
I'm lighting the flame
My life rearranged
I'm taking the stage
To be dancing free

Now I know you are a restless soul
Now I know you have so much to
give
A life unlived

Please don't leave, 'cause you've
got a sad regret
Your story needs to be told or you
won't rest
Take a chance, what haunts you will
make you blind
Only you can forgive yourself this
time

Gentleness and Permission

Over the years, many doctors and therapists have taken my classes and have studied how JourneyDance maps directly over or similarly resonates with other important therapies, including movement therapy, expressive arts, and music therapy. JourneyDance is a wonderful companion to traditional therapy. As in any therapeutic practice, you will be growing, learning, and discovering. Please be gentle with your mind, gentle with your body, and gentle with your heart. I'm emphasizing gentleness because self-love is my guiding principle. Your defenses have been active for a very long time, so give them love as you transform them. The most important thing to watch for is that you are going to experience your feelings as they come up. You can finally choose to stop pushing them down. And afterward, you may feel a sense of complete and total calm, and peace.

Give yourself permission. I cannot say this enough! Permission to explore your body, to experience new movements and dance, to enjoy the music, to be serious, to be playful, to be creative, and most of all, to be *you.*

Remember, this process is not a one and done. You don't have to decide on a specific aspect of your life you want to work on; you only need the desire to feel embodied and more alive. Enjoy moving through each quality and do it as many times as you like. You might love it so much that you make it a lifelong practice.

Let's enter your journey.

PART TWO

The Qualities of Transformation

CHAPTER 3

Embodiment

I've had the privilege to meet the Dalai Lama, can you believe it? I was only twenty-two at the time, working as an assistant account executive at a New York City publicity firm that represented artists and architects. I was cold-calling journalists, taking them on tours of art exhibitions, writing press releases, and labeling slides. From the outside, it looked like my life was going great: I had a "great job" living in a "great city." Yet my internal life was not reflected in this external life. I had just started to pursue a spiritual life in the hopes of finding my real, authentic purpose and meaning. So, you could imagine that I was completely over the moon when, because of a surprising synchronicity, I found myself in the very same room with the most enlightened person on the planet.

It was opening night of "The Sacred Art of Tibet," a gallery exhibition of Tibetan art. My job was to give out name tags and check in journalists. It was a star-studded event, attended by celebrities including Richard Gere, Cindy Crawford, Robert

Thurman (Uma Thurman's father and a renowned Buddhist scholar), and a couple of Kennedys; you get the picture. There were so many journalists and photographers, camera lights were flashing, and everyone was talking over one another trying to get to ask questions of the Dalai Lama. I felt completely overwhelmed just watching! Yet he wasn't fazed at all. He didn't let the noise of the experience upset him. Instead, he chose another path; he was calm, collected, and present.

Just before beginning the gallery tour, he walked over to my boss and asked if the two of us would escort him through the exhibit. He linked his arms in ours, she on his right and I on his left, flanking him as if to shield him from the crowd. Yet it felt as if he was protecting us with his profound, beautiful energy field. And off we went. Mic drop.

We walked slowly through the gallery, quietly chatting. Remember, this is twenty-two-year-old me, insecure and always trying to prove myself. I was starstruck. I never thought I was actually going to meet the man himself, let alone get to spend time with him! With the Dalai Lama on my arm, I became totally relaxed and grounded, not nervous, tense, or worried, and I was able to get my thoughts under control despite the chaos that surrounded us. He was complete *presence*. Everything about him was available. He was kind, open, attentive, deep, and willing to share his knowledge. I expected that he would be ethereal, untethered, "above" us all. Yet he was grounded, unflappable, undistracted, and even kind of funny and relatable. We were walking along, and he would make playful comments, like "Can you believe all this hubbub?" Then he would shift right back into his elegant, serene presentation.

It wasn't until years later that I realized that what set the Dalai Lama apart from everyone else I had ever met was that he was completely embodied. And he was able to transmit this feeling to me through his gentle touch on my arm as we walked.

Physical touch from another is one way to bring us back into our bodies and become more present. From our earliest moments of life, we crave physical contact, inherently knowing that it gives us comfort and connection. Sometimes, all we need is a touch or a hug to reground ourselves.

I met a brilliant friend, Joshua Rosenthal, twenty-five years ago. Joshua went on to become the founder of the Institute of Integrative Nutrition (IIN) and has trained tens of thousands in his holistic health coaching philosophy. Back then, he and I would dance together and go to lunch. I was in the final stages of healing my food and body image issues. I told him I struggled at the buffet line with what to eat, what not to eat, my old conditioning flaring up. His reaction really surprised me. He said, "Well, let's hold hands for a minute." As we held hands, he continued, "Can you feel how you're just dropping into your body so much more as we touch our hands together?" As we sat together, I could feel more present in my body.

I was able to sense when I was full and complete, instead of eating to the point of almost discomfort. When you're disembodied, food becomes a way of literally feeling pressure against your body. I often wonder if that's what makes us eat so much as a culture. Is it because we have lost touch with our bodies and dismiss the need for regular physical contact? Have we relegated physical touch to only sex and primary relationships?

Yet once you're embodied, your body will start talking to you, giving you signals all the time about what it needs, likes, and doesn't like. When you are in your body, you will be able to read the signals: does this food, touch, situation feel good? When I was healing from my eating disorder, I recognized that my body didn't feel good when I was either totally full or extremely hungry. It felt best when I was eating what my body really needed and not following my mind's suggestions for sugar and foods that gave me an instant high. My body showed me that it didn't like it when I'd consume large amounts of sugar because I would have a burning hot sensation in my face, or I'd feel completely exhausted right after eating.

When I wasn't paying attention to what my body needed, I would overwrite my body's message and continue eating from my mind and my emotions to shut down or hide or stuff or numb. As you become embodied and grounded, and have the skills to better navigate your emotions, you will be able to stop numbing and start nourishing. Positive, consensual physical touch and the lessons of the Embodiment quality can help you stay grounded.

If you have people in your life that you can touch and be close with, enjoy it regularly. No? Not to worry, we can keep ourselves embodied. By creating contact—or touch—with our skin, muscles, bones, and the floor, we are learning another way to become grounded.

How I Learned to Be Embodied

Not long after I met the Dalai Lama, I became disillusioned with my life in NYC. I felt purposeless and wanted to do something more, something meaningful. As one of my many explorations into the healing world, I went to see a homeopathic doctor for guidance. I told him about my lack of clarity and fulfillment. He gave me a remedy and pretty quickly I became very ill and had to go home to my parents for a few days. I had a super high fever, like 105! He told me not to take any pain relievers and just sweat it out.

I vividly remember my recovery, almost like an awakening. I realized I had to make a big decision, though I wasn't exactly sure what that would be. I knew I had to quit my job and trust my intuition. I knew that the corporate world was not the place for me, even though I had a cool and interesting job. I had applied to a graduate program but deferred it for two years. I never thought the university would take me, but I got up the courage and called. The admissions counselor literally said, "What great timing you have! Classes start this week, and we can still accept you."

I went back to grad school, took on massive loans, got my master's in secondary education, and taught English and drama in the New York City public schools. A few years in, I realized I needed to make a much bigger change and leave NYC. I loved my students and we deeply bonded, but something was still missing. I remembered the feeling of being in the mountains and nature, and it somehow soothed my soul when I camped in my sister's backyard, so I fearfully yet courageously moved to Massachusetts and applied for teaching jobs.

Unbeknownst to me, I moved to one of the modern dance hubs of New England, and "the capital of embodiment." Northampton, Massachusetts is a home base for the School for Body-Mind Centering (BMC) founded by Bonnie Bainbridge Cohen. I became totally intrigued by Contact Improvisation, a dance technique in which physical contact provides the starting point for movement, improvisation, and exploration.

When I wasn't teaching and doing theater club with the students, I was dancing and learning. Contact Improv taught me how to use the sensation of touch to get me out of my messy, intolerable mind. I started falling in love with my body and its capabilities. I was able to be tender and powerful, soft and spontaneous, flexible and aware, and eventually, quiet enough to really listen to my body.

While Contact Improvisation requires a partner, you don't have to have a partner in order to experience embodiment:

You can use the floor and your own body. That's why I practice this series of movements rolling on the floor.

I thought leaving NYC and starting over in a new environment would change me, my old ways left behind. But you know the expression, "Wherever you go, there you are" . . . I still had work to do to heal myself and come back into my body fully. This embodied epiphany is how I created the work you are about to experience.

Embodiment Starts with Grounding

When you are embodied, you may notice for the first time that your body is a nice place to be. You will be fully aware of yourself whether you are on the floor or in a chair, or when you are with other people. With practice and intention, you might start to be a little kinder to yourself or less stressed about the way you look or act. This is how we learn to release perfectionism: we are becoming aware of ourselves, instead of self-conscious. What's the difference? Self-consciousness is intrinsically questioning, judging, and uncomfortable, while awareness is noticing, nonjudgmental, and reflective.

You might not notice this energetic shift right away, but other people will. They can sense your ability to be in the moment and will want to be with you. They're responding body to body, not just mind to mind, in a state of complete presence: total attention in the moment.

Embodiment starts with a conscious *grounding*. You are literally connecting yourself to the earth, letting go of the tension we normally carry, finding the safe space that is right inside you. This allows us to create more space in the body, mind, and heart; we feel so present that the to-do list and worries that are typically swimming around can be momentarily forgotten and take a back seat to what's really important.

Grounding helps slow the racing thoughts in the mind, leading to a deep sense of relaxation. We give the critical mind a rest, allowing us to perceive ourselves differently. Your mind has less influence over your decisions because you also have your sensations to rely on. For example, if you're totally exhausted but your to-do list is 8,000 items long, you might ignore the signals your body is sending to take a nap or rest so you don't get run down or burn out. If ignored, eventually your body will send stronger messages, and if you dismiss those, you may end up getting sick or injuring yourself; then you'll be forced to rest. When you're embodied and grounded, you'll hear messages earlier, and you'll be able to make a better decision: *I know I have a ton to do, but I won't be able to do it well because I'm so tired. I need to rest; I just can't do one more thing.* Parents are conditioned to be doers, caretakers, and fixers. When you start listening to the needs of your own body, you might just stop dragging yourself around and start meeting your needs, setting appropriate boundaries, and nourishing you.

On a physical level, grounding feels like an embrace. Some people feel like they just got a big hug or are wrapped up in their comfiest clothes when they are embodied; it's a wonderful cozy feeling. Yet I also know that this experience can feel different for everyone. If you have been "out of your body," living only in your mind, you might feel heavy, weighed down, or fatigued at first, and that's perfectly normal. You might even find release, and be overcome with tears when you let go into the safety of the floor, and that's okay too. Remember, any emotional response means that you finally feel safe enough to experience your body and all its associated feelings.

On an emotional level, grounding teaches us trust. This conscious support can help you let go of stress and tension and begin to trust your body and feel safer in your own skin. We often hold our emotions in safe little compartments, in our psyches *and* in our bodies. If we've gotten the message that we are not safe, these emotions get stuck, almost like a holding pattern. Feeling grounded allows us to also feel safe, and when that happens, we can drop the defense mechanisms that no longer serve us. Then, we can open the compartments of emotions and let them surface, be felt, be fully expressed, and pass through us like a wave.

On a mental level, you are completely letting your thoughts go into the earth, releasing them, letting go of your mental chatter. You will be noticing the sensations of your body touching the ground, but you aren't actively thinking.

On the spiritual level, grounding allows us to connect with our authentic self, source energy, and the great mother of us all, the Earth. And when we tap into it, we are connected to a sense of present-ness. And when we can tap into our soul source energy, the body becomes our sacred home, and we can establish a new relationship within.

The Embodiment Experience

Grounding can occur when you spend time in nature, literally putting your bare feet on the ground. Or it can be done through embodied movement, which is what we will focus on in this quality. Being embodied means our focus is available to our physical structure and on its sensations. The Embodiment quality includes slow floor work that softens the body so that you can relax and open the mind.

At first, your mind might be telling you that this type of movement seems weird or a waste of time. The mind does not want the body to be in charge, because if the body ran the show, everything would be much slower. The pace of the body cannot match the speed of the mind, and it will never catch up with its lightning-fast processor. If the mind was a MacBook Pro, your body would be a typewriter.

When we live in our minds, we can think as quickly as our imagination can conjure. And because the mind is always pushing the body, telling it what to do, the idea of rolling on the floor without specific direction takes a little adjustment time. Yet something wonderful happens—in just a few minutes, your ruminating thoughts begin to dissolve as you become aware of how you are interacting with the ground.

When you move in the Embodiment quality, you will come into a sense of flow and fluidity. You will be literally pouring your body onto the dance floor, like water. The fluidity of the music reminds us that we're not as solid as we think. The truth is, the human body is made of roughly 50 to 60 percent water, down to the cellular level. There has been interesting research done regarding the intelligence of water, and the power of thought and feeling and its effects on water. In *The Hidden Messages in Water,* Dr. Masaru Emoto proposed that water understands language and emotion. Dr. Emoto's team took photographs of water under a microscope to determine if crystalline patterns were influenced by language. I know it might sound impossible, but his study showed what I and many others have always believed: When he used words that were loving, positive, inspiring, and kind, the water crystals were beautiful and complex, like snowflakes. No crystals formed when the words were demeaning, punishing, or altogether absent.

Dr. Emoto extrapolates his findings: "If we consider that the human body is a universe within itself, it is only natural to conclude that we carry within us all the elements."

Because we are basically a fluid system, our bodies carry the intelligence of water. I know this concept is pretty out there but stay with me for a moment. You have nothing to lose, except your negative self-talk. If you believe your words and thoughts matter, it's so much more beneficial to speak positively to yourself about yourself. Whenever you catch yourself speaking negatively about you, remember that your body, your cellular awareness, is listening.

Our breath itself is grounding, and the way you will breathe in this quality is different from all the others. You will move with your whole self—from your core center—and breathe into every cell. You will feel each inhale and exhale as you become aware of the fullness of your body and breath. The breath is connected to every movement, inhaling to expand, and exhaling to release so we can synchronize to our own flow, feeling and hearing our breath. Then as we stretch, it feels as though our body could extend a mile. It's a slow, deep awareness that creates that lengthening sensation.

Dr. Steph, who danced with me for many years and did a scientific analysis of what is happening in each of the qualities, noticed that in Embodiment, the gentle rocking and rolling generates a state of balance by activating the parasympathetic nervous system. This allows for more flexibility, increased lung capacity, and increased access to right-brain activity.

Though you might not think that getting down on the floor is helpful, occupational therapists do similar work with children on the autism spectrum. For example, the therapists wrap them up in carpets to provide a feeling of compression. They do skin brushing, horseback riding, and swimming in order to give them a tactile sense of their body. These are all ways to embody from the external to the internal, soothing the nervous system.

Most people do not like to get down on the floor, but I promise that once you learn how to do this embodiment work, you will fall in love with the floor. You'll find that touching all your body's surfaces to the floor feels totally grounding and even pleasurable. The dance grounds and cleanses us on every level from the physical to the energetic. When you stretch and expand, you'll notice and feel every part of you. And when you contract and twist, it's as if you're rinsing and wringing out the flesh and tissues to allow your blood to flow, making you more flexible and supple.

Music: Access Embodiment with Me!

The music I have chosen for the Embodiment quality will help you slow down and connect with the earth so that you can feel grounded to the floor. It is deep, slow, luscious, thick, and heavy. It features slow drums with long tones of the didgeridoo, slow vocal toning, and an electronic slow pulse. It's deeply relaxing and inspiring. These sounds work perfectly together to create the sensation of connecting into the force of gravity so that you can let go.

Start the music as you read your invocation and begin your movement practice. This playlist is over an hour's worth of perfect music for this quality. You can play as many of these songs as you like, in any order you want. There's no prescribed beginning or end.

These are the songs that have been specially chosen for this quality. Remember, this is the beginning of the playlist:

- "Tabla Breath" by Benjy Wertheimer and John de Kadt
- "Eastern Slide" by Dub Sutra
- "The Sheer Weight of Memory" by Bob Holroyd
- "Cosmic Flow" by Maneesh De Moor
- "Ecstatic Grounding" by Liquid Bloom
- "Snake Charmer" by Desert Dwellers
- "Sensory Skin" by Lis Addison
- "Koyangwuti" by Deya Dova

Find the full playlist in the *Embody* portal.

An Embodiment Invocation

Changing our relationship with our body takes time. Many of us have been mean, unkind, or even abusive to our bodies. But we can shift the old patterns of thinking to find

peace and love in our sacred body. When you change how you think and speak about yourself, it becomes possible to fall in love with yourself. Read the following invocation to start the shift; you may begin to think about yourself in a whole new way.

> Say aloud, and feel the power of your words:
>
> Dear Body, Earth, Gaia, Mother of all,
>
> I know that I come from you, my natural mother.
>
> I am part of nature, like my mother, and her mother before her, and all of my ancestors.
>
> Thank you for bestowing upon me this natural beauty.
>
> I deeply love and appreciate my body. More and more, day by day, I love my body exactly as it is. I accept the changes and shifts my body makes as I travel the path of life.
>
> My body allows me the pleasure of being alive.
>
> I deeply and truly forgive my body for any ways I may have felt betrayed by it. I deeply and truly forgive myself for any ways I have hurt my body consciously or unconsciously.
>
> I love you, my body. I love my cells, my blood, my skin, my bones, my muscles, my organs down to my very core.
>
> I love myself on a cellular level.
>
> From this moment forward, I see myself and love my body fully and completely.

The Embodied Movement Practice

Very soon you will put this book down and slowly come to the floor beneath you. I know this sounds strange, but here you are, so let's do it. Notice that there are no photographs for you to model a specific movement. I want you to be able to move organically where your body needs to go.

First, read the following description so you understand it. Prepare yourself with a mat or blanket if needed for comfort. The simple illustrations serve as inspiration to guide your shapes and movements.

Then, anytime you want to close your eyes while you are dancing this quality, please do. Your proprioception—*the perception of the position and movement of your body*—can increase when your eyes are closed as you rely on feeling where your body is in space.

It's time to enter your sacred container and begin.

Sit in a comfortable position, and bring your hands to your heart and move in easy circles. Use your breath to bring your body to a calm state and begin to let the mind relax. Inhale with long, slow breaths. Release your hands and allow them to follow the movement of your torso as you reach, stretch, or expand, and exhale to release, soften, or contract. Slowly circle the hips and pelvis. Feel what needs more opening and circle and stretch by leaning into what feels good.

After you circle the hips and pelvis in both directions, move to the chest and create more circles, letting the chest and heart lead. You can allow gentle half circles of the neck,

moving from one side to the other. Notice your body becoming warmer. Slowly open and widen the legs, sitting in a comfortable V-shape. Inhale as you expand and widen your legs, and exhale as you contract and bring your legs back together. Repeat a few times bringing the legs close together and then apart, warming the hips.

With legs in a moderately wide V, let your upper body lean right and left, and gently trace the edges of your body with your fingertips to bring your awareness to your body. Flow like water, side to side, reaching for your feet and back to center; keep it flowing and moving by feeling your weight shift and return to center and to the other side. Notice your breath inhaling to reach and exhaling to release. Move intuitively and organically, staying in this slow space. Play in this space until your legs are touching again, and then bend the knees and roll slowly down to the floor onto your back. Feel your body against the wood, carpet, or flooring. Feel your weight as you let go to gravity.

Now, on your back, slowly raise your legs and bend your knees. Circle your knees in the air. Gently massage your back and your sacrum into the floor. Slowly start rocking side to side. Explore your hands and feet in the air. Warm them up, making circles, pressing one up and one down, stretching and rocking onto your sides and back. Allow yourself to stretch gently in this side-to-side motion. You can create long diagonals, leaving your legs on one side, gently twisting. Then bring the legs back to center.

Next, fully expand to form a wide X like a snow angel, with your arms and legs splayed out as far as you can from your body as you take in a breath, and then fully contract into a fetal position, lying on one side, as you release the breath. Stretch out and then ball up, open and close your whole body a few times, alternating from one side to the other. Make this movement slowly—move like a sea creature oozing and waving—and enjoy letting your body move as it wants, rolling, pouring, and getting acquainted with a new sense of your skin and the back and sides of your body.

Next, add the belly. Start to roll, pouring yourself onto the floor like honey or a slower feeling of molasses. When on your belly, notice yourself connecting deeply with the earth, pouring your body across the space, and drop into the sensation of the fluid body. Release the belly to the floor and notice and ask yourself, *Can I soften into the earth and roll my body to increase the flow of fluids to my tissues and organs?* Move organically, feeling your belly, your armpits, the backs of your feet.

Initiate slow rocking any time you want to stay for a moment. Rocking soothes the nervous system and brings warmth to tight areas. Touch every part of your body to the floor while you listen to your breath and the music. Connect with the surfaces of your skin and explore the structure of your back and front. I call this *total surface area dancing*. As you move slowly in the flowing, pouring, rolling, you will begin to feel every last part of you as if you were connected to the earth itself. You may notice your skin, muscles, bones being gently massaged and touched by the floor. Lead your movement with your hand reaching or from your big toe and allow your body to follow its lead.

Once you get this rolling and pouring sensation movement going, you can begin to sense and feel your *fascia*, your body's connective tissue. The fascia is like a soft rubber band connecting your bone to your muscle to your skin. It feels similar to the sensation of stretching, but the fascia is layered deeper than the skin. It helps hold our structure in place, so if you are stuck in an old pattern, this kind of practice can release some of the stickiness. As you've learned, "Your issues are in your tissues," and your fascia may be holding onto your emotions. By engaging your fascia with stretching and softening, you can begin to release what you are storing. Allow yourself to feel your entire body moving so slowly and connected, every inch a mile.

In time, you may feel as if your body is doing these movements all on its own. If you can let go of the idea of movement as a specific pose or exercise, your body will explore movement on its own. Don't be surprised: when the fascia is engaged it begins to unwind and takes you to where it wants to go.

While moving in all the ways I've described, see if you can let go even more into the experience and become a creature, as if you were a snake moving across the floor. Allow your body to lose its normal thinking of different body parts and become one organism, totally present in all parts at once. Try an *ssssss* sound to stimulate the spine and see if that helps you slither or creep on the floor. Feeling your belly against the floor like a snake gently moving through the grass, allow your senses to sink deeper into the earth and move with the great Mother Earth herself.

That, my dear friends, is the beginning of embodiment. If you did this exercise for five minutes or more you would probably start feeling a little more fluid, maybe even a little more flexible. If you are in any pain, please put some cushioning under you so you can experience as much as possible; if you are enjoying this feeling, try adding more movement and slide and roll and pour, softening your flesh over the bones and becoming more supple, flexible, grounded, and present.

Movement Suggestions for Embodiment

Keep these movement phrases in mind as you practice the movement section of embodiment:

- Feel your weight as you let go to gravity.
- Slowly roll and pour.
- Massage your sacrum into the floor.
- Explore your hands and feet in the air.
- Feel your belly, your armpits, the backs of your feet.
- Pour your body like you are made of honey or molasses.
- Feel the floor with your total surface area.
- Imagine and feel the slowness, "every inch a mile."

Messages for Your Body

After your dance, say the following to yourself:

I love you, body.

My body loves me.

I take care of my body because it is my home.

I love my home.

My body is a beautiful place to live.

I thank you, body, for every day of life.

I am Alive!

Mystical Inquiry: A Grounding Visualization

The mystical inquiry of embodiment is truly about releasing your sense of control as you merge with the music, the floor, and your body. Now that you have completed your movement practice, contemplate your relationship with trust and presence. Embodiment is about trust. Deep trust requires a sense of inner safety. Feeling you're in oneness with your body and that you are deeply supported can transport you into a sense of complete trust.

Continue playing the music from the playlist, and read the following a few times before you begin. You can do this visualization with your eyes closed, if that's available to you.

Stand with your feet hip-width apart and slightly bend your knees, or sit on the floor or in a chair as straight as is comfortable. Take a few relaxing breaths and allow your body to settle. Gently notice your legs and feet and imagine them connecting more deeply into the floor. Sense if you feel your weight in the space, or if you can hardly feel your feet on the ground. Imagine you are standing on dirt or sand, and sink your feet in, just a little bit.

Now, imagine a cord or stream of color coming down from the sky into the top of your head and down into your body. This will become your grounding cord. Let it be whatever color you see. Let it be straight, wavy, curly, springy, solid, thick. Let it be what you personally need it to be.

Now, drop your cord down through the center line of your body and into the earth. Let it slowly sink down through the floor of your house or apartment, down, down, down until it touches the earth. Let it sink into the soil, the rocks, and the deeper layers of the earth.

In your mind's eye, see the dirt and rocks, and imagine a beautiful crystal. You can attach your cord to it, or allow your cord to grow and spread out like tree roots. According to *Your Aura and Your Chakras* by Karla McLaren, if you feel very grounded and you need a cord that moves with you, make it springy. If you feel very ungrounded, make it a thick cord and root it down and wrap it around the crystal, giving you a stronger sense of connection with the earth.

Now, gently breathe and *sense* your presence. Feel your feet on the ground again. Notice how your weight in the space may have shifted. Gently open your eyes in this grounded state.

You can visualize different versions of this experience and change the colors, thickness, or shape of your grounding cord, based on what you need in the moment.

Embodied Awareness Personal Practice Journaling

Reflection is a key ingredient to growth, personal development, and transformation. While we can do all the movements and visualizations listed throughout the practice, it's reflection that allows us to develop awareness that will help us away from the dance floor.

Becoming present and mindful, we can notice and respond differently to our old activations and limbic responses. I can't change what happened to me, or you, though I wish I could. I can't take away the conditioning that has made us react in our particular way. Yet embodiment brings me the presence to pause and sense what is happening in my body moment to moment. For me, I've come to the awareness that when I feel angry, a physical heat rush comes up through my body, and I know that I've been activated. Your sensations may be different.

Once you can recognize your body cues, you don't have to react to them, or try to shut them down. In fact, if you can recognize when that feeling is first coming, that split second, you have the potential consciousness to make a different choice in the moment. That's true awareness, which is the whole key to growth.

The following questions will help you tap into your awareness. Journal your answers.

- How are you feeling after this first practice?
- Can you feel love for your body, exactly as it is? How it looks, how it moves?
- What was it like to merge into the music and become pure sensation?
- Can you notice what takes you out of your body, and when you are "in" or "out"?
- When you are caught in a mental or emotional loop, what happens to your body?
- When you slow down and follow your body's natural movements, what happens to your breathing and your nervous system?
- Were you able to let go into the earth and feel supported?

Close the Practice with the Embodiment *Prayer*

Read aloud:

I feel fully connected to my body and to this earth.

I am a beautiful, fluid creature, in touch with every part of my body.

I inhabit my body fully.

I see myself through the eyes of love.

I allow all my judgments of my body to fall away like leaves falling from a tree.

I ask that my mind only compliment and care for my body.

I treat myself with total and complete compassion for my body.

I honor my body for all that I've been through, all my experiences, this body's lifelong development.

I honor its growing, changing, and s[age]ing process, and I nurture it with all my heart.

I love my body in a mature and confident way as I learn to appreciate myself anew.

CHAPTER 4

Awakening

Awakening is a new dawn, a new day. It's that moment when you look at yourself and the world differently, where everything comes together in a new way. You gain a deeper understanding of who you really are. You already have a self-concept, an identity, and ways of being, yet there's always much more to discover.

After completing the Embodiment quality, you may already feel a new sense of being present and aware. The Awakening quality begins to open your sensual nature, your energy, your vital life force, all of which are associated with feeling good about yourself. This quality is about getting into the body in a way that is total ownership, where you feel comfortable and confident in your own skin.

Our physical body generates energy like a battery, and we have energy to spare. We want to move and circulate our energy, get it flowing, and be in contact with it. We don't want it to be stagnant. Many energy medicine systems, including traditional Chinese medicine and Ayurveda, recognize that our primal energy lives in the base of the spine. In Awakening, we bring this energy up and through the sexual organs. The spine, along with the nervous system, acts as a conduit, bringing this energy to the rest of the body. In this practice, we're purposefully moving our energy up through the body so that we can use it for creativity and to feed our passion for life and purposefulness.

You'll probably have many awakenings in your life as you learn new insights about yourself. But if you don't have the vital energy force to move forward and create change, you might remain stuck with your old ways and beliefs. Personal growth requires energy and effort, and this quality awakens your energy.

In the Embodiment quality, you learned the beginnings of fluidity, of pouring yourself on the floor. Now we're going to explore how to organically move from the floor up toward standing. This in-between stage or midlevel location is where there's so much potential for movement exploration, and what we call sensationality, that is, the ability to awaken and feel all your sensations. In an elevated prone position, you will see where your body is relaxed and free, and where it is tight. Later on, you will learn about the Sensual quality, where you'll explore moving with sensuality, expressing yourself in this very powerful way. Awakening is the first quality that helps us get there.

OUR PSYCHIC ENERGY

Every one of us is psychically intuitive. You might think this phenomenon is limited to tarot or akashic readings, yet there are many different kinds of natural psychic intuition. You may have heard of *clairvoyance* or met a psychic reader who "sees," a *clairaudient* who "hears," or a *claircognizant* who "just knows."

There is also a *clairsentient* who is a person who "feels." Being clairsentient is much more common than people realize. Many people have this psychic sense in their bodies. Have you ever had a "gut reaction" to something, or a change in your energy, or feel a physical sensation, like chills, tingles, or sweats, and thought, *Maybe I should pay attention to this?* The truth is, your body sends these signals and reactions all the time. As you become more aware of your energetic senses, you can tune into your body's messages and make new choices more quickly to take care of yourself, energetically, emotionally, and physically. You will also know when and with whom you want to spend your precious time and share your life force.

We also interact with the energy of others, and our body takes an instant energetic reading. The vibes we feel, our attractions or aversions, are part of this energetic screening process. Although these first impressions might be decoded as thoughts (anything from *I feel uncomfortable* to *I feel safe here*) they are really informational downloads from your energetic body. This is why it's so important to understand your energy—both physical and energetic—and how to read, work with, and replenish it. A clairsentient tends to feel drained or inspired by people and situations, so knowing that you are actually affected by someone else's energy is a real thing. Stop doubting yourself when you have a strong knowing in whatever way it appears to you. As a clairsentient, I have learned how to listen to my feelings and sensations, how to trust what I'm sensing, and know that this is a psychic ability of mine.

Take a moment and think about the following:

Do you have a sense of your energy?

How are you impacted by other people's energy?

Do you take up a lot of energetic space, or do you contract around others?

Are your interactions conscious or unconscious, highly sensitive or generally not?

You can find your type in the book, *You Are Psychic,* by MIT scientist Pete A. Sanders Jr.

Awakening My Self-Confidence

It took me years to own my power and find my confidence. I was afraid to feel amazing in my own body, and to really love myself. I was very shy and insecure, which most people don't believe because I'm such an outgoing person. In a room of dancers, I'm confident because I know how to move my body and I can follow and connect pretty quickly. But at a schmoozing networking party, or anything social, I really never felt comfortable.

I trace the way my personality developed back to two distinct incidents that happened around the same time. When I was twelve going on thirteen, it seemed like my body changed overnight. I woke up one morning and I was 5'2" with a 38DD chest. I was way too innocent and immature to be able to handle the comments and reactions I received about my body. My self-esteem was impacted immediately by the way the rest of the world started treating me. I suddenly felt objectified, and uncomfortable, and I know that the same is true for many women at this turning point.

Shortly after my body's transformation into full female development, I was attacked in a swimming pool. I remember the incident clearly. It was a hot day at the town pool, and I was wearing my first womanly bathing suit since I could no longer fit my tween suit. I was playing a child's game of "catch the key," thinking that I'm twelve, but looking sixteen. I was diving underwater when I got attacked. A man grabbed and touched me inappropriately. In my effort to get away I kicked him as hard as I could, and then swam and struggled to get out of the pool as quickly as possible. My father was relaxing poolside, quietly reading his book about Mozart, completely unaware of what had just happened. I don't blame him for not watching; he knew I was a good swimmer.

When I told my father what happened he was so distressed he began running around the pool looking for the guy, yelling and shouting. We reported the situation. I needed him to hug me and say, "Everything is going to be okay, honey, everything is going to be okay. You won't feel like this forever. You won't always feel this scared." But he was so distraught, he didn't realize what I needed at that moment. Later I learned that to heal, each of us has to take on that inner parenting role, reassure ourselves, and give ourselves what we need. That reparenting is repatterning.

Back in that moment I was terrified, not just because of the incident, but that earlier in the day my father and I had to go to the pool office to get our passes and gave our address and phone number aloud to the clerk. I realized that the man who attacked me was sitting there in the office at the time, and I also remember him looking at me and I felt my body's alarm go off, warning that I was not safe. I was terrified he was going to come to my house and do something more to me because he didn't get what he wanted.

As soon as we got home, my mother made an appointment for me with my first therapist. I was so scared to go to therapy and talk about what happened, as I was so fully embarrassed to say the words and describe what happened. I don't know whether it was this incident that propelled my mom to make a huge career change, but the next thing I knew she enrolled herself in social work school. All through my teen years I became her guinea pig, her homework buddy. She read everything out loud. I was basically in graduate school with her. Through osmosis, I became obsessed with personal growth.

At the same time, this trauma not only affected the way I carried myself but it created certain behaviors. I was forever slouching as if to disappear. If a man looked at me in a particular way, I became extremely nervous. In junior high and high school, I wore baggy clothes because I didn't want anyone to see my rapidly changing body. By the time I was in college I was getting a lot of attention and became more confident in my sexuality, but there was still a scared little girl inside me. To protect her, I learned to use my sexuality as a way to assert my power; I became "the hunter" rather than "the hunted." Yet it was unfulfilling. In both of these strategies, I was still not in my body.

It was a significant challenge for me to get back into my body and feel safe inside myself. I was in the escape hatch, which we talked about in Chapter 1, for much too long. I wanted to be able to have a real relationship, be vulnerable with someone, and have deep intimacy.

Eventually, and with a lot of personal embodiment work, I regained my confidence and got back into my body. I focused my personal dance practice on how I felt instead of how I looked, and I never danced in front of mirrors again. The space between the floor and standing became my favorite area to explore: It became a place where I could open up and feel the joy and freedom of my flowing movements. I could embrace the pulse of my own expressive body, sensually, safely, and on my own terms. It totally changed the way I feel about myself, and I want the same for you.

I created Awakening by weaving together everything I was studying, from tantric breath work to recirculating sexual energy to Vinyasa yoga, aikido rolling, and modern dance. When I added music to the experience, the movement became transcendent.

Too many people have stories like mine, or worse, and are working through and healing childhood sexual trauma. Whatever you've been through, whatever you've experienced, you deserve to reclaim your body. This Awakening practice may provide an important first step for you, as it did for me.

READY TO TAKE A RISK?

I've worked with thousands of people who have experienced some type of childhood sexual trauma, and they often leave the dance floor feeling a sense of reclamation and joy. The reason that they're successful is because they become reconnected to their body through JourneyDance. They needed to feel all their feelings—the joy, the pain, the sadness, the angst, even the shame and the forgiveness—and start to experience themselves as a whole being through movement.

Awakening requires that you go outside your comfort zone to move into a new story about your sensual body. It may feel a little risky compared to Embodiment, because you will do the movement practice in a very intimate, animalistic posture. If it feels a bit edgy for you, you can titrate your experience. You may at first feel inhibited because of the physical position, but if you create your sacred container and practice a couple of songs each day, you can get comfortable. I want you to have a good experience with these movements because it's the best way I know for you to get to know your pelvis, hips, belly, and chest. It's both sensual and purposeful. You've got nothing to lose except your inhibitions, and you've got so much to gain: you can embrace the entire terrain of your body and your vital energy.

Matt Licata, PhD, is an embodied psychotherapist who writes so eloquently about self-discovery. Here is a quote from one of my favorites of his writings, to inspire you.

> "Something new is being born inside you, but something else is dying. The invitation before you is to stay present to the uncertainty, the chaos, and the groundless

reorganization. While it may be terrifying and disorienting to the density of the mind, the creativity of the sensual world is overwhelming and outrageous. Trust in the fires of disintegration."

The Awakening Experience

Awakening is about rekindling the fluidity of the body, finding freedom, and giving yourself permission. On a physical level, you're going to be bringing your energy to the spine through breath and pumping action of the belly. We let go of rigidity and breathe into the tight places that need space, warmth, and attention. The movements are done in a midlevel prone position (like a tabletop or cat pose in yoga), where you can be totally sensual and expressive in a very safe way. These movements take you out of the constraints that society has put on us about our bodily expression. Many people have been told the body is a source of sin and a problem. I want to change that. I don't want the body to be the problem; I want the body to be the answer. I want the body to be where we go to get wisdom, not the place where we shut down. By doing these freeing movements, you're breaking out of the box, letting yourself express, explore, and connect with the parts that are often shamed by society. Through these movements you can build confidence, because if you feel good about moving in this particular way, you can feel good about yourself in all kinds of spaces.

On an emotional level, the mind has a lot of opinions about the body! Whatever fitness state you're in, whatever age you are, and whatever aches or pains you may have (physical or emotional), it's time to learn to love your body. Though it has changed in shape, size, and form, through all of your experiences, it is still uniquely yours. Yours—my friend—YOURS. You are on a journey to see and feel your body through the eyes of compassion, empathy, joy, and passion.

On the mental level, you may notice your comfort and discomfort with this kind of physical expression, and become aware of your associated thoughts, how you judge yourself, or give yourself permission to be sensual. You'll notice your inner dialogue and if it is loving and allowing, or unkind and critical.

On a spiritual level, Awakening is a rebirth where you are rising up to a new awareness. You claim ownership of yourself, unlocking divine sexual/sensual energy, and when liberated, your creative channels will open. Your intuition becomes more available, and that energy can lift your spirit.

Music: Move and Awaken with Me!

The music to access Awakening has a watery quality: pulsing, wavy, melodic with light percussion, slow to medium tempo. It has a distinct energy that your body can respond to.

Start the music as you read your invocation and begin your movement practice. This playlist is over an hour's worth of perfect music for this quality, ranging from light and slow to more intense. You can play as many of these songs as you like, in any order you want. There's no prescribed beginning or end. For this playlist I start on the slower side and progress to faster rhythms.

These are the songs that have been specially chosen for the Awakening quality. Remember, this is the beginning of the playlist:

- "River Goddess" by Maneesh de Moor
- "Don't Forget to Breathe" by Bitter:Sweet
- "Resonant Migration" by Liquid Bloom
- "River" by Ibeyi
- "Beauty Beats" by Beats Antique

- "Saraswati's Twerkaba" by Desert Dwellers and David Starfire
- "Rubedo" by Drumspyder
- "Liquid" by Share the Light
- "Ohm" by SOOHAN
- "Tribal Trap" by Peace Sine

Find the full playlist in the *Embody* portal.

An Awakening Invocation

Say aloud, and feel the power of your words:

Dear Source, Creation, Energy,

I invite my vital energy to be awakened.

I am willing to explore parts of myself that I have left dormant, suppressed, or shut down.

I am open to feeling my energy and expanding my movement potential.

I am excited to bring movement to places I don't normally move.

I am ready to feel sensual, creative, and confident.

I trust my body to give me insight as I awaken to more energy.

I give myself permission to feel fully alive in my sensuality.

And so it is.

Awakening Movement Practice

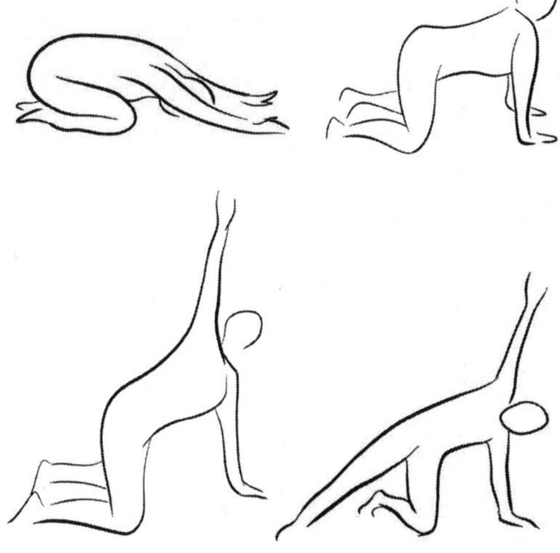

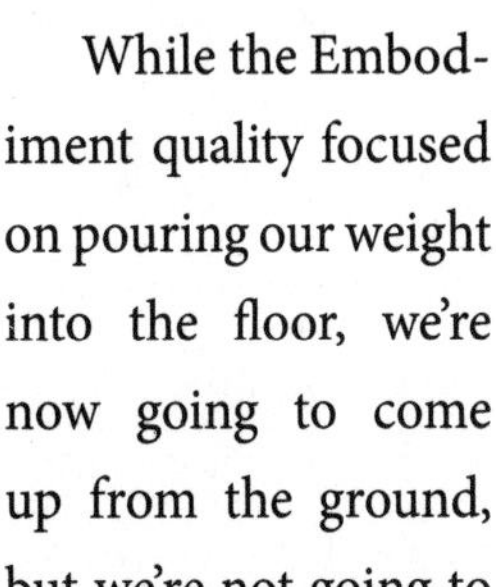

While the Embodiment quality focused on pouring our weight into the floor, we're now going to come up from the ground, but we're not going to stand. Let's stay in a middle zone and focus on what I call the *animal body/primal movement*: the hips, pelvis, spine, tail, and butt. For those who have experienced certain traumas, including sexual trauma, these areas may feel blocked or tight. This practice is intended to open your body, which may bring up dormant feelings. Take it slowly and move at your own pace.

Moving in the table position will help you determine where you hold tension, especially in the hips and shoulders. In this elevated prone position, you have a different relationship to gravity. Movement increases blood flow and the circulation of synovial fluid to the joints to keep them supple. The more you move, the more movement you'll have available to you.

Awakening is a feeling of being like water, emerging with flow and pleasure. I call this *feeling your liquid body*. Your body is a vessel, and the vessel contains water. You can move

with slow fluidity that warms the body and brings flexibility to the spine. You can stretch the back and torso to stimulate and strengthen the abdominal muscles. You can open the chest so that you can breathe more deeply. At the same time, the movements of lifting and lowering will stimulate the kidneys and adrenal glands, which, in combination with deep breathing, relieve stress and calm the mind. This can help to develop postural awareness and balance.

Dr. Steph explains that the gentle undulations simultaneously relax and invigorate soft tissue in the core. This allows for increased circulation, which oxygenates and detoxifies the tissue and muscles. Your range of motion is enhanced, which allows for higher levels of sensory awareness and nervous system communication. As you increase the speed and range of your movement, you create oscillations and waves so the lymph—the fluid system that detoxifies the body—can flow. The lymph is the only pump in the body that doesn't have an actual pump, so we have to move in order to pump the lymph to detoxify. As we're detoxifying, we can shed toxins, negative feelings, and old, stored emotions.

Make sure you have enough space to get comfortably into a table position. If you have trouble or difficulty being on the knees, place a thick mat, folded towel, or other cushioning under your knees. If you cannot access this position, explore the movements sitting in a chair. Anytime you want to close your eyes while you are dancing this quality, please do.

It's time to enter your sacred container and begin.

Begin lying down with your belly on the floor. Lay your head on your hands and wiggle gently, feel your belly connecting to the earth and notice your spine moving. Take a few breaths here, wiggling to warm the spine, making a little space. Slowly lift your head and bring your hands and forearms under your shoulders. Stretch and breathe. Slide your shoulders side to side.

Bend your knees and carefully come up into child's pose, folding your knees under your chest. Slowly breathe into the pelvis and exhale gently, then breathe into the chest and exhale. Notice how your body moves with the breath, and begin to lift up slightly to a low table position, with your elbows and forearms on the ground and your chest slightly lifted. Begin making a small wave from the pelvis to the chest, gently awakening the spine. Feel free to pulse the spine up and down, lifting and lowering a few times, allowing your pelvis and chest to move accordingly. Feel the music and move organically. There is no right or wrong here, just remember my rule: "no mistakes, only learning," and there's no need to try to look a certain way.

As you feel a bit warmer, slowly rise up to full table, hands underneath your shoulders, knees and shins still facing the ground. Keep your head in line with the torso, not dropping it too far forward or back; let it be part of the spine. Begin to breathe deeply, and on the exhale, gently pull the belly to the spine. Take a few deep breaths with a forceful exhale. Expand the belly with the inhale, and then pull that belly to the spine on the exhale. Keep a gentle contraction of the abs throughout the practice in order to support your lower back. Don't worry if you let it go now and then, just be conscious of your body and don't do anything that hurts.

Let your spine move up and down in a wavelike motion, from small to large, starting with a pulse at your tail, and follow it, traveling up to your head. If you are familiar with the practice of yoga asana from India, this movement will be like cat-cow as if dancing. Imagine you are a cat, stretching and exploring. Feel the pleasure of the body moving gently as you let your spine, pelvis, and chest pulse and flow. Allow your breath to move with your body, sometimes sounding the breath aloud, whenever you feel the impulse. If you can roll your tongue in a purring sound, go for it, *rrrrrrrrrrrr*. Gently move in circular waves, both parallel and perpendicular, as you undulate and wave side to side and up and down. Focus on your pelvis and gently rock up and down. Let yourself move and explore your tempo and range of motion as you feel the music. Let the hips move side to side, making small or large circles.

Allow your spinal waves to slow as you focus on your chest. Let your chest pulse up and down, making space in the shoulders. Feel free to rock the chest side to side, making circles in both directions. Keep your neck relaxed and let it move with the spine. Feel the pleasure of your liquid body moving from pulsations to waves and back again. Imagine for a moment that you're a wave of water, a flowing river. If you were water, how would you move?

Continue to be aware of your breath flowing with your body as you move in circular waves, parallel and perpendicular. Let the water in your body flow, ooze, and pulse. Explore what feels good, notice your sensations, and pause in those spaces to open up and feel into it. Notice if there are any numb or tense areas, and gently bring movement there. Energy may begin to unlock, you may start to feel uninhibited, and you may feel much warmer.

Let's go a little bigger with our movement and explore balance and freedom. Staying in table position, let one arm rise and fall as you enlarge your dance. Feel what's possible to gently open up. Then try the other side. After a few explorations, bring both hands back down and lift one leg off the ground, open your hip, and make some exploratory circles. Remember my other rule, "don't hurt yourself"; just see what's available to you. With experience you will develop more range of motion. Switch legs and open the other side.

Now you have more possibilities. You can crawl a bit and lift your knees off the ground. You can "walk" on your hands and feet, building upper body strength. Feel free to explore being a dancing four-legged creature.

Place one foot on the floor in front of you so are in a low lunge. Move your arm up and down to open the space, extend your arm like a branch moving in the wind. Try the other side a few times. Allow this movement to grow and explore your animal body.

As we rise, lift your knees off the floor. With your hands and feet still on the floor, gently come to your feet by walking it out, stretching out the backs of your legs, calves, and ankles, pressing one foot into the floor and then the other. Back up your hands to move slowly toward your feet, transfer your weight to the legs, and rise up, swaying into a standing position. Continue to flow and wave side to side into standing.

How are you feeling now? Are you energized? We used the body to increase our energy level and feel a visceral sense of aliveness. These movements are so energizing that you might want to do the Awakening quality every morning. Every time I do the Awakening practice, it transforms my energy. I feel ready, I have that get-up-and-go energy, and I'm ready to get busy living.

Movement Suggestions for Awakening

Keep these movement phrases in mind as you practice the movement section of Awakening:

- You are a wave of water, a flowing river.
- Make space in your spine.
- Envision a cat stretching.
- Send a wave from tail to head, up your spine.
- Notice feeling sensation.

- Find and move numb or tense areas.
- If you were water, how would you move?
- Let the water in your body flow.
- Think of words like: ooze, pulse, flow, wave, stretch.

Mystical Inquiry: A Visualization for Awakening Vital Energy

I'd like to invite you into a visualization that might help you sense more of Awakening's energetic flow in your life.

Sit comfortably and ground yourself with your grounding cord from the previous chapter. Close your eyes and imagine a pool of light just underground. Let it be a vibrant color that suits you, like gold or orange or iridescent. Imagine breathing this beautiful light in right through your body, coming in through the base of your spine and up into your sexual organs. Bring it up and through your body, like you could take it through your spine and out to your limbs, up through the neck, and into your face. Fill yourself with this healing energy.

Allow it to circulate all around your body like light traveling, and move it to any tight or numb areas. Linger in these areas for a moment, bringing more energy to any places you are not loving of or that you avoid embracing. Feed your body with this loving vibrant energy. If you feel yourself smile, take a moment and revel in that sensation.

Sit in this energy bath for as long as you like and then gently open your eyes.

Awakening Personal Practice Journaling

- As you begin to free the spine and pelvis, what energies arise within you?
- Can you be with these energies in a nonjudgmental way?
- What blocks or frees your ability to feel sensuality?
- Were you able to bring energy to places in your body that you have judged or been mean or critical to previously?
- How is your energy? Can you sense any change?

Messages for Your Energetic Awakening

After your dance, say the following to yourself:

I feel my energy.

I love my spine.

I love my pelvis.

I flow like water.

I am liquid light.

I am awakened.

Close the Practice with the Awakening *Prayer*

Dear Sensationality, Liquid Life, Primal Body,

Thank you for this sensual animal body that I can move in so many ways to awaken my vital energy.

Thank you for awakening my sensuality and my sexuality, and any other areas of my life that I've been holding in dormancy.

Thank you for awakening any parts of me that were stagnant or inflexible.

I take more pleasure in each moment, reawakening my miraculous body.

I love and appreciate how my sensuality directly affects how I feel about myself.

I can love myself more and more, and embrace more of me.

I engage with my body with new eyes to go deeper inside.

I am awake and alive! 

CHAPTER 5

Immersion and Expansion

The Immersion quality allows us to travel inward, to focus so deeply in the moment when there is no future, no past—just here and now. Immersion is like an entrancement: a hypnotic experience of seeing yourself, discovering yourself, and moving with every part of you. You will blur the outside world of distractions and come closer to knowing yourself. When you can immerse yourself in the moment with your mind, your body, and your movements, you develop a loving relationship with yourself that expands out into your life. Then you can discover the beauty of your own body, expand into more fullness, learn to take up your appropriate space, stop hiding, and start shining.

I invite you to see yourself, really see yourself in a new way, through the eyes of appreciation. Not through eyes of disgruntled, *I don't like myself* voices, but with new wonder and curiosity. None of us has time to waste on self-victimizing, diminishing self-talk anymore.

We have to heal our "not enoughness" and our self-critical minds so we can get out into the world and do something meaningful and life-giving with our precious life.

You'll be focusing on your body with your eyes and your inner vision, not in a mirror, and really looking, learning a new way to appreciate yourself. You are going to tell your body "I love you" part by part and slowly break down the negative, conditioned messages that you've taken in and perpetuated. The practice is not about how soft and smooth your hands are, or whether your hair looks pretty, or any other external "beauty." It's about discovering that *you are a miracle.* Your hands have done so many good things in this world, from the basics of cooking, cleaning, caring for your beloveds to working, creating, writing, and loving. This body is what allows you to live, feel, and express. It is your vehicle for your soul's journey. It's time to see yourself anew, with wonder.

Once you can embody yourself in a loving way, you no longer have to carry self-criticism and unworthiness, and you begin to find the freedom to expand, take up space, and explore the world. The Expansion quality encourages us to let go of unconscious limits so that we can explore the question, *Do I allow myself to take up space?* Many of us walk through life with self-limiting impressions of our place in this world, feeling stuck. Expansion encourages you to move freely, to claim yourself, and to feel confident in your space. Practicing taking up space can help you feel more comfortable showing yourself and showing up more fully, worthy, and whole. It's okay to be seen. It's a human need to be seen and known.

Grappling with the Body Image Wound

The most common and false limitation that seems to plague people is feeling and believing that they are not good enough, flawed, and somehow broken. I've dedicated half my life—and I mean that—to eradicating this painful, destructive belief. The concept that we are not enough is often a conditioned belief based on societal expectations.

I was teaching at a women's empowerment conference in California and heard a powerful story from a facilitator. Her mother, whom she loved dearly, was dying of cancer. She and her sisters made a video of their lives together. As the images went by, her mother looked at her daughters and began to cry, saying, "Oh my God, I was never fat. I can't believe I spent my life battling the 'fat belly.'"

That story hit me sideways, as it did most of the women in the room. I thought about my own longtime body image obsession, and I felt so sad for this woman, and for all women, who live with unnecessary expectations about their bodies that they carry to their end. If you are stuck in a constant state of "not enough" and perpetual self-criticism, then you might be missing the enjoyment of life. Let's commit not to look back on our lives and wish that we had a flatter stomach but to start loving our bodies *now*! If you commit to making the shift into a self-loving mindset, the Immersion quality can take you there.

A belief that we (or something about us) are bad, wrong, or unlovable may stem from negative childhood experiences. I remember when my sisters were teens and tweens. One was diagnosed with anorexia, and I had no idea what that meant. All I knew was that she wasn't eating, Dad was yelling, and Mom was crying. The other one beat herself up whenever she looked in the mirror, so much so that I cried watching. She was teased in school during that vulnerable developmental stage of becoming womanly. By seventh grade, kids told me, "You're so fat you're gonna break the swing," and was teased in the girl's locker room for *not* yet wearing a bra (little did I know what was coming!). The other girls would touch your back to see if you were mature enough to be their "friend." I'm sure you have your stories.

It's a sad truth that so much time and money is spent on addressing body hatred rather than healing, loving, and honoring the body we have. All the visual icons of our time are skinny and probably starved themselves to be on camera. These unnatural bodies are our icons of beauty and power. I know millions of women, myself included, who do all that we can to diminish, reduce, and shame this belly when in truth we should be revering it. The truth is, the belly should be celebrated. The belly is the home to the diaphragm you use to breathe. It is the home of our sacred softness. Our babies live here. Our womb is holy. Our belly is holy.

It can take a lifetime to grapple with false beliefs that have been instilled in us, either intentionally or by accident or abuse. Holding onto these beliefs is a tragedy that so many beautiful, sensitive souls have had to face. The truth is, *just being* is valuable. We exist, we are part of the whole, and therefore we matter, and we are essentially more than good enough; we are worthy.

Discovering that we are good, valuable, worthy, and do not have to *do something to be loved* can be truly emotionally freeing. Our wakeup call is to see our truth and become empowered to accept our *enoughness*. It is possible to heal these old, conditioned beliefs, to root them out and replace them with new overlays of love, worthiness, and self-acceptance. Whatever hardship, heartache, or heartbreak you have been through, it's time to own yourself as more than enough: You are magnificent, beautiful, and miraculous! This quality offers a shift in perspective and gives you a chance to practice this shift whenever you need it.

When I focused on and explored how different parts of my body move on the dance floor, I started to see how I think and feel about my body. I saw that there was so much more potential in me for love and transformation when I was away from the mirror: I was able to change my perspective. I realized that I really do like my hands. I love following my hands like birds or butterflies moving through space. My elbows are very interesting. I had never thought about my elbows before. When I move my elbows out and in, up or down, the rest of my body reacts and moves in a creative way. I love moving my pelvis, and most everyone I dance with loves to circle their pelvis. I feel joyful when I shift my pelvis side to side or back and forth.

I also noticed that I was still not nice to my belly. I've always judged it, criticized it because it's not flat, it's curvy. Yet when I dance with it, I can find joy and pleasure moving it and see it differently. Maybe for you it's not your belly, it's your thighs, or your size. Whatever your "not good-enough body part" is, we can shift that relationship.

Many people shut down their potential because they've been told in some way not to take up space. Now is the time to explore enlarging your presence in space, so that you can feel more worthy and whole. It's okay to feel wild and free, to stand in your essence, show up, and unapologetically be yourself. In one of my workshops, there was a woman I noticed who kept appearing and then almost vanishing in the class. I joked with her and said, "Wow, you're so good at disappearing. You must have an invisibility cloak." She told me that she was extremely shy as a child, and when she didn't want to be seen, she figured out a way to "disappear." Then, as she became more comfortable in the class, she allowed herself to be more visible, took up more space, leaping and twirling, regaining her innocent playfulness.

When I'm appreciative of just being me, I can have a new relationship with my body. I want to expand and share myself with the world. Let's bring our whole selves to the dance floor in an immersive and present way and begin building a loving practice.

How to Really Love Yourself

Self-care is not just about taking a salt bath or applying essential oils, though that can help; it's how you treat yourself both internally *and* externally.

Can you feel love for yourself? Can you say, "I love myself"? Or do you find yourself saying, "I hate myself"?

When someone says, "I hate myself," it's usually because they feel unworthy, have heard too many negative messages, and/or have been mistreated. They are so uncomfortable being in their body that they don't have the capacity to feel and process difficult emotions. Bruce H. Lipton, PhD, proved in his seminal book, *The Biology of Belief*, that thoughts repeated with an associated feeling create a neural path that over time can become a "belief." Hating yourself may be just a thought that, with enough repetition, became a belief.

What if we reinvestigated this idea of "hate"? What if hate really meant a "passionate *discomfort* in the moment that we don't want to FEEL"? Can you imagine that self-hate occurs when you are having a difficult feeling that you just don't have the bandwidth to process? Simply put, maybe it's really not "I hate myself"; it's "I hate *this feeling*." Sometimes it's easier to say "I hate myself" than to feel the uncomfortable feelings of sadness, grief, anger, jealousy, blame, shame, etc.

What if you could be with these difficult feelings and experience the discomfort and not perpetuate the cycle of self-hate? Then, you could understand what's really driving these emotions. Once you feel them, they will dissipate naturally once they are named. And when you can hear yourself, you can find compassion for yourself. And when you have compassion for yourself, you can change your perception. As Bruce Lipton says, "When we change our perception, we change the chemistry of our body." Then, we start to feel better physically and mentally.

If you can feel love for yourself and say, "I love you and I forgive you. I appreciate you and I thank you," you will be able to feel a fuller range of positive emotions. These words are similar to the powerful Hawaiian *Hono'oponopono* prayer. When I was on a plant medicine journey, working on my own self-love, the shaman told me to say the following to my own body so I could begin forgiving and restoring my relationship with myself. He explained that this practice, a ritual for reconciliation and forgiveness, comes from the Kahuna shamanic tradition. He had me say:

"I'm sorry for ________,

I forgive you for ________,

Thank you for ________,

I love you."

He asked me to fill in the blanks, and you can fill in your blanks too. We may have occasional setbacks because of our mind's old neural pathways, but keep thinking *progress*, not perfection. And, if you can remember to insert forgiveness, appreciation, and compassion into your thoughts and words, you can slowly and positively change your beliefs. I will offer you my MindBusting technique to change your thoughts in Chapter 13.

The Immersion-Expansion Experience

On the physical level, Immersion is a series of flowing movements that increasingly take up space. You will be standing, swaying, feeling the music, and focusing all your attention on your body parts. You'll discover your body's movements through isolated explorations that bring you into the present moment: exploring each body part from hand to chest, core, hips, and feet, and releasing tension along the way. As you become totally immersed in yourself, you can invite the inspiration to expand this feeling out into space, into the room, with larger movements, waves, momentum, and spirals.

On the emotional level, we are practicing feeling love for every part of us. No part of our body is left out. We become fascinated by our movements, giving love and attention to places we have not been kind or nice to. When we conjure our feelings of enjoyment, love, and appreciation, we may fall in love with ourselves.

On the mental level, we learn more about ourselves. We hear our inner voice as we move the body, and if needed, shift that voice toward appreciation and positivity. This is so essentially important because we can zap our own energy when we stay in negative loops. Yet we gain potential and inspiration when we hold a positive intention.

On the spiritual level, Immersion takes us deeper into our hypnotic container, an immersive, altered state where regular conscious thought slows down enough for us to listen, observe, choose new thoughts, and overlay the old system by entrancing the self. Almost like a moving meditation, we find a one-pointed focus to take us more deeply into the moment. In this state of total focus, we shut out all distraction and feel a sense of oneness with our body and soul.

Music: Immerse and Expand with Me!

The music to access this quality moves from a smooth, luscious, thick, melodic, moderate rhythm to one that is faster, lighter, and uplifting. The music touches our souls, and the movement allows spirit to move through us, with us, and inside us.

Start the music as you read your invocation and begin your movement practice. This playlist is over an hour's worth of perfect music for this quality.

These are the songs that have been specially chosen for the Immersion quality. Remember, this is the beginning of the playlist:

- "In the Twilight" by Phaeleh
- "A Little Deeper" by KR3TURE and The Human Experience
- "Benijo" by Yeahman
- "Cleopatra in New York" by Nickodemus and Carol C
- "I Am the Mountain" by Pardis and VFerg
- "Varshaver" by Balkan Bump and CloZee
- "Savannah Sultana" by Scott Nice
- "Boho" by Slow Nomaden
- "Dear Insecurity" by Brandy Clark
- "Scars to Your Beautiful" by Alessia Cara

Find the full playlist in the *Embody* portal.

An Immersion/Expansion Invocation

Say aloud, and feel the power of your words:

Dear Mother Gaia, Rivers, Oceans, Seas,

Allow me to flow like water and to dance as you do.

When I look at myself, let me see with new eyes, seeing the miracle of me.

Allow me to see and own my truth.

Allow me to dig in and uncover my false beliefs that hold me in a not-enough mindset.

Let me love all the parts of my body I have not been loving.

May I open myself to receive new knowledge that will assist me in remembering who I truly am.

Let me gently and lovingly move every part of me that's available.

My being is innocent, miraculous, and divine.

I open to this today as I set out on my journey to enoughness.

Whatever is revealed, I have the strength and resilience to hold it and heal it.

Let me immerse fully in the experience to remember the now.

As I love every part of my body, let me expand that love beyond myself.

And so it is.

Immersion/Expansion Movement Practice

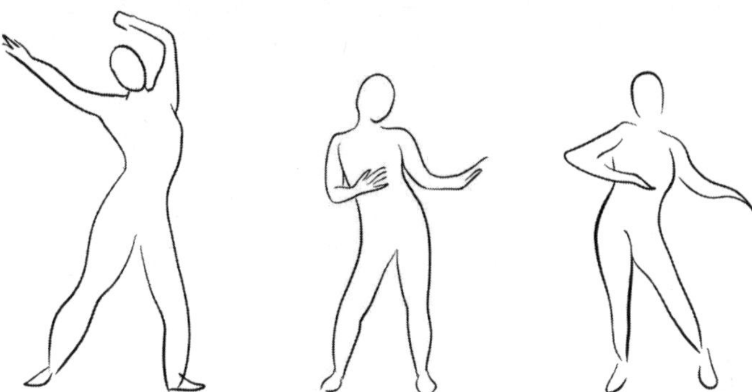

You already have more access to your entire body, your front, your sides, and your back. You've opened the spine, activated your sensory system, and awakened your energy. You've expanded your conscious awareness of your body in space. Now you can get immersed.

Dance with your eyes open to link what you see with what you are feeling. Each of the Immersion movements are meant to show how you flow in space, warming the joints with increasing and energizing movements.

Now is the time to enter your sacred container:

Let's rise up from the ground to standing, allowing your body to sway naturally as you feel the music, shifting your focus inward. Visualize yourself in water, moving slowly, warming your joints by circling each body part: shoulders, elbows, wrists, fingers, chest, hips, legs, knees, and feet. Be with your natural desire to move, staying present in the moment, placing your attention on one body part and then moving to the next. Explore purposefully, admiring yourself.

Let's start looking at your own hands for a moment. Really seeing them, let them lead the dance, let them move in space with your focused attention. Imagine your hands as butterflies or birds, and let them take you on a journey in the space.

Discover your unique ways of moving your fingers, expand your hand, open your fingers, leading with your pinky or thumb. Let your fingers undulate and make waves, feel and see how beautiful your hands are. Linger on your hands until you are ready to shift your focus on your wrists.

Notice how your body responds when you follow the gentle turning of your wrists. Feel how moving the wrists sends impulses up into your whole arm. Let your wrists lead your body and play with the shapes they can make and remember that weird is wonderful!

Then travel up to your elbows. Notice how they can lead your body in different ways. Widen your elbows apart, bring them closer together, notice how this opens and closes your chest. Allow your elbows a chance to move and explore your sensations.

Gently move your attention to your shoulders. Slowly circle your shoulders, bringing warmth there, feeling your sensuality. Lift and lower them with the music, feel your pulse and spiral, leading with your shoulders, and see your beautiful shoulders out of the corners of your eyes. Notice how you feel, allowing the movement of your hands, wrists, elbows, and shoulders to awaken your torso. Relish the moment for as long as you like.

Now, imagine you are moving in a slightly thicker substance, like honey, or become the flowing honey itself. Allow this feeling of being a "liquid body" to move into your chest and torso. Pulse your chest forward and back, side to side, and explore slow, luscious circles. Luxuriate in feeling sensual and expressive. Follow your intuitive movement and change your tempo to slow down or speed up. You can't do the Immersion dance wrong; there are no mistakes.

Let the movement travel down to your hips and have a slow honey dance with your hips. Let your hips lead you through the space with circles, pulses, and freedom. Linger here and get curious, explore making figure eights, pulse forward and back, all the while becoming present with your body and seeing yourself through the eyes of love.

Travel in this way through your entire body. Feeling your lusciousness, it's time to overwrite past thoughts you've said to your body, or parts you have ignored, and replace them with positive messages to your body and mind. I encourage you to gently and softly talk to your body, if you feel open to that, and say, "Thank you, hands, I love you," or "Thank you, hips, you are beautiful." Get creative with your personal messages.

Let your legs and feet continue this liquid body dance. See your legs, letting them make small to larger circles all the way down to your feet. See your beautiful feet and let them draw patterns on the floor as if you were painting with liquid colors. Move and follow the flow of your whole body, feeling smooth and supple.

Now, fully connecting and integrating all the isolations into a whole-body flowing movement, you are ready to Expand. Shift your gaze upward and out to the space around you. Increase the size and shapes of your movement, taking up more space as if you are swimming. Explore creating waves with your whole body, lift and lower, feel momentum and suspension, rise and fall, glide and open. Add a gentle turn or a spiral to your movements, both within your body and around the room. Allow yourself to take up even more space. Weave in and around your space, seeing yourself as if you were seaweed floating in water, or playfully moving, like a dolphin diving. Allow yourself to become more active in your movement: leap, glide, travel through space, and raise your arms. Focus on embodying and fully engaging your physical presence. As you expand, you're filling the whole room with energy.

When you feel complete, slow down your movements, come back to center and stillness. Bring your hands to your heart. Ask yourself, *How do I now sense the flow of my body and my energy?* Can you say and feel, *I love myself?*

Movement Suggestions for Immersion/Expansion

Keep these movement phrases in mind as you practice the movement section of Immersion/Expansion:

- Focus on your body parts, follow your fingers, your wrists, see how they move.
- Feel your liquid body, like water or honey.
- Rotate in circles and spirals.
- Consciously be loving to each part.
- Feel your hips pulse, rotate, circle.
- Move like water, or be like seaweed in water—light and drifting with the flow.
- Take up more space, travel, sail, spread out, explore.
- Fill the whole room with your energy.

Mystical Inquiry: Shedding a Skin

On my spiritual quest for meaning, I have often read about the metaphor of shedding a skin. "Just as a snake sheds its skin, we must shed our past over and over again" is attributed to Jack Kornfield explaining Siddhartha Gautama, the Enlightened One or Buddha. I always thought that when a snake shed its skin it would be a process, but I had no idea how truly intense it was.

Come with me, back in time, to when my children were about five and seven. I took them to a nature center to see a chinchilla exhibit where the kids could touch, pet, and play with them. If you've never seen a chinchilla, they are very cute.

Lots of children were shouting with excitement, and we parents were asked to wait in a nearby hallway so we could watch but not get involved. Patiently waiting, I heard a *thump, thump, thump* in one of the huge glass cases along the wall. I looked around but didn't see anything, so I asked one of the animal guides, "What's that noise?" It happened again, *thump, thump, thump.*

The guide came over to me and said, "Oh, you've got to see this snake. It's shedding its skin. Over here, come watch."

I looked into the glass-enclosed habitat and saw a ten-foot boa constrictor rubbing itself along the walls and rocks. The nature guide was excited: "Everyone thinks that when they find a whole snakeskin it's like the snake just slithered right out, but that's not how it works. The snake begins to feel their old skin drying out, and its instinct is to get the dry skin off. It takes much longer than you'd think because the snake needs to feel the right amount of pressure from the inside to know when to work it off. It starts the process by rubbing on the rocks, rubbing on the ground, sometimes even banging itself a bit. See how it's dragging itself around?"

As he explained the physical process, I had my own internal epiphany. I know that change isn't easy: It's not just as simple as when you're ready, you just slither out and discard your old habits of mind. It's hard work that other people don't see. It's an intense process that requires preparing for change, and then doing it with consistent action that takes time and patience, just like the snake. When I saw the snake working so hard and so diligently to release its skin, I knew I had to bring this idea to the dance floor.

I want to invite you to shed your old skin of self-criticism, the old skin of *not good enough*, not perfect

enough, not beautiful, not lovable, all of that! My dear friend, shaman and medicine man, Cristhian Cadenas, says, "In order to change we must shed a skin like the snake sheds its skin, all at once, not one scale at a time." The shedding of skin is a rebirthing process. I want to invite us to see ourselves, really *see* ourselves, in a new way, through eyes of appreciation.

Imagine what it would be like to let go of an old story that you no longer want to tell because all it does is bring you into negative feelings that aren't relevant today. What would it feel like to release a layer of negativity or a critical voice? What skin are you willing to let go of today?

We will *metaphorically* shed a skin using a transformative ritual to symbolize the release of old stories and negative limiting beliefs. Performing an action, stating your intention, and feeling the emotion tells the mind that we are serious about change. The mind is resistant to change, so we must move into the altered state of music and movement to get to the subconscious. When you commit to yourself, "I am ready to release this old critical, disappointed, mean, not good-enough voice," you are taking a stand for yourself! Then, embodying this transformative ritual solidifies your intention, telling the mind and body, "I'm making this change, now." Once your intention is embodied, if you feel, sense, or hear the old voice returning, you can notice it immediately, take back your power, and make a new choice in that moment—ending the old cycles of repetition.

Let's begin our mystical inquiry: set your intention and start the music I have selected for this piece, as you feel the music inspiring your movement. You can do this process as many times as you like.

Shedding the Skin Playlist

The songs in this playlist increase with intensity and emotion. The original ritual transformation was created with physical vigor in the song, "Rapid Cognition." If you would like to try a less intense version, use "Spiderbite" or "Smoke and Mirrors."

Then, please play the final two songs in this playlist to close the practice.

- "Spiderbite" by Beats Antique
- "Smoke & Mirrors" by ill-esha
- "Rapid Cognition" by Phutureprimitive
- "Duality" by Tumbara
- "Red Cosmic Earth" by Drums on Earth

Set your intention and say to yourself: *Today I will shed the old skin of (complaining, criticizing, feeling sorry for myself, disliking my body . . .* whatever you are ready to intentionally release). Repeat your intention three times.

Now, standing in your sacred space, visualize a cavelike doorway. Make the doorway with an archlike gesture, whatever size you need to feel comfortable. If you need a big space, make a big gesture for the doorway, or if you want a tight space, give it a small arch for the doorway, whatever makes your process more tangible for you. You may want to close your eyes to fully imagine entering an earthy cave with soft dirt and rock walls. Move your body through the doorway and into the cave you've created. See the cave as a sacred space and sense the curved walls around you.

Imagine that you are a snake that is feeling the internal pressure to shed its skin. Cascade your hands down your whole body, bringing the snake image into form. Allow

yourself to feel bound and tight, and move in that way, feeling the tension of confinement and connection to your old skin. It's okay to feel the uncomfortable emotion of what is no longer serving you. Acknowledge the discomfort of carrying an old story about yourself, the old skin you're ready to shed. It's okay to feel that discomfort so you can see and know how you treat yourself, because change is coming.

Now, dance as if you are rubbing your tight body against the cave walls, allowing yourself to feel into the urge to break free from the confined space of your "old skin." You are creating a new body memory of releasing the old skin, the old story.

Continue moving in a snakelike way, from tail to head, pressing, and pushing. Move from your core, circling, spiraling, winding, and unwinding. Move your chest and shoulders in circles and unlock and loosen any feelings of tightness. Imagine being the snake I saw, bumping into the walls of the cave, dragging itself on the ground against the dirt, rubbing against rocks to release the edges of the old skin.

It takes effort to release that old skin and then to move smoothly out of it and live into a new skin of our choosing. As the music progresses, slowly push or press one arm up through the old skin, making space to release the top of your head. Imagine you are slowly, and with consistent effort, coming out of the old skin. Raise the other arm and press the imaginary skin down to free your chest, moving more freely. Take the "old skin" down to free your hips and pelvis, moving and enjoying your body as you become totally free of old thought patterns, the old voice, the old skin. Step completely out of the old skin, rebirthing yourself into free, expansive movement.

Look down and see your old skin as a complete snakeskin. Lovingly pick it up from the ground, and step outside the cave. Gratefully hold your snakeskin up to the light of the moon or the sun, or whatever light source you visualize. Honor the past with a thank you: "I release you. I thank you for helping me become who I am becoming today."

You will return your snakeskin to the earth by releasing it in a gesture, or symbolically burying it under the soil for composting. "Dig" a small hole in the ground and place your skin back into the earth. Stand tall in your new body, one layer lighter, and feel into yourself by reaching your hands up to the sky. Bring your hands to your heart and set an intention for your new skin, telling yourself, *I love you.*

Immersion and Expansion Personal Practice Journaling

- How does it feel when you take the time to focus on one body part and follow it?
- What beliefs do you have about your body that need to be shed and transformed?
- What is your heritage/religion, and how does that culture feel/think about the body in general?

Now, write a letter to yourself to implant the new message in your mind. Choose what's most needed.

- **Dearest Body:** Write a letter of apology to your body for anything you feel it needs to hear. Apologize for the ways you have abused it or disliked your perceived flaws.
- **Dearest Body**: Write a love letter to your body, appreciating its beauty. What is your favorite part of your body and why? Describe in detail why you love it.

Messages for Immersion and Expansion

Please say the following to yourself:

I am enough.

I am spirit divine.

My being is beautiful.

I love my being.

My being is love.

I am good.

I am enough exactly as I am.

Close the Immersion and Expansion Practice with a *Prayer*

Beloved spirit, source, energy, and my personal guides and teachers,

I am water. I flow like water. I am warm, flexible, and fluid.

I can shift and change with ease.
I see myself anew and appreciate every inch of my body.

Loving myself this way, I know that I am enough in every cell of my body.

May I move through the world with a gentle confidence that pervades my being.

May I own my value and know that I am worthy of the divine abundance of this world. This beautiful world in which I am a being.

May I honor my being, that inner part of me who knows the beauty of my existence.

Please allow me to instill this message into my heart, so that I remember daily.

I am enough and I am good, across all time, space, and mind, past, present, and future.

May I continue this dance and let my inner beauty shine more and more.

I am fully immersed in this moment.

Thank you, and so it is. 

CHAPTER 6

Funky Connection

Let's turn up the joy! Now that you've gotten more deeply embodied, awakened to sensation and energy, immersed lusciously in the moment, and hopefully fallen a little bit more in love with yourself, it's time to reset your baseline emotion to joy. Yes, I said joy! Joy is that feeling of vibrant aliveness that sparkles in us when we smile, that lifts us out of our dark moods with a little laughter, a giggle, and some humor. Joy is contagious: we can share it, and we can increase it. Joy is definitely my favorite emotion, and why wouldn't it be? Is it yours, too?

You may be thinking, *Is joy possible for me?* I can't promise that every person will be able to access joy immediately, but I can tell you that everyone I've ever danced with rediscovered some sense of joy through movement.

A common theme in many personal growth practices, including the teachings of AA and Al-Anon, is the idea that when we shut down one emotion, we shut down access to all our emotions. When we try to hide from our anger by numbing out, or when we stuff or hold in our grief, our access to joy also becomes compromised. It's like turning down the volume on your life. But when you can feel and experience joy, it reminds us that emotions aren't always negative, and that fun, pleasure, and laughter are also in this mix. Accessing joy is essential to retaining some positive feeling of hope and inspiration. And once you access joy, your body remembers that you can return to it after experiencing more challenging emotions.

With this new perspective, we can slowly increase our bandwidth to get comfortable with the full range of emotions. In other words, having access to true, authentic joy gives us the insight to know that it's okay to feel and be with all our other emotions. Ultimately, knowing that you have the ability to return to joy is the beginning of resilience.

Are you a person who easily feels the pain of the world but rarely notices the joy that is equally present? There will always be reasons that diminish our joy. We don't have to look far to see injustice, suffering, and an excess of truly painful situations. Joy is not about ignoring them or putting a rainbow wash over reality. When you can feel joy without shame or guilt, you can become a shining light for others who are so in need of inspiration.

But here's the thing about joy: it's an inside job. You might have to "fake it until you make it." Funky Connection can be your gateway into joy. It allows you to get a little wild, a little snazzy, a little groovy, so you can be free to explore joy, maybe for the first time in a long while. The lessons of this quality will help you create a sense of inner confidence and trust. Feeling free and fun helps us lighten up and release stuck energy, allowing us to stand in truth without pretense. When you start to play and let go of your expectations of how your body is supposed to move, or how it's supposed to look, and allow yourself to respond to music, you start feeling better about yourself and, maybe, about the world around you.

Funky Connection provides a sense of freedom from self-consciousness. We live in a world so focused on the external image, a world of mirrors and selfies. Funky is about letting go of this inhibited self. Once you can let go of your self-consciousness, as the journey continues, you'll be better able to delve into the shadow parts of yourself. Feeling joy makes the deeper exploratory work palatable and doable.

YOU CAN TITRATE JOY

Some people find Funky Connection is their favorite quality because it can be super enjoyable and totally energizing. Others have a harder time getting into the groove.

If you are self-conscious and have felt awkward expressing yourself, you can start here in the privacy of your own sacred space. You can let go of your inhibitions and allow yourself to feel the freedom. If you grapple with depression or any mental health or personal challenge, you may have a different experience with joy. It may be really hard for you to access it or experience more intense ups and downs. If you are not feeling joy right now, please remember, there is nothing *wrong* with you. I've met many people who have had to shut down their joy in order to please a parent or caregiver or partner, or who have been taught to compartmentalize joy and only express it in "appropriate places" like at a party or with friends. In some cases, and in some extreme times in our lives, we may need assistance balancing our emotional system with the help of a doctor or psychiatrist. This practice isn't about "betterment," like there's something that needs to be fixed, it's about restoring joyful and self-loving feelings. This work is anti-stigmatizing and is an inclusive space for belonging.

Whatever your relationship with joy, see if you can give yourself permission to let some in, even if it's just a little at a time.

The Resiliency + Joy Equation

We know resilience is the ability to keep going in hard times. Let's take the definition and break it down a bit. In the dictionary, *resilience* is "the capacity to withstand or to recover quickly from difficulties; toughness." When I read this, I realized that if we perceive resilience as toughness alone, it's a lot harder to keep our hearts and minds open. Being *tough* is important in some cases, but in general, toughening forces us to close off, harden our hearts, and fall into the trap of self-protection and a defended heart. This definition of resilience keeps us from reaching compassion and empathy, and locks us in a pattern of isolation and not allowing anything to touch us.

Luckily, there's more. There's a second part to the definition: "the ability of a substance or object to spring back into shape; elasticity." That's the part about resiliency that I connect with most. I want to be elastic, not tough. During difficult times, losses, tragedies, we may have to stretch our capacity, and at times we may feel totally "bent out of shape" or "stretched too thin." Resilience provides the capacity to feel, process, and come back to center, whenever we are ready.

So how do we build resilience, stay in the body, keep our hearts open, be compassionate, and have empathy? We add a practice of joy. Joy is an energy, a life-giving feeling. When we add joy, resilience begins to feel more like empowerment. Without joy, even our best attempts at resilience can feel like suffering.

Resilience - *Joy* = SUFFERING
Resilience + *Joy* = EMPOWERMENT

I built my own resilience by reclaiming my joy through radical self-acceptance. Unfortunately, I had to start working on it when I was very young. When I was little, I was often labeled as "too much," as in "She talks too much, she moves around too much, she's too smart, she's too disruptive, she's too enthusiastic." So many of us have been told we are "too much," so this quality is dedicated to the "too much" crew! I love you, and you are family! Make some noise!

But in second grade, being constantly told to calm down would make a person shut down, don't you think? I had just transferred into a new school, and I really loved my teacher. I came in so enthusiastically; I was super pumped to make new friends and fit in. Even though I was fidgety and a little hyper, I was totally the "hand in the air" participatory student. And I talked *a lot* on the side. It's possible I was a little disruptive.

One day, my teacher asked the class, "Is that the jabberwocky?" She looked around the room and everyone slowly turned toward me. I was like *Am I the jabberwocky*? I didn't get the reference (turns out "Jabberwocky" is a nonsense poem written by Lewis Carroll that appears in *Through the Looking-Glass*, the sequel to *Alice's Adventures in Wonderland*). She would say things like, "Jabberwocky, if you don't be quiet, you're gonna have to sit next to JD," who was a boy in class who *never* spoke. Ever. So, I learned my lesson, and just shut down. I became shy. I had no more joy. I certainly stopped loving the teacher, and poor JD, can you imagine *being* the punishment? I felt sad for him too.

By third grade I was completely "well-behaved," raised my hand to speak, shut down all my enthusiasm, and was criticized by the other kids because I became the "teacher's pet." By fourth grade, I became known as "the shy girl" because I never spoke up in class. I started to hate school. I would go home from school and cry. I never spoke in fifth grade—at all. I was teased and picked on in the playground. I didn't fit in, and I felt a strong lack of belonging. I started getting migraines and spent more time at home than at school.

By sixth grade there was a shift. I finally met "my people" who became my best friends. I got myself back, not fully, but a little bit. By high school I was still considered shy by people who didn't know me, but I found a sense of belonging in my friend group.

The only place that I've ever been truly unselfconscious was dancing. Even in high school, I would go to the dances and the music would come on, and literally people would be saying, "Is that really *Toni*?" I would just go nuts. I could do the worm and I roller-skated like a pro. I didn't care about what I looked like, only what I felt like, and when I was dancing, I felt my power, my resiliency. Over time I made my own community of weird, wild, powerful, deep people through dance. And little by little, I used embodiment to turn my self-consciousness into self-awareness.

I created the Funky quality as a way to bring up the emotions and positive feelings of joy into your body, so you can feel that sense of empowered resilience. I learned not to take myself so seriously, like a "proper adult," and give myself permission to be weird and wild. Moving in a funky way allows you to "find your groove" and "jam out." It's just a ton of fun! We can't help but enjoy it! It's the best way I know how to be comfortable in my own skin and feel confident, inspired, and safe.

The Connection of Funky Connection

Funky Connection quality was birthed on a packed dance floor, full of people who didn't know one another. I wanted to create something where people interacted with one another to create some kind of unity and sense of belonging. I remember when I first started exploring this movement quality, I moved with people and observed the energy. I noticed that when I encouraged people to lightly interact, either with a side-by-side smile and glance, or a face-to-face "copy you, copy me" moment, they took on the exact facial and movement expressions they were seeing on others. The whole class LIT UP!

My goal was to create a reflective experience in which people "saw" one another, but what I didn't realize is that the work was actually tapping into real science. The brain's *mirror neurons* respond to actions that we observe in others by firing in the same way, and re-creating that action for ourselves.[3] What we see in others we can project onto ourselves and change the way we feel—instantly.

Rodrigo Gonzales Zazoya, Gestalt therapist, professional dancer, and JourneyDance trainer, studies and teaches various therapeutic modalities for understanding and healing trauma. He believes that this particular quality helps us to heal social traumas, like fears of partnering and interacting, or fears of being seen and taking up space. When we dance with others, we can change the way we feel by mirroring their expressions and movements.

I invited people to say positive compliments to one another like "You're so funky!" or "You're so amazing!" and they started to connect

3 Acharya S., Shukla S. Mirror neurons: Enigma of the metaphysical modular brain. J Nat Sci Biol Med. 2012 Jul; 3(2): 118–24. doi: 10.4103/0976-9668.101878. PMID: 23225972; PMCID: PMC3510904.

even more. Yet, I noticed that most people would hear the compliment and then say, "No, *you're* so amazing." They brushed off the compliment instead of internalizing it.

So, I added an instruction for a response, where each person would have to say, "Thank you very much." These simple words give us the permission to take in positive messages, and really allow ourselves to feel them. The energy completely shifted and elevated from normal to alive, and the whole room was buzzing with positive vibration.

One way to jump into the spirit of Funky Connection is to join me dancing on Tuesdays through the website portal. Another is to practice giving and receiving compliments. What if we saw the good in others before we judged them? Giving and receiving compliments helps us see the best in others, and then we can see the best in ourselves.

Can you receive a compliment without rejecting it, brushing it off, or negating it instantly? This is an act of self-deprecation that many of us do because we were conditioned to believe that it's rude or prideful to feel good about yourself or be confident. Try an exercise of giving ten honest, heartfelt compliments in a week. How do you think that will make you feel?

Then, think about how you would feel if the ten compliments landed on you?

The Funky Connection Experience

On the physical level, pain is easy to locate. Let's find where in your body you feel *joy*. Is it in your hips, in your feet, in your bounce, in your shake? Is it in your pulse, your step, your face? Is it in your heart? Or in your belly? One of my dance teachers from the early Kripalu days, Nateshvar Ken Scott, used to say, "Joy lives in our feet."

On the emotional level, joy feels like laughing on the inside. I know when things aren't easy, the first thing we do is drop the joy and focus on the other emotions. What if we could create a baseline of joy and decide, *This is where I live*? If we choose to inhabit joy, the other emotions will come and go, be felt and processed, and we will always have a home base to return to that is positive and nurturing.

On the mental level, we are letting go of inhibitions and thoughts of *I don't fit in* or *I'm not doing this right*. We build a positive mindset by playing with affirmations and compliments. We take a little risk and find our confidence and openness.

On the spiritual level, I believe that Spirit just might be joy! In this quality we lighten up and reconnect with play, our innocence, our essence, which are all parts of authentic joy. We've all had the experience of connecting in our pain; what if we connected in a universal sense of joy? The truth is, we tend to think we are alone, but we are essentially connected to everyone when we access joy. Strangers become friends, and the Funky quality brings forth this sense of unity, community, and belonging.

Music: Get Funky with Me!

The music to access this Funky Connection is fun, wild, and uplifting, funky, chunky, remixed, four-on-the-floor, playful, horns, percussive, steady beat. Every song in this Funky list is awesome, uplifting, and seriously fun.

Start the music as you read your invocation and begin your movement practice. This playlist is over an hour's worth of perfect music for this quality. The songs are short, and they are all very different, so find the ones that resonate with you.

These are the songs that have been specially chosen for the Funky Connection quality. Remember, this is the beginning of the playlist:

- "Ghost Dance" by Captain Planet
- "Chunky" by Format B
- "Good to Go" by LONIS and Daphne Willis
- "Yeah I'm Feelin' All Right" by Rayelle
- "Baianá" by Bakermat
- "Feels This Good" by John Mero and LONIS
- "Faith" by Stevie Wonder and Ariana Grande
- "Delight" by Jamie Berry and Octavia Rose
- "Booty Shake" by Timmy Trumpet and Max Vangeli
- "Freak Flag" by Laura Love

Find the full playlist in the *Embody* portal.

A Funky Connection Invocation

Say aloud, and feel the power of your words:

My Dear Body,

May I walk this life with more joy.

May I feel and express my joy freely and easily.

May I feel joy as commonly as feeling all my emotions.

As I dance, may I feel a new joy-filled space inside me and elevate my emotional vibration.

May joy be my baseline that I return to again and again.

May I get wild, weird, funky, and free to see beauty all around me.

The Funky Connection Movement Practice

Funky Connection is a pivotal shift from self-focused attention to an outward exploration. The movements allow your body to experience what it's like to have fun in an unselfconscious way, where you don't care about what you look like, only what you feel like. It's a bounciness, a joyful feeling of being in your body in a way that's different from anything else we've done thus far. The movement is all about creating shapes and pulsations with your muscles, joints, and even in your bones.

According to Dr. Steph, the faster pace of Funky Connection movement creates a state of internal arousal; you might find that you start to sweat and elevate your heart rate. As you tap into your joy, your positive feelings stimulate your brain's activity, and the way you think about yourself can begin to change. Your internal focus, combined with external guidance, activates your ability to see yourself in a new light, expanding your possibilities.

Enter your sacred practice container:

Standing up, sway from side to side and start to feel into this new style of music. Notice the beat and the rhythm and allow your body to wiggle, shake, or shimmy. Snap your fingers and let your body experience what it's like to bring this music to life. Let the music pulse in your core, feel the weight of your body connecting with the ground. Pulse, bounce, and feel your feet. Find a little joy in your feet as you walk, skip, and lightly jump up and down. Integrate all parts of your feet: the toes, ball, and heel. Lead with each part and notice how it makes you move in different shapes: on your toes, let your hips swivel; on a heel, lean back into your weight.

Bring the movement into your knees and thighs, allowing a full, funky expression. Come to your core and feel your chest and pelvis beginning to move. Circle your chest to the right, left, all the way around, making big and small circles. Swing your hips and pelvis side to side, making space, and begin circling in one direction for a little while, and then the other direction. Notice that you may have one direction that's easier than the other. This is caused by habitual movement and fascia patterns. You can shift these patterns by softening and staying with the tighter side or direction for just a bit longer. Make the circles bigger and wider, let your face express and enjoy the moment of freeing your pelvis. Then, pump your pelvis forward and back, freeing any stuck energy. Touch your body, placing your hands on your heart and solar plexus or belly, and say, "I own myself."

Move to the beat, walking through your space in a fun and funky stylistic stride. Roll your shoulders back, one and then the other, as you walk. Try amplifying your movements and letting them grow bigger.

Now let's start a body conversation where you are going to focus on different parts of the body and have them "talk" to one another. Let your hands and feet lead the movement, moving together, exploring, creating new shapes in the space. Use the music to influence your movements and get "weird" and let go. Find your joints and pulsations. Let your wrists talk to your ankles. Allow yourself to make strange shapes that animate the music. Enjoy being playful; it doesn't matter how it looks. Let your elbows and knees talk. Notice how these joints move, explore their pulsations. Move your elbows toward your knees and away from your knees, open and close your knees as you open and close your elbows, all the while feeling the beat in your body.

Now, responding to the music, allow all your body parts to talk to one another in any way you want. Set your whole body free to do exactly what it takes to feel good. Let the music make you smile and see if you can move this energy to every cell of your body. Allow your creativity to fly: make shapes, angular, jazzy, smooth, weird, wild, whatever feels good. If it's available to you, let your head dance, bop, and pulse. Maybe even swing your hair in the air. As Laura Love says in her song, "Let your freak flag fly."

Movement Suggestions for Funky Connection

- Pulse, bounce, and feel your feet.
- Feel the weight of your body connecting with the ground.
- Find your joints and pulsations.
- Amplify your movements and let them grow.
- Animate to the music.
- Get weird, funky, and let go.

Mystical Inquiry: Funky Affirmations for Increasing Self-Love

Do affirmations really work? In Chapter 2, we discussed that affirmations work if you can actually feel and own the message. Guess what? Funky Connection brings you into the place where joyful messages about yourself feel real.

I remember in my early twenties reading the book *The Only Diet There Is* by Sondra Ray and it was a wonderful help to me. Her book is full of exercises and practices to help people learn to love themselves exactly as they are. There was one exercise—to fill yourself with positive, loving affirmations—that I found to be very difficult. When I was feeling super crappy and I looked in the mirror and said, "You're so beautiful, you're so wonderful, you're so great, you look marvelous etc., etc.," it did not stick, and I felt stupid. I began to feel worse for not feeling the affirmation positively affecting me.

Funky Connection transformed this mental practice and brought it to the physical level. It was my key to owning my affirmations and really feeling good about myself, and seeing others in a wonderful light. I have found that when you are feeling so good in your body, the affirmations you say can stick, and you can transform your mental patterning.

In this mystical inquiry, take your funky affirmations to a mirror. I know I said that there are no mirrors in JourneyDance, but for this specific exercise, please bring one into your container. You'll be using it for the following self-love practice.

Originally taught by Louise Hay, a mirror practice is a form of self-healing, where you sit with yourself for periods of time, just being with yourself, or repeating specific scripts in front of a mirror. The purpose is to accept yourself fully and love your image as you are.

In my exercise, you will be dancing just as you did in your funky movement practice, adding the affirmations script below and enacting the affirmations in the mirror for your own positive reflection. Saying these affirmations and compliments out loud as you animate them can begin the process of real transformation. You may begin to notice your mental blocks, where you are hard on yourself. Don't worry and keep dancing, allowing the joyful music to assist you. You might feel totally inspired to honor yourself in this new way as you own each affirmation.

To begin, continue with the playlist, or choose your favorites from the list of songs, and start dancing in front of a mirror. As you dance with your own image, chant to yourself. If any of these affirmations don't work for you, skip them and add your own. It's most important that you hear what you need to hear:

You're so funky! Thank you very much.
You're so amazing! Thank you very much.
You're so adorable! Thank you very much.
You're so creative! Thank you very much.
You're so glorious! Thank you very much.
You're a little wild! Thank you very much.
You're so luscious! Thank you very much.
You're so smooth! Thank you very much.
(Add your own or repeat whatever you need to say and hear!)
Thank you very much.

Now, check in with yourself. How do you feel? It's okay if you felt silly at first; you can learn how to receive a compliment, especially from yourself!

Funky Connection Personal Practice Journaling

- Do you enjoy the playfulness of the mystical inquiry?
- What phrases really landed for you and what do you need to work on?
- What brings you the most joy in your life and why?
- What activities always energize you?

Additional writing prompts:

- My definition of inspiration or joy is . . .
- Joyful expression to me is . . .
- I sparkle and glow when I . . .
- My perfect day is (include all the senses) . . .

Messages to Stay Funky

After your dance, say the following to yourself:

I am inspired.

It's okay to feel good.

I allow joy into my day.

I create joy. I share joy.

I am filled with joy!

I spread joy.

Close the Funky Connection Practice with a *Prayer*

Oh, Great Beloved, who delights in all things joyful and free,

I open my spirit to receive more joy now.

I open my body to feel the exuberance of life.

I allow my emotional flow to touch joy on a daily basis.

May my mind be filled with new, positive, uplifting thoughts.

May my smile be infectious so that I spread as much joy as I feel.

Thank you for this gift of life.

Thank you for the gift of feeling good.

I feel deep gratitude for all the joy I am about to experience.

And so it is!

CHAPTER 7

Evocative Emotion

Now that you can access joy, it's going to be easier to get in touch with all your emotions. The Evocative Emotion quality is where you'll explore your different emotional states, and then tell your story through movement so that you can access past hurts and traumas on your own terms.

I think of emotions as *e-motion*, or energy in motion. We tend to think of emotions as thoughts or feelings, yet emotions are far more than that. They're a form of energy that propels you into an action, because emotions literally move through the body. As you learned in the last chapter, when you feel joy, you laugh and smile and there's a bounce to your step. There's a totally different energetic reaction when you feel sad or angry, and sometimes these difficult emotions get expressed in negative ways. For instance, rage can feel like heat moving through the body, and it might make you want to explode verbally or physically. But you know that if you do explode, it can have terrible consequences. Yet if you don't express your anger in a healthy way, it will be internalized, and that also has its own set of consequences. If your emotions are expressed without consciousness, it's like a child having a tantrum.

Sometimes, people suppress their emotions because they're afraid of them. They may worry that their emotional reaction is never going to end, or that what they will feel is going to be too painful or will hurt someone's feelings. Instead of letting the energy flow, when there's too much stimulus from the outside world, a loss, a traumatic event, or too much emotion moving through us, we turn to our brilliant defense mechanisms to protect us.

The first line of defense is shutting down by going quiet or numbing out with distractions and addictions. Being super busy is another way of numbing: you aren't giving yourself time for self-reflection and being with your feelings. All this repressed energy creates stagnation that shows up as pain, illness, or emotional limitations, including the inability to enjoy love, happiness, and peace.

I've also found that it takes much more energy to repress an emotion than it does to express one. When I felt sadness in my chest and I wanted to cry, I taught myself how to literally hold my emotions in because I didn't want to be embarrassed by them. Yet by the time I got home in a safe place to let my feelings out, I couldn't access them anymore, and it was even harder to tap into them. If I just let myself cry in the moment like a child would, the emotion would be processed, and I would be able to move on.

The truth is, it's healthy, normal, and common to feel and move through emotions relatively quickly, actually in minutes. As Harvard neuroscientist Jill Bolte Taylor, PhD, explains in her book *Whole Brain Living*, "When a person has a reaction to something in their environment, there's a ninety-second chemical process that happens in the body. After that, if you continue to feel fear, anger, and so on, you need to look at the thoughts that you're thinking that are restimulating the circuitry that is resulting in you having this physiological reaction, over and over again."

In Chapter 13, you'll learn my MindBusting technique to teach you how to assess your thoughts and not fall down the rabbit hole of retriggering your emotional response. But for now, just know that your emotional expressions don't have to last long. What's more, this Evocative Emotion practice gives us a space to uncover our thoughts, those that are creating these reactions that we have become so accustomed to. Not only do we learn to feel, we can see our emotional reactions from an observer's perspective and gain the mindfulness to shift our thoughts.

Another way we hide our emotions is by wearing masks that conceal what we're really feeling. Sometimes the mask is "the nice girl, the good girl," or "the angry one," or "the bitch" (feel free to add your pronoun/gender). Have you ever felt angry, but reacted with passive aggression instead of letting someone know how you feel? If you've been taught that you can't experience anger or hurt, you will take it out another way. There could be a lot of anger or sadness behind the face of the nice girl. The bitch could be the most wounded, sweet person, but they are afraid to be seen as vulnerable. Our masks are acquired over years of practicing where we got the most attention, be it positive or negative.

Masks also create unconscious crossfirings of emotions through conditioning. For instance, the cultural concept that "boys don't cry" has created generations of men who express their sadness as anger. Girls were taught "don't be angry," and then learn to express their anger as sadness. But then where does the true anger and sadness go? Bingo—into the body!

Your conditioning is not your fault. I want you to honor why you wear a mask, and provide a space that's safe to feel, express, and process your hidden emotions. When you can recognize and feel your emotions on the dance floor, you'll be much less likely to mask them. Then, you can open yourself to true vulnerability through honest communication. Vulnerability also requires trusting those with whom you share your life. Whether this is family, friends, coaches, or therapists, it doesn't matter; what matters is that you feel safe to allow emotional flow.

We have to find a healthy way to get in touch with our emotions and move the energy through the body, and I do it through movement and dance. In this practice, we create a supportive space where you can be vulnerable with yourself first and then you can be vulnerable with others. Together we will build that foundation by moving to music that evokes different emotions for short periods of experimentation. In your container, your sacred space, you'll be with your emotions on your own terms. We allow ourselves to stir, mine, and excavate our stories, our repression, so that release and maybe even catharsis can happen here, or in the later slower movement qualities. When you can feel, process, express, name, and release these emotions, you no longer fear them. Then, the next time you feel difficult emotions, you can become more resilient when they come up.

Once you can be with your emotional range more fully, you become empathetic, loving and supportive to yourself and your beloveds. When we expand our bandwidth and honor our emotional nature, we can hold space for others, be more connected to ourselves, and be much more present humans. We release the energetic charge of stress and start to feel more at home in our own bodies. Resilience is built by feeling your feelings, getting through the experience, and arriving at the other side. I know this sounds simplistic, but if you can express your anger in a safe way while dancing, if you can allow the tears to flow, express your grief, even feel your joy, you know that you can be with all your feelings and be empowered.

If you are numb and are going through a time of needing to hold back the dam, I completely understand. That said, it's essential that you also make space for feeling. This segment can be a powerful therapeutic tool to honor your stories so that you can come back to center, back to trust. So many of us carry deep wounds that may be present for the rest of our lives, but our attitude toward them, our ability to embrace, digest, and process our experience, makes us resilient and strong. If we can feel, we can heal.

How I Learned to Repress and, Finally, to Let Go

Growing up in my household was a mixed bag. I deeply love and genuinely adore my father. Since my earliest memories, he was exuberant, buzzing about life, highly intelligent, and wanting to share his world with us. I inherited many of his traits. He also had uncontrollable and unconscious outbursts of anger that were deeply terrifying, confusing, and alarming. I remember my mother screeching at my dad to calm down, yelling, "You're gonna have a heart attack!" or "You're turning purple, you're scaring the children!" I must've heard my mother say these things thousands of times. It would be indiscriminate, screaming about a bill arriving in the mail or something in the living room that fell over. We literally didn't know what was going to cause a complete and total eruption, and when it came, we were terrified. All three of us kids would run to our separate rooms, close our doors, and just hide until it was over.

My response to my father's anger created a systemic pattern in my body, which I have been working on for thirty years. It is so deeply ingrained because I was born into a family where this behavior was already operational. After many years of my own deep work, I'm certain his behavior came from his own childhood that was filled with intense pressure and emotional neglect.

It's interesting that the word *scared* and *scarred* are so similar, because my sisters' and my nervous systems were scarred by this indiscriminate and abusive anger, leaving us scared and wired for fear, then anger, then shame—just like him. My father's explosive emotional behavior caused all of us to have different issues going forth, either being super angry, or shutting down emotionally, or impatiently waiting for the other shoe to drop, or being guarded to avoid being hurt. My mother either yelled at him about his behavior or emotionally numbed out. I became an emotional observer, repressing all my emotions until I couldn't hold them in any longer, and became an expresser on the dance floor.

In my family, I only got attention for the emotions that my parents could handle. I learned not to express too much anger or sadness in front of anyone, because if I did, I would take up too much space, so I learned to compose myself as positive, happy, and controlled. I shut down my emotions, except for joy. In truth I was an extremely emotional child who yearned to cry and laugh and yell and shout and be that expressive emotive being. I have learned that my sadness and anger wires were crossed. When I was sad, I acted angry. I didn't cry very easily, because crying was not the emotion that got attention in my family. It was definitely anger. If we were yelling, we got yelled at. If we were crying, we got the infamous headshake of disappointment from my father who just didn't know what to do with us. Our mother would comfort us in an attempt to bypass and get us back to happy as quickly as possible.

To actually free myself of my repression, I had to learn to express myself and tell my stories. Luckily, I found theater and dance. Nothing has helped me more than processing and releasing my anger both in theater and on the dance floor. Once I release the energetic charge of my anger, I can not only observe my sensations as they arise, I can make a new choice in that moment to respond, rather than react. Becoming acutely aware of our emotional body's signals can save us from perpetuating dysfunctional family dynamics, and free us to become conscious of the words that come out of our mouths, or our reactions that create pain.

I discovered that with an effective movement process, I don't have to tell the same story over and over again. After my divorce, I was so angry at my ex-husband. I carried my anger onto the dance floor for years. I beat myself up about failing at relationships. I beat him up about it forever. I could not let it go. I kept telling the same story. I was full of rage, blaming him, shaming him, and shaming myself, too.

I processed it on the dance floor, week after week. I let myself express my anger through my body with my pulsations and my elbows and my fists and my face and my knees and my guts and everything. During one "Tell your story to the dance floor" moment, I was telling my same old story, and an inner voice sounded within me: *What if today is the last day I'm going to tell this story?* So, I brought it to the dance floor one last time, in my most dramatic fashion. And when I was done, I was *done*. I knew I would change the relationship to my story, and my ex, forever. I would no longer allow myself to be activated as I had been before. I transmuted this story and took my power back. I made this choice for my healing, because I have a choice.

I never told that story again. I had processed the emotions enough to move on to the next stories of life. Since then, when grieving a loss, I was able to sit with, feel all my emotions, and freely move with and release my tears and my anger, and it has changed me.

The dance floor is waiting and available for your stories. You can tell them as many times as you like and in many different ways. Asking yourself, *Is this the first time, or the last time, I need to tell this story?* will give you the freedom to tell your story until you're done.

The Evocative Emotion Experience

On a physical level, we'll be invigorating our bodies with movement, breath, sound, and embodied storytelling. You'll ride the waves of whatever feelings come to the surface, let them move through a process of physical repetition, and let them express in shapes and patterns. You will feel the visceral release of stuck energy as you add vigor and sound expression to the dance and the music, anything from a sigh to a cry to a wail.

On an emotional level, we invite the emotional energy to come alive, feeling, sensing, rising, and stirring. We may feel glimmers or waves of sadness or grief, empathy or compassion, anger, or frustration. We will be riding the wave of our emotions, knowing that we'll process them in our own time, and that they may not come to their fullest expression until we get into the slower-moving qualities.

On a mental level, we are mining for what needs attention. When we ask ourselves to tell our story to the dance floor, we can see what stories and thoughts need to be processed: old stories, old repetitive thoughts, old limiting beliefs, and thoughts we would not choose to think if we knew we had choice in our thinking.

On a spiritual level, we open ourselves to healing and learning. We know we are more than just a body or a messy mind. When we can consciously become aware of our emotional bandwidth, we can open ourselves to the possibility of greater awareness of our spiritual life. Even when we lose our faith in this wild world, we can still tap into the desire to live more fully in THIS BODY, to live our passions and mission, and stay present with it, as Ram Dass put it so perfectly, to *"Be here now!"*

Evocative Emotion Invocation

Say aloud, and feel the power of your words:

I am a multifaceted being. I love that about myself.

I can feel my feelings and move through them.

I intend to be both a witness and a friend to myself as I go through this experience.

I will observe my triggers, my emotions, and my expression.

I will notice what choices I make in the face of difficulty.

And I will honor those choices knowing that I always do what is best for me in that moment.

I am willing to grow.

I am willing to know.

I am willing to love and accept myself more fully each day.

I gain resilience by expanding the bandwidth of my own emotions and I learn true empathy.

The Evocative Emotion Movement Practice

This practice creates emotional flexibility in a mindful way by combining improvisational theater and dance. There are feelings we are comfortable expressing and feelings we are not. There are feelings we hang on to and feelings we run away from. By combining a dramatization influenced by the music with your movement shapes, you can access all your emotions, and let them move through you. You are now invited to dance in three powerful ways: you can tell your story to the dance floor, process sadness or grief, and/or release the charge of withheld anger or rage. You might want to try everything available to you, or you might want to avoid some of the emotions for now and skip one of the dances. Whatever is happening, let it be okay just to have agency to choose and have your own experience. You deserve to *feel*.

During the movement practice, you may find places in your body where you might have physical or mental reactions, or places you have become activated. As humans, we all have acquired certain "activators" or "triggers," which is just another way of saying *strongly conditioned responses* to feeling unsafe or traumatized. Please remember that you can always titrate your experience, by going slowly, choosing your music, and using your breath and grounding for self-regulation.

Dr. Steph says that this stage of the flow encourages our brains to overwrite old thought patterns and create new neural pathways, so that we can fully express ourselves and feel safe in our bodies again.

Now it's time to choose a pathway and begin. This practice has four separate playlists that offer a great range of emotions and textures. I invite you to dance with whatever feelings come up, allowing the songs to touch you and inspire movement. Let the music move you and let yourself express fully. It ranges from strings, full orchestral, introspective, sad, passionate, angry, with lyrics, with voice, weird, emotional, intense to folk songs that tell stories.

You only need to move to three or four songs from each section. You'll tap into the emotions with dramatic, honest, and authentic expression. You might cry, express rage, or grieve. Whatever emotion arises, let yourself feel it.

Keep in mind that the body doesn't lie. When you feel the music deep within and you are compelled to make shapes of sadness, or pulses of anger, remember that there's nothing wrong with you. You may want to do the anger dance twenty times before you move onto another dance, especially if there is so much held inside that you can let out in this way. Or you might not think you have any anger, yet the music makes you feel uncomfortable. Each person will have a different reaction to the same music, and that's okay. The music shows your body what's inside, and my responsibility as your DJ is to provide you with a choice. I know that this music could stir sadness, and that's why I'm choosing it for this quality. I know that music manipulates energy, the emotional tone, the physicality, so I chose the music carefully to awaken the emotional landscape for your feelings.

1. Tell Your Story to the Dance Floor

Use your body, without words, to tell your story. There are no specific instructions; the lesson is recognizing how music can activate different emotions. You choose how to move to express that feeling, discovering what you are holding inside you. The expression of your emotions and stories, if done in a creative, artistic, safe, and sacred way, is the key to healing and thriving. By telling your stories without the limitation of words, you begin to feel heard in a new way.

Your story can be your struggles and successes, the limiting beliefs, and the inner longings. Here is the place where we express everything we need to express. The pain, the sadness, the wordless, the angst, the frustration . . . whatever we are feeling that doesn't get any space for release! By dancing, moving, grunting, shaking, expressing it, we turn our ANGST to ART! By dancing it freely, we release a discharge valve inside us, feel relief, and move the energy.

Keep in mind that some stories take a very long time to process. You now have these techniques and tools you can return to again and again. You can tell the same story as many times as needed or move on to other stories that need expression and listening. Think of the dance floor as the listening universe.

It's time to turn on the music and enter the container:

Let the music lead you as you slowly warm up the body with a sway as you stretch and soften. Feel the melodies and allow the emotional tone to touch you. Invite your emotional body to express through the physical body.

Start moving your hands, leading your body through your space. Travel with your feet and take up more space. Add your chest and shoulders to the dance.

Begin to tell your story to the dance floor. Hold the idea of the story you need to tell lightly in your mind and allow your body to do the talking. Make shapes and pulses that express your story to the music and let yourself feel the emotion of your story. Lift and lower, rise and fall, soar and sink, expand and contract, move fast and slow. Remember to keep breathing. Listen to your breath, and any other sounds that you make: all are welcome. Notice how the music grows and changes and let your movement and breath do the same.

Feel the power of emotion in your body. This dance represents the ordeal part of your Hero's Journey, being with the emotions, the stories, and things you can't control. Lean to the back, the side, or forward, animating your emotions. Feel your full range of movement and, keeping the story alive in your intention, say, "I'm telling my story to the dance floor, the dance floor is listening to me."

You might feel inspired to leap off the ground or sink into the floor. Follow your emotional body and freely give it this time to express. Take all the time that you need. Keep moving in this way until you feel complete.

When you are ready, slow your movements down and stretch, breathe, and soften. You can close your dance with the prayer that follows, or head to your journal and allow your answers to the questions to flow.

Tell Your Story Playlist

This is the beginning of the playlist:

- "Rains of Castamere" by Break of Reality
- "The Arena" by Lindsey Stirling
- "YaYaYa" by RY X
- "Opéra" by Emmanuel Santarromana

- "How She Bends" by Toni Bergins

Find the full playlist in the *Embody* portal.

2. Dancing with Sadness and Grief

JourneyDance facilitator Jean Trewhella, who uses this work to help others move through grief and loss, reminds me of the most beautiful description of grief she once heard: "Grief is love with no place to go."

The gifts of grief are hard won but deeply transformative. As painful as it is, many people who have gone through the grieving process acquire truly compassionate and open hearts. Grieving requires vulnerability and an emotional range that expands our capacity to feel.

Societally, we are not taught how to process sadness and grief. We live in a culture where wellness is a business and everybody's trying to feel good, get fixed, improve, and achieve betterment, to the point where any emotions other than joy are shunned. Yet we need a space for grief. We can't just be a feel-good culture, it's just not honest. There's a point in every person's healing journey where the grief is ready to be felt. Whether it's loss of a loved one, loss of a childhood never fully experienced, grief from trauma, or the ending of a relationship once deeply treasured, grief will come up.

How we choose to process and/or carry grief impacts our lives and our attitudes toward the past, our present, and the future. Grief is the great tenderizer for the hardened heart. It's okay to feel your grief, our history's grief, the collective grief, the Earth's grief. When grief is held in a sacred space, we can let the tears flow and wash through us so that our hearts and bodies can open more fully to the present.

It's time to turn on the music and enter the container. Let's see what is needed to release, and experience the relief that comes from finally letting go into grief, into the loving mystery of the divine.

Listen to the music and let it move you as you slowly warm up the body with a sway and easy movement to stretch and soften. Feel the melodies and allow the emotional tone to touch you. Invite your emotional body to express through the physical body.

Start moving your hands, leading your body through your space. Travel with your feet and take up more space. Add your chest and shoulders to the dance. Allow your grief or sadness to surface and move it with the music. Make the intention "if I can feel this, I can heal this," and let your expression and movement become the grief itself.

It's okay to be dramatic with your shapes, lift and drop, expand and contract, or be a wave of emotion, rising and falling. Keep moving, even if it's more slowly. Let your feet take you as if on a slow waltz with yourself. Make shapes that show the pain, anguish, sadness. You may hunch over, you may touch the floor. You are enacting these emotions as part of your ordeal, the challenge. You can even collapse to the floor and rise up again. Keep your emotions in motion.

Move until you feel complete. Find your breath and let it deepen with a big inhale and exhale. Find stillness as you close the practice.

Dancing with Sadness and Grief Playlist

This is the beginning of the playlist:

- "Nuvole Bianche" by Ludovico Einaudi
- "Lion Theme" by Dustin O'Halloran and Hauschka
- "Heal" by Tom Odell
- "On the Nature of Daylight" by Max Richter
- "Closer" by Ane Brun
- "Breathe Me" by Sia

Find the full playlist in the *Embody* portal.

3. Dancing with Anger and Rage

Anger is real, it's natural, and it needs an outlet. Anger transformed is power. Anger transformed is motivation. Anger transformed is energy to accelerate your empowerment. We can physically be with, feel, discharge, and move through anger. What relief you can feel! Remember, it takes much more energy to repress emotions than it takes to express them. So once expressed, you actually feel more powerful as your energy is flowing. Tamping down our anger creates tightness and constriction in the body. To be clear, when we speak about letting anger be expressed, we don't mean "being" angry, we mean releasing any repression of our personal power, and allowing the expression of the repressed energy.

Reevaluation Counseling (RC) was a liberating practice I studied in the early 1990s. We learned many processes and then we engaged in "counseling" with a partner. The most powerful thing we learned was how to be with and witness another person's anger so we could "hold space." When anger came up, we would each take a strong stance position and press our hands into each other, pushing with force toward the center of the connection. The "angry" person could let go of the charge by pressing and feeling their hands connecting with the other, releasing the charge and feeling such a flood of energy that was freeing. I learned that expressing the anger was much healthier than keeping it in, or even just talking about it.

It's time to turn on the music and enter the container:

Feel into the music and the strong beats and sounds. Pulse and bounce a bit to warm up. Allow yourself permission to create vigorous, edgy, and intense movements. Remember my rule: *don't hurt yourself!*

Do your dance and stay IN the body, present with your feet, your hands, your head, your guts. Take up lots of space to expand and move in one direction or the other. Make shapes with your elbows, be sharp, jagged, and forceful. Freely release with big sounds. Please don't judge yourself, just let the movement come. It's okay not to be pretty! Keep moving and discharge by pressing on the space with your hands, with your body, your chest, your pelvis, whatever parts want movement, as if you are making an impression on the space. Express the anger charge from anywhere held in the body. Don't hold back from yipping, grunting, gibberish, whatever wants to come.

You may be able to identify what you are angry about, or you may not. Just notice any thoughts and keep moving: let them influence you and play with the size and shapes of your movements. Try getting small and contained and move your core, activating your viscera by making sounds. Increase your speed and vigor and feel your blood pumping.

It's okay to feel the awakened power of your anger. It's your power and you can give yourself permission to feel it and own it. Once you have discharged enough of your anger, and begin to feel empowered, you diminish your story's hold over you. In this state, you remember who you are without your story, and see your anger as potential energy.

When you feel complete, take a walk through the space, slowing down your movements until your heart rate decreases. Stretch and soften, and then you can go to your journal for some reflection. Or, you might have a ton of energy to fuel your day and go forth.

Dancing with Anger and Rage Playlist:

This is the beginning of the playlist:

- "Persia" by Matisse and Sadko
- "Groove" by Oiki
- "Rollstar" by Dom and Roland
- "Brym Al Mar" by Häana and Dimond Saints remix

Find the full playlist in the *Embody* portal.

Movement Suggestions for Evocative Emotion

- Allow whatever needs to be told to come through.
- Let the music lead you.
- Tell your story to the dance floor.
- If I can feel this, I can heal this.
- Expression is emotion released.
- Lift and drop, expand and contract.
- Be a wave of emotion, rising and falling.
- Take up lots of space or get small and contained.
- Release with big sound.
- Make sharp, jagged shapes.
- Discharge the emotion to reduce our story's power.
- Make sounds whenever you feel moved!
- Don't hold back from yipping, grunting, gibberish, whatever wants to come.

A Song I Wrote for You

To deepen your practice, listen to my song from the Tell Your Story playlist, or read the following out loud:

HOW SHE BENDS

They say you're good if you bend
toward the light
feel the warmth on your skin
just when you're ready to bloom
night sets in

Reaching out through the shadows
To stars so far away
craving my moment to open
but feeling afraid

Who will I be if I let go
who will I be if it ends
how she bends

Bends
how she bends
broken stems
on the mend
heart of gold
can't be sold
I am whole
never will forget how she bends

I take off my mask of perfection
What will be my reflection?
I'll lay it here on the ground
I don't care who is around

Who fill all the cracks with honey
Make me look sweet just the same
Hiding under the pain
The rain
The strain

Who will pick up the pieces?
If she's just playing pretend.
Oh how she bends

Bends
how she bends
broken stems
on the mend
heart of gold
can't be sold
I am whole
never will forget how she bends

Sun comes up in the morning
the light always appears
can I stretch out my petals
without fear

What if I break into pieces
falling to the ground
it's okay if you feel broken,
you can bend

Bends
how she bends
broken stems
on the mend
heart of gold
can't be sold
I am whole
never will forget how she
bends

It's okay if you feel
broken, you can bend

Mystical Inquiry and Transformative Ritual: Break Out of the Box

Rodrigo Gonzalez, JourneyDance trainer, was teaching about trauma and how it shows up in the body. He explained how in Sensory Experiencing trauma-release work, when the body cannot complete the stress response of fight, flee, or protection, it stores the residual energy. This trapped energy becomes part of the trauma itself and needs to be released in an action of completion. Movement and dance can close the loop of uncompleted action.

My father would express his anger freely and sometimes explosively, but we children didn't get to express our anger back at him, so we just shut it down. For me, anger was an incomplete physical pattern that needed to be completed, so I've always been very expressive with my anger on the dance floor, and have since been able to close that loop.

The following transformative ritual can be an act of completion. In this practice, we create movements that are different from our normal ways of moving. We take up more space, and dance bigger or wider. We expand or extend, are vigorous and powerful. This is how someone who felt trapped gets to break out of their box. Someone who felt small gets to feel big. Someone who felt frozen gets to run. All these changes are possible when we dance toward completion. If you've got anger that you've been holding onto, this is your chance to move that repressed energy! We'll kick, punch, jab, elbow, all in a dramatic expression that hurts no one, so we can discharge the energy and complete any incomplete action. As a dance we'll establish the box, break out of the box, dismantle the box, and prepare for an alchemic fire ceremony in the next chapter.

Let's start by asking: What are your limiting beliefs, about yourself, the world? Where do these beliefs come from: your family of origin, religion, society? Do your current beliefs serve you? Is there a cost to yourself or others by holding on to these beliefs?

We create boxes in which to live that are made from our limiting beliefs. For some of us, this box serves as a protection, and for others, their box condemns them to live in a limited way, through conformity or repression. When we investigate by putting the thoughts "outside ourselves" and onto the dance floor, we may see that even though we didn't intend to live inside this box, it is now our comfort zone, so we perpetuate it, even if it's unhealthy and unloving. But once we recognize it, we can change, dismantle the old negative judgmental pattern, and find our own way to truth.

The Break Out of the Box process comes from the idea of ending perfectionistic thoughts, self-abusive chatter, and keeping the limiting beliefs from running your life. Ready to release your limiting beliefs and repressed anger? Play your powerful, evocative music from the Break Out of the Box list and enter your container.

Music for Break Out of the Box

- "Proxy" by Martin Garrix
- "Bruk Bruk" by Dillon Francis

First, we create the box as if we were doing a mime story. Place your hands in front of your face, palms outward. Now slowly move them up, down, to the sides, and to the ceiling to see and feel your "box." Applying a bit of pressure, assess how strong your box is and ask, *Is my box made of sticks, elastic, or concrete?* Some of our minds are more flexible and fluid, others are more tight and rigid. No judgment, it is what it is; just feel it and sense it.

Now we can dance inside our box. Feel what it's like to have the box constricting us, feel the ceiling, feel the walls you've created with limiting ideas, judgments, and repressed emotion. Move to the music in small, powerful ways inside the box. Feel the tightness of this small space.

Once you've gotten the sense of the power of the box, notice what thoughts make up the box. Any of these thoughts could be part of your box: *You're not good enough, you're too big, too small, too old, too young, you're a failure, you can't do that, you'll never make it, you shouldn't have done that, this is the best you can do, you are nothing . . .* We carry so many of these limiting beliefs. I know it's unpleasant to think about these, but once we can name them and recognize them, we can CHOOSE to think about ourselves differently!

Can you see what's holding you back from your possibilities? Feel it in your body. It's time to break out of this box.

Start with your elbows; jab and press them outward as if you are elbowing the box to crack it open. Try punching motions with your fists upon the walls, kicking with your feet and knees, grunting and yelling if needed. Once the walls are weakening, don't forget to smash that imagined ceiling. You can do it! *Only you* can do it! Keep at it until you feel almost tired of punching, elbow jabbing, and kicking.

Now, notice a "crack" in the box and step outside through the crack. Walk around the box. Look at it and say out loud, "I see you, box, I've got your number, I see how I've allowed you to confine me!" or something that feels right to you.

Now you can dismantle the box, literally taking it apart. Pull the high parts down and throw them on the ground, pull the foundation up, get all the pieces of the walls and make a pile on the floor. Take a moment and feel your power.

All that's left is to transmute the remains of the box by composting it into the ground. Jump on it a few times, stomp on it, or you can bring your hands downs to the floor and drum on it. Then, clap your hands together and make a big sound to finish this transformative ritual.

Say out loud:

Thank you and I release you, old box.

I was safe and comfortable in there, but that was the old me.

Now I am free. I am powerful.

I choose what I believe from this moment forward.

And so it is.

Evocative Emotion Personal Practice Journaling

- Where were you blocked, and how do you feel after moving your body?
- What stories need to be told, and retold, in order for you to heal?
- What old story do you need to reframe for your life to improve?
- What negative thoughts, relationships, foods, habits, addictions need to be transformed so you can feel free?
- What emotions arose inside you?
- Was this difficult for you? Do you find you gravitate toward joy? Sadness? Anger?
- How do you feel after expressing your feelings?

Messages to Embrace Your Emotions

After your dance, say the following to yourself:

I am emotional.

It's safe for me to feel.

It's safe for me to know.

I am resilient.

Vulnerability is my strength.

Close the Evocative Emotion Practice with a *Prayer*

Dear Beloved, Sacred Masculine, Sacred Feminine, Masters of Light,

Teach me, oh wise ones, how to weather the storms and ride the roller coasters of my life.

Allow me to embrace living in my full experience of my body, emotions, mind, and spirit.

Allow me to not fear living!

May I feel my anger and not judge it.

May I forgive myself if my unexpressed anger has become resentment.

May I give myself permission to express this power in safe ways.

Allow me to remember that living requires strength, risk, and vulnerability.

Show me the way to take risks and reveal my vulnerability.

Show me the way to honor myself, instead of being hard on myself.

Guide me to transform my angst into art, turn my pain into expression, and put my emotions to creative use.

Remind me that I am resilient and that I am good.

I love myself more fully each day.

Thank you, and so it is.

Move Right into Alchemy Transformation

The qualities of Evocative Emotion and Alchemy Transformation are deeply linked. I don't want you to stir up all your emotions and then have no place to put them and transmute them. So as soon as you complete this practice, go on to Chapter 8.

CHAPTER 8

Alchemy Transformation

Now that you're getting comfortable expressing your feelings on the dance floor, what can we do with all the emotions we're tapping into? I say we use this knowledge for our highest healing. This process starts by transmuting, or transforming, our old subconscious patterns, traumas, and hurts, and turning them into wisdom. You may be a product of your past. But you are NOT your past. You are in the present and can create your future.

I call this Alchemy Transformation because the process almost seems magical. It is a deeply mystical inquiry that will lead you toward real change through a true altered-state experience. You'll be going into peak or heightened states through vigorous movement where you'll get completely out of your head and become embodied. We process our negative feelings and come out the other side with a whole new outlook. You will be able to see your past pains and make the decision to process them so that you can heal. You will be shifting your energy, literally turning your angst into art.

I believe each of us is connected to a source of key knowledge that is true for us and only us. In this practice you will tap into your highest, wisest, powerful, centered, loving parts. You will meet your wise one, your healer, your knower. In this practice you will tap into your intuitive power, your deepest truth. Not your story, but the authentic power that is already present within you.

The truth is, no one knows you better than you know yourself. You are your greatest healer. You can read thousands of books and have a thousand therapy sessions, yet at the end of the day you are the only one who decides if you will end a pattern and open your heart to become transformed. No one can do this but you. No one can live your life but you. You can reframe your life story into one of the hero.

The pain you carry may be from your own past, or from your generational or ancestral lineage. It can also reflect your relationship with the world, as imperfect as it is. Any of these pains can be transformed into power if you face it with the understanding that you are an integration of all your experiences. This concept may be difficult to hear, but it's true: you are the integration of all your past experiences, like them or not. When we acknowledge and learn to love and accept our past, we can move forward from a place of self-love and self-forgiveness rather than neglecting, abandoning, or rejecting the difficult parts of us.

Are you ready to shift and let go of the past, as well as release your doubts, fears, worries, and shame? This practice is a sacred time to "burn"—or energetically transmute and clear—whatever you are ready to release. I strongly believe that you will feel your full empowerment once these patterns are processed and old energies are cleared.

To me, being in your power means gaining a sense of personal sovereignty. You will no longer feel like a victim of your circumstances when your mindset becomes positive and you act from love and clarity. When patterns return, as patterns will do, you'll have a choice, and that choice is power. You can express yourself, get your needs met, set good boundaries, and have healthier relationships. Let's become more powerful by owning ourselves, releasing judgments of our negative patterns, and moving powerfully into acceptance and transformation!

As we continue on this journey, I wish you your highest healing now.

My Energetic Clearing

I love all the qualities, but Alchemy Transformation is by far my favorite. It resonates not only because of the peak experience and the incredible heat, joy, celebration, and power that comes up through movement, it matches my personal need to burn, to release, to let go, to be free, to be untamed, so that I can return to my true nature.

I've studied many different forms of psychological and experiential psychodrama, other philosophies of why we perpetuate overt cycles of abuse and violence, and the subtler forms of dysfunction that can influence our sense of self. I've learned that all our hurts, burdens, and unconscious loyalties (the secrets and unsaid agreements we keep for our family) affect our personality, and the way we show up in the world. We often subconsciously carry the emotional and energetic burdens of our family as an act of caring, in a loving attempt to assist our parents. These energetic patterns and imprints can survive across generations and have been influenced by the way we were raised, the time period, and surrounding culture. If you feel an inner disturbance or an inexplicable weight that has no apparent reason, you might be carrying burdens and loyalties that are affecting your energy.

After years of unpacking my story in therapy, taking ShadowWork programs and training, and participating in family constellation work, I discovered that my inner sadness was an energy that came from an unconscious need to help my mother carry her pain and grief. Ever since I was a small child, I subconsciously helped my mother hold her sorrow following the loss of her mother. I wanted to be with her, connect with her, so I carried some of her sorrow for her.

I also had few and poor boundaries when I was growing up. As I mentioned, my father was an indiscriminate screamer, and this violation of boundaries left me with little guidance on how to hold appropriate space for my own feelings. My mother and I were emotionally *enmeshed*; we were so entwined in taking care of each other's feelings that I had trouble identifying mine and separating from her. And if that wasn't enough, school was literally exhausting for me: by the time I got home I would feel emotionally wrecked, yet I never understood why. I found out later that I was a *clairsentient* and had real empathic and psychic abilities. During the school day I was literally picking up on and actually absorbing other people's energy, as well as dealing with my own issues.

Carrying these burdens was really unhealthy for me, and I had to find a way to purge all the sorrow and grief and stress that I was carrying. All I knew was that I just didn't want to feel my feelings. From the time I was sixteen to twenty-four, for eight solid years, I was bulimic, purging my emotions in this self-destructive way.

I created Alchemy Transformation as a healthier form of purging. I realized that whenever I danced and really got vigorous, I felt amazing afterward. I felt like the real *me*, unburdened and unencumbered. I was so present I could hear a pin drop in my mind. With intention, I could clear my energy and take the dance even deeper into explicit process work. I was able to release and process on the dance floor instead of in words in therapy or with my friends or family.

Think of this as *energetic hygiene*, where you cleanse yourself from all the attachments that are weighing you down. It's influenced by various forms of energy work, shamanic teachings from many different traditions, and the concept of energetic cords, which are the connections that we have to people, to our ancestry, or to the stories from our past. Sometimes, you have to cut these ties so that you can be a free, sovereign being. When you are energetically clean and clear, you can make new choices for yourself and free up new energy. Once I became conscious of the burdens and loyalties that I was carrying, I could see how I was affecting my own children, and I intentionally ended that cycle.

Now, I can use my energy for my highest good, and when I clear, I burn like a flame, and you can too. We are the energy of our own transformation. Then, we become another type of flame: a clean, bright, shining light of inspiration, the light that can be seen in the darkness when we need it most.

The Alchemy Transformation Experience

On the physical level, this dance is high intensity and vigorous. You're increasing your heart rate as endorphins are being released; you may feel an energetic rush. This vigor, combined with the music, may put you in an altered state.

On the emotional level, Alchemy Transformation plunges us into deeper states of emotional awareness. In the last chapter, we mined the grief, anger, and sadness, and now we're going to process it.

On the mental level, you'll focus your intentions like a laser to transmute whatever you want to work through. You'll use psychodrama to create an inquiry where you dance the

seen and unseen, the outer and the inner landscape. You tap into your truth and notice where attention is needed in your most intimate relationship: the one with yourself.

On the spiritual level, you strengthen your intuition and inner awareness, providing the power to transform negative beliefs into positive personal change. You receive messages from your highest self in the form of images, thought blocks, auditory information, and more.

Music: Cleanse Your Energy with Me!

I'm sharing this particular playlist to take you on a transformation that feels empowering. I've used this practice and taken people who were painfully shy to being seen for the first time. I've witnessed people processing childhood sexual trauma and getting back into their body. I've witnessed people release old voices of unworthiness and begin to sparkle like a diamond!

This music is more beat driven than any music that we've danced to so far; it's very intense. It is multirhythmic, layered, evocative, powerful, and expressive, and features a variety of vigorous styles—from electronic to drumming to world rhythms—that create the transformative experience. The songs will help you move, shake, bounce, pulse, and rebound.

You may be surprised by how much you connect to this music and your reaction to it. The purpose of Alchemy Transformation is to help you connect with and feel your power. In this practice, you're going to be learning about yourself, and I want you to be able to have the freedom to express whatever comes up without shutting it down because you're worried that your movements aren't acceptable to others. Besides, you're in your sacred space, your container! You may find that you love to "burn" and get completely wild and chaotic and free, which may be a part of yourself that you never allowed to be seen or experienced before.

In my classes, I've seen that when some people tap into their deep angst, they break down into tears because they have never been able to feel their truth freely. And I've seen others who have guarded themselves so carefully that they revel in displaying their feelings. No matter what comes up for you, don't allow judgment to shut down your natural inclination of expression. Keep moving, move with it, and move some more!

Remember, this is the beginning of the playlist:

- "Yigi Yigi" by David Hudson
- "Loggy" by Si
- "Amma" by James Asher, featuring Sivamani
- "Fundamentally Floored" by Wild Marmalade
- "In the Fire" by Tribal Dance
- "Simcha" by Airtist
- "Macha" by Sagi Abitbul
- "BigBamBoo" by Yomano
- "Didgedelik" by Hilight Tribe
- "Dualis" by Ataya

Find the full playlist in the *Embody* portal.

An Alchemy Invocation

Say aloud, and feel the power of your words:

I am wise. I am strong. I am whole. I belong.

I know that I have power over my mind, though sometimes I allow it to run wild. I forgive myself for that.

As I strengthen my connection to my power, I can listen better and better to my mind and decipher what I truly need and what I can now release.

I know that what I used to believe about myself, and others, can change.

I know that I can teach myself new ways of seeing and holding my story.

During this process of shaking things up, I'll be letting go and reframing my past.

I am now ready to look deeply within, feel my alchemic power, and make space for new energy to emerge.

The Alchemy Transformation Movement Practice: The Fire of Release

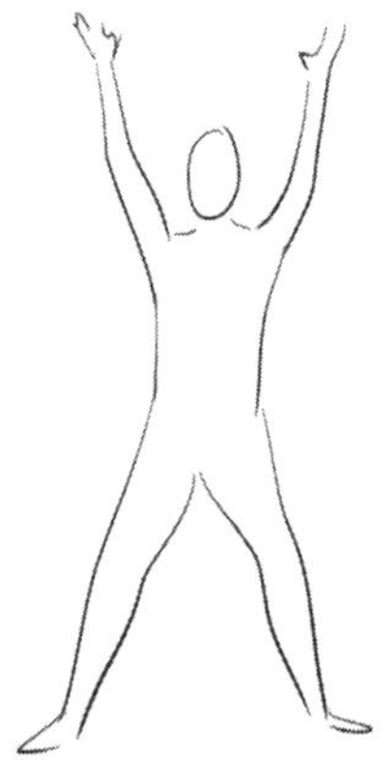

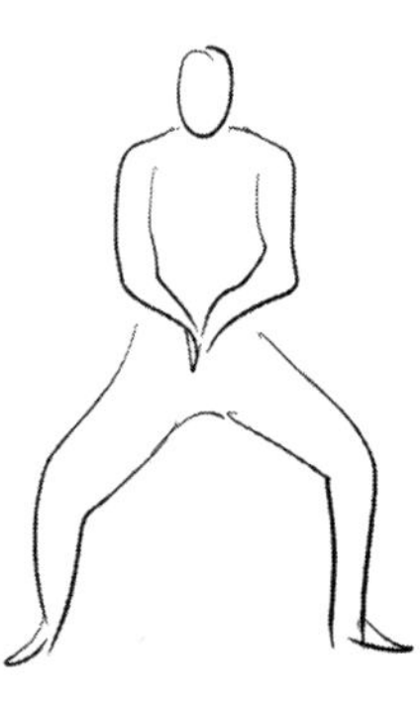

The centerpiece of the entire journey is the Fire of Release, a creative visualization and movement exercise designed to purge and transmute. Dancing with closed eyes may give you the freedom and safety to do deep release and ritual work. Making sounds is powerful here; feel free to release through your voice.

There are three parts to this movement practice: the Energetic Clearing, the Fire of Release, and Gratitude Wisdom. The process begins by assessing and intentionally clearing your own energy body. We create an opportunity to clear regrets, resentments, doubts, worries, burdens, negative messages, negative mindset, abusive thoughts, old patterns, addictions, whatever is needed in a catchall phrase I call *glunk*. When you are cleared, you embody the flame in the Fire of Release. Fire has been revered since its discovery; people have gathered around fires for all time. Fire is a powerful, transmuting element that permanently changes the form of whatever it touches. Without fire, you can't have alchemy, so in this dance, we enact the flame itself. Finally, you give thanks, as gratitude is an acknowledgment of the wisdom you have gained from the past.

Dr. Steph says that during Alchemy Transformation, our brains begin to have a peak experience, similar to a runner's high. This is the ultimate creative space for generating insight. The brain is having an *aha* moment, and the ground is fertile for new ideas and behaviors to be created.

Ready to move? It's time to enter the container:

Part I: Energetic Clearing

Walk around your space and feel into the music. Imagine you are walking in nature or climbing a mountain, seeking your sacred space. You can be in a forest, the desert, the

beach, under moonlight, whatever feels good to you. This space is where you will create a sacred circle to do your work. Only you know what your work is, and you don't ever have to tell a single soul what you're working on.

Focus your walk into a circle. Walk your circle a few times with one hand gently pointing to the middle. Establish a spot that will be the top of your circle; you will return to this spot after each clearing.

Let yourself shake and move, feeling the music as you assess your emotions and your energy in your body. Keep a gentle to moderate body pulse going throughout the practice as you explore your relationship with different emotions and thought patterns, one at a time. To start, let's look at fear, one of the most destructive thought forms that we pick up from so many parts of life.

Pump your body with breath and sound, *Ha!* Place your hands in front of your core or stomach, where sensations of fear, excitement, or butterflies are felt. Using your hands, express the act of physically pulling from your core the memories of any time when your power was taken away from you, any time that you felt someone pulling on your energy or taking your energy from you. You are releasing that person's energy and those feelings.

Think about any fears you may have and imagine that they rest in the center of your body. Fear of loss, fear of the world, fear from our lineage, fear of being alone, fears go on and on. Keep your feet moving a bit as you intentionally pull your fears out of your body and toss them into the center of your circle. Shake off your hands. Make a clapping sound. Feel your power growing.

Keep your feet moving a bit as you move your hands to your back and release any blocks from the low back, any areas where you feel loss of your power. You may want to make sound here too. As you move and dance and release old energies with big gestures and sound, you may begin to feel your power awakening. Pull your blocks out of your back, and toss them into the center of your circle. Shake off your hands. Make a clapping sound.

Now, bring your awareness to your shoulders, and start to shake and wiggle them. Shoulders are where we can carry the weight of the world. Worrying can diminish our energy and put us in perpetual mental loops. Let's make a change! You can release doubts, worries, regrets, and the heaviness you are carrying. Think of your worries as energy and just release them from your shoulders. Move as if you could take them off with your hands, like lifting a heavy weight, and plunk them into the center of your circle. Shake it off, clap your hands, and walk your circle once again, feeling more powerful. You are making a choice to change, you are taking an action, telling your mind and body: this is real.

Now, let's attend to our mindset. Place your hands in the air near your head as if you are reaching for your thoughts in the space of your mind. Muss up your hair, move your hands in the air. We're going to clear out the negative mindset, any thoughts that diminish how you shine brightly, any thoughts that bring you angst. Vigorously pull and draw away the negative thoughts or messages in your conscious and subconscious mind, and toss them into the center.

If you have a very upsetting thought that feels old and sticky, you can dramatically extract those thoughts by plucking them out with your hands (remember in the Harry Potter series, Professor Dumbledore would pull out thoughts like silver threads with his wand). Or, wrench them out in a grand gesture, claiming your sovereignty over your mind's patterns. Remember, this active visualization tells your mind you mean business. Gather, pull, and toss these thoughts you no longer desire into the center of the circle. Find the ones that are repetitive, old, destructive, or that don't belong to you anymore. Once you've put all your thoughts in the center, shake your head and hair out again, clap your hands a few times, and walk your circle and come back to the top once again. Excellent! Let's keep going.

Finally, let's root out the *glunk*. You don't have to know what your *glunk* is to clear it, you just have to feel it and move through it. *Glunk* can be anything that blocks you from living your mission, your dream for your life, your vision, your voice, your vitality, your love—it's all up to you. It could be a harmful message from the past. It could be a story that's affecting you right now. It could be a recent breakup. It could be something with your child, it could be any situation. *What old story do you need to reframe for your life to improve? What limiting messages, negative thoughts, old voices, unlived dreams, relationships, habits, addictions need to be transformed so you can feel free?*

Take your hands and swipe down your arms and legs, holding them about two inches away from your skin, and consciously draw out anything that blocks your ability to trust yourself and your intuition. Any old judgments that blocked your voice, told you not to speak your truth or that you should be quiet. Toss all that into the center. Consciously and intentionally release shame, guilt, judgments of self and from others or society, collectively. Move through what you can in this moment, knowing that you can do this exercise again if you feel there is too much for one clearing. Now, toss all your glunk into the center. Stand tall. Claim your space and your powerful intention. Gently yet firmly, stamp your feet on the ground and say twice or more, in your mind or out loud, *I am Here and Now!*

Toss everything and anything that's come up for you that no longer serves who you are becoming. Once you have released all that, walk your circle one more time and come to the top and clap your hands and let your body shake and move. Now we will begin the Fire of Release and transmute all the energy you placed in the center and alchemize it into power and love.

Part II: The Fire of Release

Now that all your old thoughts, patterns, imprints, fears, doubts, worries, and glunk are in the center of your circle, we become the flame itself so that we can alchemize our angst. First, you have to transform your circle into a pit that has a solid boundary, so take a moment to remember your image of being out in nature and gather some rocks to place on the edges of your circle; this will be your firepit. When you are finished, rub your hands together vigorously until you feel heat growing between your hands. Imagine that you are creating a spark, the tiniest flame. It's starting, and you're going to blow that spark into the pit with a *whoosh* sound. Feel and sense the spark's heat and power.

Dance around your circle, making it wider. Sidestep around the fire circle a few times, moving faster into a sashay, around some more, until you feel a sensation of a swirl or a vortex of energy.

Bring your hands up to the sky and imagine that you are reaching for a flame from the heavens. What color is it? Magenta, gold, silver, orange? Bring your hands down to the ground and pull up another flame from Earth's deepest core. You are ready to "become" the flame itself. Slow your dance down to a still point, reaching your hands to the sky, and say aloud, *I am the flame.* Now, move, dance, and enter the center.

You are the flame, so move as much as you need to in order to transmute your material in the circle. Dance freely and wildly, keeping the fire going for as long as you need.

Just let it all go. Burning, being the transmuter, changing this energy with the element of fire. Shake from your feet to your knees to your hips and let that shake naturally travel all through your body. Bounce by pulsing your heels off the ground, up and down, bringing your internal heat upward. Let your shoulders rebound and pulse your core, chest, and pelvis. Let your body tap into what it needs as you dance with it. Powerfully shake and shake some more. Sweat and breathe and sound! You can chant, "Fire in my belly," or "Power in my belly." Play with making powerful shapes, hold and pulse your shapes, feeling the power build in your body. Travel sideways around in the circle, moving inward. Continue shaking, jiggling, pulsing, wild, chaotic, free dancing.

Step out of the circle and take a moment and assess your alchemy. If you want to add any additional glunk to the center, you can, saying aloud: "I release and dance for my highest healing now." Then jump back in and burn a little bit more.

When you feel that your alchemy is complete, that the intensity of the energy has been dissipated from your dance, and that your fears, doubts, worries, and glunk have been transmuted, step outside your circle, and take one of the very highest tiny sparks of flame, and say, "May this be my inner flame that I may burn and compost, whatever I do not need, at any time," and place that small flame in your body. Place it anywhere you like that you will remember for later use.

Now, complete your energetic alchemy. Reach your hands up to the sky, and start physically pressing the energy of the dance down. Press from the sky to the earth a few times. Bring your body down to the ground. Let yourself feel your innate power. Drum on the ground, pound on the earth with your hands. Feel the beats and the pulses. Let the power move through you and put your last remaining flames out. Imagine the ashes, the smoldering soot, all the glunk that you've burned, and press it into the ground.

When you feel complete, rise up slowly to table position. Gently pulse the body. Allow yourself to feel clean energy being restored back into your body. Pulse your spine, your chest, and then slowly come up to standing, taking your time.

Then rise up to clear the remains as if they were ashes. With intention, release the ashes out an open window or door, or remove them in some simple way. Send the transmuted energy to the sun, or place it in a plant as compost. Come to center, bring your hands to your heart, and say, "Thank you, fire."

Part III: Gratitude to Wisdom: Thank You, Past

Speaking aloud and truly feeling your gratitude is the final step to fully integrating the past into appreciation. Stand still at the top of your circle and lift your hands high into the air to thank the past, which is always being integrated into your present. If you feel ready, say aloud, "Thank you, past."

Now say aloud, "I release you and I thank you," as many times as you like, to thank those old patterns, thoughts, and behaviors for keeping us safe, for shaping us into who we are becoming, because now we are ready to move in a new way—shifting our direction. At one time, those patterns developed to protect us. Now that they no longer serve us, we release them with intention so we can move forward with happiness and strength! I have come to know that not all of the past needs to or can ever be forgiven. But, if we can process, acknowledge, and find ourselves ready to honor our past, change and transformation become our next step—and for that we find gratitude.

Now you can choose to ask, *What are the gifts I've received? What are the lessons? And what is here for me now, in this story, all processed, that I have alchemized into my personal medicine?* Honor you, with a closing self-embrace.

Movement Suggestions for Alchemy Transformation

- Rub your hands together.
- Feel the energy coming from your hands.
- Shake, bounce, rebound, and pulse.
- Release fears, doubts, worries, and glunk.
- Dance your flame.
- Burn up your "stuff," moving wild and free.
- Feel your innate power.
- Say, "I release you and I thank you."

Mystical Inquiry Transformative Ritual: Meeting Your Inner Guide

Many books have been written on working with our "parts" or "the inner child." In this inquiry, we use a psychodrama technique to create splits, where you "become" and enact two parts of yourself. You'll be creating an investigative conversation with yourself, fueled by your imagination and enacted with music and movement. The goal is to dialogue with ourselves, learn from our parts, heal, embrace, integrate, and empower ourselves as whole.

To do this, we invite our inner guide to share knowledge. Your inner guide can be one of many archetypes, including the Warrior, Lover, Goddess, Sovereign, King, Queen, Magician, Alchemist, Mystic, Spirit Guide, Wild Woman, Medicine Man/Woman, Higher Self, Sacred Rebel, Healer, Wounded Healer, Sage, Saint, Shaman, etc., and can extend to animals, elements, nature. Choose whatever image or construct resonates for you.

Find a place to stand with three to six feet in front of you so you can step back and forth between two positions, *Me,* and the *Inner Guide*. Start the music from the playlist.

Standing tall, bring one hand to your heart and the other to your belly. You are now claiming your space, the Me. Asserting this as your space, say aloud, "I am Me, standing here, authentic and present."

To establish the second position, take two steps across and turn and face the Me position. Invite your Inner Guide to come and be with you. Bring your hands down to touch the ground. Feel your connection to the earth. Slowly lift your hands up to the sky and make a powerful gesture, widening the legs and lifting the hands into the air in a star formation. Make a loud sound with breath, like *Ohhhhhhh,* anchoring you to the Inner Guide position. Say aloud, "I am the Inner Guide, the Inner Healer, the One Who Knows." Close your eyes and feel into this being you are becoming; ask yourself open-ended questions to deepen the visualization: *What am I wearing? What does my body look like? What is my skin like, my hair? Am I wearing a headpiece? What does it look like? What resources do I have with me? A staff? Crystals? Magic fairy dust? A wand or sword?*

Start moving as if you are the inner guide and feel what your dance is like in this part of you. This dance could be different from your regular dance, your shapes, and your movements. Just let it come.

Then, walk back to the Me position to acknowledge that you are ready to begin the movement conversation. In the Me position, touch your hands to your heart and your belly, and say again, "This is Me." Dance freely, creatively, artistically, slowly, deeply, showing the Inner Guide whatever you need to express. Be as

open as you feel comfortable. Through movement and gesture, ask for what is needed: release, clarity, healing, resolution, or guidance. You can offer up a situation to the Inner Guide; a pain, a belief, a feeling, or anything that wants to release or needs attention. Show and express through a wordless conversation. For example, if you feel ungrounded, wildly busy, dance very fast; if you feel exhausted, sink into a slumped-over position and move slowly; if you have pain or aches or illness, show your Inner Guide where you need assistance.

After a minute of this expressive dancing, bring it to a pause, take two steps across, move back, and anchor yourself into the Inner Guide position. Put your hands on the ground and lift them up toward the sky and make your sound, *Ohhhhhh!* You can look across to the Me position and inwardly nod or acknowledge, *I am the Inner Guide and I'm here to work with you energetically.* Take a slow walk around the Me position, where you were just dancing, and as you walk, assess what is needed. Intuitively work on your energy body with your hands, give sparkling light energy to the exhausted, give love to the broken heart, remove the energy around physical pain, give yourself the answer to a long-awaited question, share the instructions you've been looking for. Just let it happen and be a channel for your highest healing. Trust your role—whichever archetype you may have chosen—as the Inner Guide. If you need to have magical fairy dust, light, flames, crystals, a sword, scrolls, tools, books, you're going to know exactly what you need, and you will have it at your disposal. Everything is available to you in this imagistic energetic clearing.

Intuitively work on your energy body with your hands, clear energy, give love, remove obstacles, delve deeply into what's unseen, give yourself the answer to a long-awaited question. Just let it happen and be a channel for your highest healing. You can bring energy to your heart to directly give love as a balm for grief or loss. You can cut dissonant cords that don't serve you or drain you. You can unplug from an unhealthy attachment.

Let all of the energetic debris fall away, and take two steps back, completing your role of Inner Guide. Then step back into the Me position, anchor yourself and touch your heart and your belly, and say, "This is Me." Assess how you feel. Embody, move, and dance what it feels like to have all that energy cleared, cords cut, unplugged from everything that you don't want or believe in, answers provided, love given. Feel this free dance, enlarge your movement as you let go and express.

Now you will merge back with your Inner Guide to represent the unification of yourself. Keep stepping back and forth between the two positions, and say aloud, "I am Me, I am the Inner Guide" a few times until you feel complete and merge back into one.

From this newly empowered sense of self, gather all the debris from the process. You can create another Fire of Release, or put it all in an imaginary basket to pour into one of your plants or outside, or send it up to the sun, out your window. Be sure to move and clear that energy in a final way. Then you are complete with this process.

Transformative Ritual: Meet Your Inner Guide Playlist

- "In Search of a Lost Past" by Huun-Huur-Tu and Carmen Rizzo
- "Mother Taiga" by Huun-Huur-Tu and Carmen Rizzo
- "Cuzco" by E.S. Posthumus
- "Jawsharp" by Rishi and Harshil
- "Unibeat" by Nanigo
- "Tenfold" by Tommy Brunjes and Layne Redmond

Alchemy Personal Practice Journaling

- In my life I haven't been able to express or even feel my power because I was afraid that . . .
- After I release all of this, I am excited to experience more . . .
- What do you need to "burn" in your next Alchemy Transformation dance?
- Did you notice your ability to work on yourself energetically? How?
- Do you believe that you can heal yourself?
- What, or who, showed up as your Inner Healer, Inner Spirit Guide, Inner Teacher?
- Can you accelerate or amplify your power?

A Song I Wrote for You

To deepen your practice, listen to my song from the playlist, or read the following out loud:

UNDER THE TABLE

You suck on me like a vampire
take a little bit at a time
you don't take it all in one long pull
leaving me desperate and divine

No you don't, no you don't, no you don't, no you don't

You pull on me bit by bit
And I learn to like it
Need the pain, I take the blame
I cannot fight it

No I don't, no I don't, no I don't, no I don't

She is a little girl hiding under the table
waiting for the storm outside to pass, she's just a little girl
hiding under the table
she doesn't know that it's the past
She's not hiding from you

The rage comes back and haunts me
I fight it as it grows
Echoes of my father
I want the tears to flow

But they won't no they won't no they won't

Dragon with my mind on fire
Stirring out of control
I don't want to burn you
or cause you to go

No I don't no I don't no I don't

She is a little girl hiding under the table
waiting for the storm outside to pass
she's just a little girl hiding under the table
she doesn't know that it's the past
She's not hiding from you

The rushing rains come down
And wash away the fire
The storm has passed
He's out of breath
there's nothing more to shout about

No he won't, no he won't, no he won't

Can I forgive you?
Love you all your wrongs
doesn't matter who I could've been
because of you I'm strong

I'm no longer hiding under the table
I'm strong as hell and I'm feeling free at last
I'm no longer hiding under the table
and I am gonna dance
and dance
and Dance

Messages to Unleash Your Potential

After your dance, say the following to yourself:

I am wise. I am strong.

I am whole. I belong.

I am the flame.

I am free. I am powerful.

I am alchemy.

I am the phoenix, rising from the fire.

Close the Alchemy Transformation Practice with a *Prayer*

Beloved Source, Spirit, God, Goddess,

May I empower myself now.

May I feel my power and sovereignty.

May I release difficult emotions through movement, sound, and writing, just for me.

May I know that I can heal, even if I don't share these feelings with others. Just by accessing and releasing my stuck energy, I will free up new energy for my personal use.

I access my inner alchemy, my inner guidance, with ease, joy, and gratitude.

I can turn my angst into art, my past into my personal medicine.

I now unplug from all that held my energy bound to the past or kept me stuck in any way. In all areas of my life, across time, space, and mind, I set myself free for my highest path and purpose always.

And so it is.

CHAPTER 9

Empowered Celebration

You now know that you have the power to shift your mind's patterns, move through your emotions, and evolve your body's reactions to life intentionally and consciously. This knowledge is the gift that will set you free, because it opens up the possibility for you to decide what you want and who you want to become, instead of resisting and staying attached to your old patterns.

Like a butterfly going through a metamorphosis, you alchemized your life experiences, trials, and triumphs into your personal medicine, distilled into a potent elixir of wisdom, resilience, and purpose, ready to heal and inspire yourself and offer the same to others. And just like the butterfly effect, which suggests that one small action can affect a much larger chain of events, when you flap your vibrant new wings, your medicine will affect change far beyond what you can see.

Honor that you are a deeper being because of all that you've been through. Now that you've intentionally become conscious of and begun to release the old patterns and imprints that were pulling your vibration down, you can refill yourself with visceral joy and a fresh perspective. It's time to galvanize all your joyful power into a new vision, zooming in on what you really want.

You've felt and expressed all the emotions, and now you are left with a clear and empty vessel. Let's fill this new void with your dreams and overlay them with the pure joy of existence and gratitude. It's time to celebrate your new possibilities and take full ownership of your energy. You are now in your power, bringing yourself and your personal medicine to this world that needs you.

You may feel like the world is such a crazy place that you don't have a right to embrace celebration or dream your own dreams. But I'll never forget when my very first soul counselor and my lifelong mentor, spiritual teacher, psychic, and channel, Ariana Shelton, said, "Earth is where it's at. There's a line around the block to get here. It's the only place in the universe where you are in a body and you are experiencing Life." So, here's permission to start celebrating this one gift of being. If you ever needed permission to celebrate, permission is granted.

The Empowered Celebration quality is all about giving yourself permission to be completely uninhibited so you can let go and dance with wild abandon, bringing joy into every cell of your body. As you've already learned, accessing joy helps create new memories to overwrite the past and become a reservoir for the future. This time, we're going to create joy in our bodies, celebrate ourselves, manifest, and dance with our dreams. In her book *Excuse Me, Your Life Is Waiting*, Lynn Grabhorn uses the expression "buzzing positively" to describe the feeling state needed to connect with and bring forth our desires. In the channeled teachings of Abraham, Esther Hicks calls this state "tuned in, tapped in, and turned on." This ideal feeling state is one where your joy and desire are aligned with inspired action and are the key to manifestation, because that alignment enhances celebration, dreams, wishes, longings, and desires, further fueling the alchemy of transformation. I can't think of a better way to achieve this state than with celebratory dance.

There have been many books written on the power of manifestation that dive deeply into the Law of Attraction—the idea that we intentionally (or unintentionally) manifest our reality at all times with our thoughts, feelings, imaginations, and energy. When I focus all of my attention on my fears, doubts, sorrows, and sink into my suffering, I find myself in a mess of my own swirling negativity, and I attract and create more of the like. I might unconsciously snap at my most beloveds, causing them to feel these same emotions. Yet when I feel real joy or pursue my passion in service to others, my desire, my positivity, and their effects on those around me inspire me to make the changes I need to make, and from there, I attract more good into my life. Arriving at the vibration of joy perpetuates more joy. For me, dance is the fastest way to embody the feeling state necessary for manifestation rather than sitting, contemplating, and thinking my way into it.

My dream is that you have joy at your fingertips, a feeling that you know so well, available to you at the snap of a finger. And when you feel joyful sensations in your body, take this as a ripe opportunity to dream big and look at your life with gratitude. The Empowered Celebration quality will put you directly into this ecstatic, joyful feeling state, where you become more intentional with your mind and your power, free to celebrate yourself, your life, your body.

Claiming Empowerment

When you know who you are, stop second-guessing and diminishing yourself, you'll find your power. It may be the still, small voice within, your calmest energy. Or it could be the full force of your love, your passion for change, or your wild, expressive dance.

Empowerment is a feeling, not an action. Empowerment is knowing that you can change, and that you have a choice, even if you choose *not* to. Having this knowledge puts you in the place of sovereignty. When we are empowered, we don't use our power *over* others; instead, we use our power to support love and purpose.

The thought of stepping into your power might be a bit scary. You may have never accessed your power, claimed it, or met it. You may have had to shut it down or hide it in relationships or work to please others or maintain the status quo. Marianne Williamson's famous quote from her book *A Return to Love* reminds us, "Our deepest fear is not that we are inadequate. Our deepest fear is that we are powerful beyond measure. It is our light, not our darkness that most frightens us." Does this resonate with you?

In this quality, you can feel your power expansively and ecstatically. Of course, you'll still feel sadness, anger, frustration, joy, grief as part of life, but from this new empowered place, you remember that emotions are impermanent and will not relentlessly engulf or paralyze you. You have the power to come back to celebration and rediscover your intrinsic joy when needed.

Being in our power, and staying in our joy, takes a level of awareness and practice. Are you ready to move and dance your power, to be the open conduit for the change you want to make, and manifest who you are becoming and what you most desire? Can you say what you need to say, and feel the power to stand for yourself, and shout to the universe, "I am ready now!"?

CHANGE CAN BE BIGGER THAN US

So many of us have been conditioned to always want for ourselves first, but the truth is every single one of us is woven together. We know that there's so much to dismantle in our world; there's so much to reevaluate. The righteous anger, grief, and indignation about the current state of the world is palpable. So what can each of us do to make an impact? How are you going to use your power for sacred activism?

We can use our power for collective change, and from an empowered state we call ourselves out of the small self and into the web of humanity. Whenever we manifest, we can create for ourselves *and* for the highest good of all: we want to be mission-driven to change the culture from *me* to *we*. Utilizing our personal medicine as a guide, we can ground our manifestations in authenticity and compassion.

If you want to change the world, then create your vision as visceral and doable as possible: dream into it, commit to it, love it, dance it, plan it, and take inspired action to embody it. You can do it!

How I Danced into My Dreams

Ever since the "Toni puddle," I had a single vision, and I held that vision without hesitation for the last twenty-seven years because I love this work so much. I got the imperative message that this was what my life's work was going to be, but I certainly had no idea that this vision would become a reality. I was all in with my passion, so I put myself in places where I could share my work, help people get embodied, process their pain, and find their joy. The more I did it, the more I wanted to do it. And this vision has taken me to lead thousands of others in transformational movement.

It can take a leap of faith to make a change. But for me, it wasn't that simple. At first, I was working full time teaching, creating other businesses, and dancing on the side. Slowly over the years, I found myself spending more time on my dream, and eventually, I took a risk and made a full commitment. Now, I've danced with over 200,000 people, and I want to dance with a million. So I'm holding my vision.

Sometimes, manifestation takes years and that level of commitment. And sometimes it's more immediate and quirkier. In 2004, when my children were little, I had a tiny car, an old VW Golf, and it was not going to work with the strollers and all the kid stuff I needed to lug around. I needed a bigger car, so I decided to manifest a Toyota Sienna minivan.

I tested out my process in a manifestation dance while leading a movement workshop. I got myself "buzzing positively" and I pictured a gold Toyota Sienna in my mind. I imagined "the works": automatic doors that open with a button, cup holders, places for their stuff, the kids laughing and smiling in the back seat. And then I did the dance. I was moving, gliding, and careening around; I was embodying my imaginings on the dance floor like I was driving my new car. Of course, no one knew what I was actually manifesting. And I thought the whole business was pretty funny.

The very next week, I decided to *do* something. I couldn't just wait for a gold Toyota Sienna to arrive in my driveway. I went looking at tons of used cars, test drove a bunch, but I didn't see one that I really wanted. I ended up thinking, *Maybe I'll get this Silver Honda Odyssey instead. This one is all right.* So I changed my mind, and I began looking exclusively for the perfect silver Honda Odyssey.

After a few months, a friend gave me the name of a man who goes to Florida to buy used cars for resale. I met with him and told him exactly what I was looking for. He told me he'd be in touch from Florida if he found anything. About two weeks later I got a phone call from the car man. He said, "Hey, I found you a great car. I don't know if you're going to want it because it's not a Honda Odyssey and it's not silver." I asked him, "Okay, what did you find?"

And no joke, he said, "It's a 2002 Toyota Sienna, and it's gold." I had a moment! I had literally forgotten all about my manifestation dance until that moment. My mind went BINGO! So I said, "Oh my God. Yes, yes, yes. I'll take it!" I was so excited, he probably thought I was a little nuts by my wild reaction! And I drove that minivan for more than ten years!

It took six months to manifest what I had asked for, and I had pretty much dropped my original vision. But I had set my intention for it and then *wham,* it was in my driveway! Was it a coincidence? You could say it was, but I don't think so.

Of course, in life there are many more important things you will want to manifest than a car. The point is, you are powerful, and your desires, your dreams, and your visions for this world can happen. You are a manifestor. You are building, you are becoming, you are constantly evolving if you choose that mindset. When you dance this dance, you can celebrate the you that you are right now, *and* the you that you are creating. Every moment that brings you closer to that holds great potential for celebration.

The Empowered Celebration Experience

On a physical level, you will dance full-bodied freedom. There are no rules, no expectations, no performance; just pure movement. Run, leap, jump, bounce, pulse: your

shapes can pour out of you naturally when you move to the music. You may get hot and sweaty; this is the time to dance full on!

On an emotional level, you'll experiment taking on an attitude of confidence and ownership, joy, and freedom as you reach ecstatic celebration. When we move in this way, we feel the ineffable truth of spirit.

On a mental level, you get out of your mind, letting go of all thoughts, feeling the ecstatic state of your body. If you want to do a manifestation dance, you can bring your energy and your intentionally focused thoughts to your well-loved dreams and desires, picturing them in your mind's eye.

On a spiritual level, you ground all your transformative potential into your body; expanding and uplifting your energetic vibration. You hold this vibration for as long as you can, knowing that from your soul's point of view, you can always find it again.

Music: Feel Your Power and Celebrate with Me!

I love this playlist for its pure thumping power, fun, joy, and groove! Choose the pieces that inspire you to feel motivated and powerful. This music is electronic, organic, pop, ecstatic with a strong beat. If you find a favorite, feel free to sing along with the positive messages as part of your dance. Remember, this is the beginning of the playlist:

- "We Can Dance Again" by Armin van Buuren, Reinier Zonneveld, and Roland Clark
- "Catgroove" by Parov Stelar
- "People (Get Together)" by Pink Panda and Silverland
- "Welcome to the People" by JADED
- "The Spirit" by Bakermat (with Aretha Franklin)
- "Brighter Days" by Emeli Sandé

- "Cutting Shapes" by Don Diablo
- "Khatwet Serena (Serena's Step)" by Hossam Ramzy
- "Joy" by For KING & COUNTRY
- "Can't Stop the Feeling!" by Justin Timberlake

Find the full playlist in the *Embody* portal.

Empowered Celebration Invocation

Say aloud, and feel the power of your words:

I have surrendered what needed to burn, so that my soul can thrive in gratitude and celebrate my time on this beautiful plane of earthly existence.

I am ready to touch my power, embrace it, get to know it, meet that part of me that is the manifestor and creator of my life.

I am ready to own my power. I am excited to celebrate all that I am, all of who I am becoming.

I will treasure these moments of self-discovery, and as I open to possibility, I know that a whole new world awaits me.

When I celebrate and move, I create a joyful vibration and am energized by it!

No matter how massive my power is, I know that my heart is big enough to hold it.

The Empowered Celebration Movement Practice

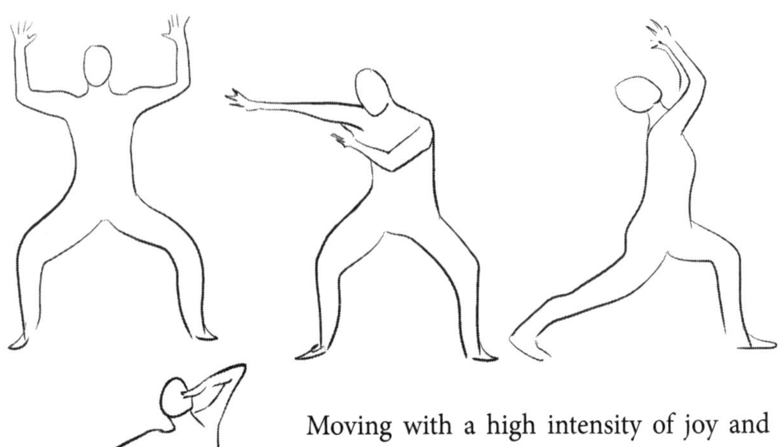

Moving with a high intensity of joy and freedom helps you embody the sensation of our celebration. We free dance and let loose; we raise our vibration and take the chance to dance big. When we can let go and move with wild abandon, joy, freedom, and personal expression, we get out of our minds and might even lose track of time, having a blast!

We feel empowered in a joyful way. This kind of power is not about the size of your body or physical strength. It's about your personal energy field, your intentions, your focus, and your presence holding a positive vision of yourself and your world. When we add joy and celebratory movement to your process, your felt sense of empowerment and full-on spiritedness grow exponentially.

Dr. Steph says that after the peak experiences of Alchemy Transformation, it's important to solidify the information that is being processed. This dance is about firing up the new wiring and embedding the connections of our intentions and creative power. During the Empowered Celebration phase, we are reiterating new ideas and adaptive behavior. Ecstatic and euphoric feelings can occur here, as well as the deepening of emotional release.

It's time to enter your container:

Let the lively music fill your body with good vibrations. Make sure to get your "thump" on, and really feel your body moving and amplifying your energy. Play three songs and see how you feel; if you want to commit to five songs, go for it. If you just *can't stop the feeling*, play them all!

As you dance, feel the power deep inside your body! Remember, power doesn't have to be hyperactive . . . it can be steady, strong, and bold! Feel the exuberant rhythms and move with them freely. There is nothing to do but move. Pump and pulse your body, from your feet to your core, from your shoulders to your hips. Rock and groove from your arms to your head. Feel your energy and expand as you travel around your space. Let your body find a sassy walk, then try another. Get a little wild and say to yourself, *This is my dance*.

Shake when you feel like shaking, bounce when you feel like bouncing, then shake and bounce some more! Do what your body wants to do. Make shapes that come effortlessly, and move whatever wants to move! You might even skip, leap, glide, or bound through your space. Allow for the elevation of your vibration through the music and your wild expression. Celebrate your life, your body, and your feelings. Celebrate your success, your dreams, your self-love. You might even jump and kick a leg in the air, spin, whirl, or twirl! By expressing yourself without expectations, moving without performing, you set your body and your mind free!

Pause occasionally to hold the joyful power within and refill your energy! How much more joy can you hold? Let's

see. Let your body tap into what it needs as you dance. Feel your joy. Feel your power. Get physical, move bigger, move powerfully, move faster, turn up your internal heat! Feel your breath moving in your body. Feel your sweat and let go. Keep moving! You can rise up, lifting your hands in the air and bop and rebound. You can get low and pulse your pelvis and let loose.

When you must stop, after you're dripping with sweat, slow your body down and take a walk through your space to cool down for at least a couple of minutes. Revel in the feelings in your body.

Bring your hands to your heart and say to yourself, *I bring this joy into every cell of my body and being. I receive this ecstatic celebration in my every cell. I love* me!

Movement Suggestions for Empowered Celebration

- Bound, leap, jump, spring, bop, skip.
- Spin, whirl, twirl.
- Find a sassy expressive walk.
- Elevate your vibration.
- How much joy can you hold?
- Dance with your dream.
- Celebrate the "you" you are becoming.

SMILING KEEPS JOY FLOWING

The simple act of smiling ignites a cascade of positive effects within your brain. It's been scientifically proven that when the muscles in the face contract into a smile, they send signals to the brain that trigger the release of dopamine, serotonin, and endorphins, which all make us feel good and reduce stress. According to Ron Gutman, the author of *Smile: The Astonishing Powers of a Simple Act*, "British researchers found that one smile can generate the same level of brain stimulation as up to 2,000 bars of chocolate."

If you start noticing yourself slip into fear, doubt, worry, and/or glunk, see if you can muster a smile and let that empower you. Let it shift you! Joy is your power! So, make smiling your practice when you're not dancing wild and free.

Mystical Inquiry: Manifestation Dream Party

This mystical inquiry can help you create, with purpose and attention, your desires: love, relationships, family, career, abundance, art, your mission, your vision, your sacred activism for the world. If your dream is an old one that weighs you down or makes you feel regret and bad about yourself for not achieving it, then please don't focus on that dream. You can always bring that story back to the Evocative Emotion and Alchemy Transformation qualities. This moment is here for you to connect with the loved dreams of the present and the future. There's a part of us that knows what to manifest; we know when we are in right alignment because we feel a sense of purpose, intuition, and joy.

Let's begin by exploring these clarifying questions:

- How do I want to wield my power?
- What am I ready to create with my power?
- What am I ready to bring forth into this world?
- What parts of me want to be seen and known that I have yet to share?
- What do I want to do with this precious life?

For this inquiry, you'll need a few light, flowy scarves, anything that floats when you move it through the air will

do. When you're ready, press play on Transformative Ritual: Dream Manifestation playlist, and enter your container.

Bring the scarves into the center of your container and place them on the floor. Face the scarves and lift your arms to heart level, palms facing toward the center.

Invite an invocation from your energized higher self to assist you in your dream party, saying to yourself: *May I manifest this vision for my highest good and the highest good of all.*

Slowly move in a circle, following a grapevine step. Keep moving around the circle and feel the energy build. Imagine that the scarves in the center of your circle are in a beautiful vessel or basin. Move your arms in a circle facing the basin as if you are stirring ingredients in a delicious recipe. Stir the vessel, adding your dreams and desires. Throw into the basin all that you wish to enliven your dream, like love, joy, delight, freedom, abundance, expansion, whatever feelings this dream brings to your heart and soul.

Now acknowledge the scarves as representative of your dreams coming to life. As the pace of the music picks up, pull a scarf out of the center to represent your first dream.

Dance with your scarf, your dream, your desire. Hold it in your arms lovingly, let it dance playfully, throw it up in the air, run through your space with it, leap, glide, be right there in the moment with it. You will know just how to dance this dream and give it your love and attention. Dance and move to the music with your intentions held lightly in your mind, and stay "buzzing positively"!

Leave the circle and move around the room, nourishing the dream, dancing the dream, imagining it to be true, here and now, existing, happening, feel the feelings of experiencing this creation. Then, return to the center of your container so that you can honor the dream you danced. Place your scarf back in the center.

Take a moment to see if there is another dream you want to explore. If so, exchange the scarf for a different scarf—another dream. You can have as many dreams and as many aspects of life you're working on. Don't be afraid to dream! Dreams are inspirations for your life. It's okay to dream, it uplifts your spirit. Let your final dream be totally personal.

When you are complete for now, as dreaming never ends, place the scarves back in the center and bless your dreams. Close your sacred space with a gesture of gratitude to the Dream Party. Stand at the top of your circle and lift your arms to the sky, or place them on the earth, and say, "Infinite spirit, bless these dreams for my highest good and the highest good of all, I receive the manifestation under grace with my deep gratitude."

Repeat this dance whenever you feel it's time to create something new in your life, or bring in the celebratory energy for your dreams.

Off the dance floor, take an inspired action toward your dream. Take another and another, and let me know what happens!! It may take a minute or more than six months, so be happily surprised when it comes to pass.

Transformative Ritual: Dream Manifestation Playlist

- "The Buzz" by New World Sound and Timmy Trumpet
- "Banghra"—Short Vocal Mix by Krid P
- "Jolie Coquina" by Caravan Palace

Empowered Celebration Personal Practice Journaling

- How do you feel when you move freely, exactly as you wish?
- Were you able to feel and claim your power and your ecstatic energy?

- How can you bring your personal medicine to this world?
- How will you shift your vibration so that you can manifest your personal vision?
- If you were to commit to your vision, what top three action steps would you prioritize? Why?
- Did you notice any attachment to old dreams that you might need to release in order to feel more daily joy and elevate your vibration?

Messages to Connect You with Your Power

After your dance, say the following out loud:

I choose love over fear.

I choose possibility over fear.

I know my deep inner power.

I celebrate me exactly as I am.

It's time for me to live my dream.

What am I waiting for?

I smile!

Close the Empowered Celebration Practice with a *Prayer*

Infinite spirit,

I am ready to own my power and celebrate all that I am.

My inner passionate spirit is my power.

I claim this power to serve life in a new way, fortified with my own essence.

My deeper knowing and my journey of self-discovery is my true power.

Transmute my anger to compassion, love, and freedom. Teach me my power in all its forms, so that I can use it for the most authentic manifestation I desire, for the highest good of all.

I now understand that my power is a positive thing and I don't have to be afraid of it.

With deep humility and gratitude, I thank you for teaching me how to wield my power in a positive direction for the greatest outcome of all.

I commit that my power be used for the highest good and I ask for your guidance in how to do this daily.

I can joyfully dance my way to my aligned path.

And so it is.

CHAPTER TEN

Sensual Freedom

Each of us comes to the Sensual Freedom quality from different places along a wide spectrum of perspectives and experiences of our bodies. You may be completely at ease, open, relaxed, and expressive, or you may have a difficult or complex relationship with your body, your sensuality, and your sexuality. These different outcomes may be related to sexual trauma, highly restrictive or identity-harming environments, or a sexually positive upbringing, and all points in between. Wherever you fall on this spectrum, this quality is an invitation to enjoy the sensual nature of your body, experiencing it from a new perspective that's positive and beautiful for you.

You are capable of being sensual, whether you experience it or not. Sensuality is human nature, it's how we enjoy nourishment, pleasure, and connection. It is the anticipation of flavors and textures hitting your tongue; it's the first bite. It's the enjoyment of life's moments. It's about enjoying your body shamelessly as you embody a total appreciation of what's possible. Engaging in sensuality strengthens our mind-body connection as we pay attention to our physical sensations and listen to our body's feelings and needs. This practice can become an act of self-love and compassion, affirming our worthiness and value.

Your connection to your sensuality and sexuality can deeply affect your self-esteem *and* how you feel about your physical body. Imagine what it would feel like to have a sensuous love for yourself, completely on your own terms, without having to consider other people's expectations or the external gaze. We could cast aside the false and harmful assumptions about which bodies are beautiful and which aren't, and once and for all transform the societal burden we carry. This shift to enjoying our sensuality from the inside is game-changing work.

You are your own aphrodisiac: just dancing and moving sensually can make you feel wonderful. When you dance sensually, you naturally increase your proprioception and your interoception, which we talked about in the earlier chapters, because you start to see and feel your body moving in space in a slow, smooth, luscious way. And when you do that, you turn on a sensory perception that I call *embodied intuition*. This is intuition that leans on your body's wisdom in tandem with your mind. You begin to have a deeper insight and develop a new sense of boundaries and begin to say *yes* to what truly feels right for you and *no* to what does not. When we're not connected to our sensual body, we can miss the subtle cues of what "good" feels like, and when we have access to our sensations, we can pick up these sensory signals much more easily. When you practice this Sensual Freedom state, you can feel a visceral sense of self, and may notice when your personal, and even sexual, boundaries are being encroached upon and make new choices.

So how do we find our right relationship, our alignment with our sensuality? In this quality, you'll engage with your sensuality in a deeply personal and private experience. It's not about performing or adhering to old societal expectations; it's about connecting with your own authentic movement and pure sensation.

Sensuality Is Just for You

I have always been a very sensual being. I love being outdoors, feeling the sun, the wind, the trees, and digging in the dirt with my bare hands. I love swimming and gliding through the water, walking barefoot on the sand. I'm drawn to tactile activities, making clay into pottery, playing instruments, touching the keys and the strings. I love everything physical and sensorial about cooking: the chopping, seasoning, smelling, and sampling, and then enjoying the delicious food. I feel most alive when I'm fully embodied in a sensory state.

Being a sensualist like me doesn't make you outrageously sexual, but it certainly can enhance your feeling of sexiness. Sexuality without sensuality is like eating without tasting. But here's the thing: sensuality and sexuality are different. Yet so many of us have limited our access to our sensuality because we confuse the two, and worse, because sexuality is so often connected to feelings of shame.

Sexual shame has been boiled into us, stemming from the religions we grew up with, the traditions of our home and culture, the puritanical heritage of this country, and the systematic, patriarchal control and suppression of women and others who don't conform. As women, we are shamed if we are too sexy and shamed if we are not sexy enough. We have been shamed because of our sexual preferences, identities, and desires. When I hear someone in one of my classes say, "I just don't do that kind of dancing or movement because it's not safe." I know that shame has been holding them back for years, and they haven't even noticed how much of their life force they have shut down.

I remember running around naked when I was a very young child, and it all seemed perfectly natural. Friends would come over, we'd rip off our clothes, and run around the yard. By age eight, we were told, "Put your clothes on!" As I got older, I felt less comfortable with my own body. No one taught us as young adults about sensuality or sexuality, except for the eighth-grade sex ed class where we were educated with silly videos on how to make (or not make) a baby, and how not to get sexually transmitted diseases. It was a comical, shaming, and fear-based lesson plan that left a bunch of hormonal teenagers running around with blindfolds on, trying to tame our sexual selves. We knew what was taboo, we knew what we should avoid, but we really didn't know how to access what was good, healthy, sensual, and natural.

For me, as a young adult, it was heartbreak hotel. After an awful breakup with my first love, I avidly explored my sexuality almost as a power play. I had been hurt by someone, so I tried to use my sexual power to regain my sense of self-esteem. Sometimes the experience was good, and sometimes it wasn't. Especially during the college-age years, I used my sexuality as a provocation. I believed that I could so easily get hurt or be taken advantage of, so I decided to use my sexuality as the hunter/provocateur/seductress. Yet in my effort to reclaim myself, I found that my misguided power play hurt both myself and others. There was no sensuality in my sexuality; sex had become a dissociated performance. Years later, I regretted those encounters and had to face another layer of sexual shame.

I've since learned that getting in right relation with my sexuality was ultimately a sensual experience. I intentionally stepped out of seeking power and moved into pleasure. And where did I learn this? Again, it was on the dance floor. Dancing my sexuality and exploring my sensuality in a safe container was a critical piece that helped me understand that these two worlds are intertwined but are not the same. When I began to really know my body and could sense and feel what I liked and didn't like, I could embrace sensorial pleasure in every aspect of my life, and then make the right decisions for me as to what is a healthy sexual relationship. For me, I need both pleasure in my body *and* pleasure in my heart to feel complete. The two must be connected or I feel out of alignment.

Your sensuality and your sexuality belong to you and only you. I have no judgments regarding your sexuality—you do you—but whatever you do, I invite you to respect your expression in the context of self-love and right alignment. The challenge is to find what really serves your heart and soul. We all want to feel good about ourselves on a sexual and sensual level, so we need to learn how to esteem ourselves from the inside, and not give that power to a partner or lover, which means getting our value from the outside.

When we understand ourselves and our desires, we are operating from the inside, and we can let go of our shame and shift our love dynamics into Sensual Freedom, where you will know what you want in many different aspects of your life. For instance, while you may feel sexually attracted to another person, when you are using your embodied intuition, you may recognize that a relationship is or isn't conducive to your well-being. With this embodied intuition, you can assess what's really healthy for you in relationships. Some people can have casual sex, some people cannot. Some people can do polyamory, some people cannot. Some people need monogamy and commitment while others thrive in open relationships.

Understanding both your sexual self and awakening your sensual nature are both essential for a vibrant life because they are so connected to your energetic life force. In order to explore your sensuality, you'll be going into your container with a bit more consciousness and intention around the sanctity of your space. I want you to have a chance to dance sensually, without fear of judgment or shame. You may feel liberated to express yourself freely without fear of judgment, focusing on sensuality and self-awareness rather than performance. It can change the way we dance, maybe more freely than ever before.

If you are a survivor of sexual trauma, or carry a heavy cloak of shame, this quality may require a very gentle approach for you to safely journey through and embrace this opportunity to reconnect and mend your relationship with your body. If you can honor yourself and recognize, respect, and prioritize your own needs, values, and well-being, over time you may experience a major shift in your sensual expression. I have worked with many people who have been able to rediscover a sexuality and sensuality that they are comfortable with through this intentional movement practice. When they come to the dance floor and go through each of the qualities, layer by layer they reclaim their body. By the time they arrive in Sensual Freedom, they are able to sip the experience, drink it in, slowly at their own pace, instead of being inundated.

A special note to women and LGBTQ+ folks, whose bodies have been assessed, valued, or devalued on a regular basis. This dance is for you.

The Sensual Freedom Experience

On the physical level, you'll be invited to move slowly and lusciously, feeling and rediscovering every part of your body. You'll have a complete sensate experience, focusing on the moments before sensuality becomes sexualized. You'll allow energy to build and subside.

On the emotional level, you can gently or playfully open to your own receptivity and softness, you might even feel your own desires awaken. You may feel joyful, wistful, longing, "yummy," passionate as you explore this terrain.

On the mental level, you become so embodied that the internal chatter quiets down, allowing you to feel and recognize your unique beauty. You might notice self-judgment, or critical voices, or an appreciation of yourself in right alignment with your sensuality. You might even begin to love yourself from the inside out.

On the spiritual level, you are connecting spirit to the flesh, you are allowing love and passion to live within your every cell, and allowing yourself to develop a deeper inner knowing and embodied intuition.

Music: Dance Your Sensual Freedom with Me!

The music for this quality is thick, sensuous, and flowing, with an occasional saxophone, or vocal for deeper effect. The songs feel expansive yet internal, drawn out, extended, sexy, or jazzy. Remember, this is the beginning of the playlist:

- "Unthinkable" by Damien Escobar
- "Kundalini Rising" by Mant Monaco and Activation
- "Reclaim" by Malka Russell
- "Tincture" by Feral Fauna, KR3TURE and Heather Kristie

- "Espejos" by Symphony and Kompass
- "Love Me Like a River Does" by Melody Gardot
- "Special" by Lizzo
- "Got It" by Marian Hill
- "The Little Things" by Big Gigantic and Angela McCluskey
- "Woman" by Amber Lily and Lily Fangz

Find the full playlist in the Embody portal.

The Sensual Freedom Invocation

My being is innocent, miraculous, and divine.

I open to this today as I set out on my journey to Sensual Freedom.

When I forget that I am part of this sensual world, please help me to remember.

Allow me to sink deeper into my body and its beauty rather than get caught up in the mind and its driving forces.

Let me take pleasure in each moment, in my breath, in my senses, and open me up to more delicious yumminess than ever before.

I am ready to reawaken my miraculous body, experience that sweetness like honey, and allow new possibilities into my life.

The Sensual Freedom Movement Practice

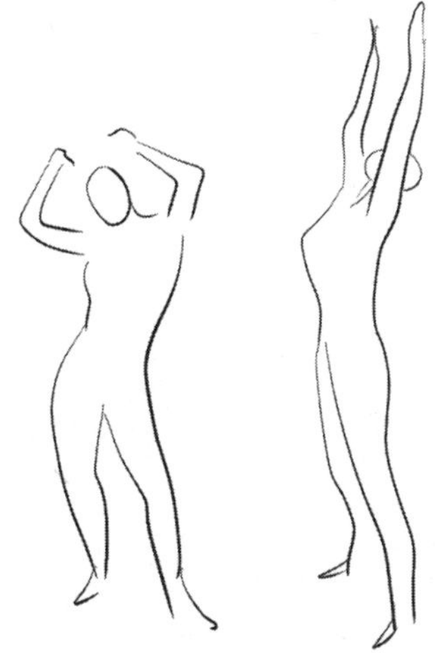

The Sensual Freedom quality invites us to celebrate our bodies in all their diversity and uniqueness. Rather than viewing our physical selves through a lens of criticism or judgment, we learn to appreciate and honor these magnificent vessels that carry us through our life's journey. As we release societal standards and expectations, we can truly embrace our bodies with love, acceptance, and gratitude.

By taking time with our movement, making it feel delicious, slowing everything down, we can delight in the pleasure of feeling, savor our sensory experience, and relish living in our bodies. We can learn to nourish, cherish, and celebrate ourselves. We become more attuned to our bodies' signals, developing an aliveness and an empowered self-awareness.

The dance is super slow. Focus on feeling every part of you with a new perspective, now that you have a different relationship with your body from when you started this embodiment process. Expressive movement with the intention of achieving pure sensation can bring you into your most primal body. If you feel your sensuality reawaken and you want to share it with others, then you have the freedom to do so. But for now, this dance is just for you. From a trauma-aware lens, let's do this work in private, without a viewer.

Dr. Steph says this is the quality of resolution, relaxation, and satiation from a nervous system perspective. We are still acutely aware of mind/body interconnection and sensory experience. In this phase we can experience heightened sensory and tactile reception.

Enter your container.

Let's start standing, grounded and present, feeling the bottoms of your feet connecting to the earth. Very simply take a few invigorating inhalations, feeling the sensuous music inspiring your body. Notice what parts of your body want to move first, and just follow your personal flow. You can let your chest glide, side to side, around, diagonally, just moving freely and softly.

Begin to sway side to side to the luscious rhythms and vocals. Explore the delicious sensations and stay with yourself. Pulse your pelvis and chest, rock your body, stretch, elongate, and contract your muscles. Feel free to touch your fingertips to your skin, your clothes, and cascade gently up, down, across, and over. Slide and spiral, expressing your sensuality, taking your time for each exploration. Playfully lead your whole body with different parts of you: your nose, your mouth, and anywhere in the body that wants attention.

Move to your shoulders, roll them around in smooth circles up and down, feeling every sensation. Tenderly contract or expand, relax, and stay with soft repetition, feeling an easy liquid-body effortlessness.

Now, feel your edges, your sides, your back, all the places where your body connects to space. Imagine you are made of liquid light, golden honey, or a sweet-scented oil. Let the music lead you deeper into that liquid sensation, loving yourself with the image. You are moving like honey, or moving through honey; let it slow you down and see the golden colors in your mind's eye. You can close your eyes and feel the music; you can move and stretch, oozing and undulating.

Come home to your hips and pelvis, swing slowly back and forth, pulse gently side to side, and swirl around in a circular motion. Then invite your chest to join in, slowly in undulations and spirals. Lovingly touch your head, caress your face, your neck. Touch your hair with your hands. If that feels good and sensual, rub your scalp, bringing more sensation to your head.

Have a playful, yummy conversation with your whole body, let your shoulder talk to your hips, let your chest talk to your pelvis, let your head move carefully and slowly in soft circles. Feel your luscious body fully and with all your attention. You might smile and bring your joy into the body.

If it's comfortable for you, close your eyes and let go a little deeper into your own personal private dance moment. Express yourself freely and fully moving exactly as you wish, truly dancing sumptuously like nobody's watching. Feel every cell bathed in golden light and bring healing light to your whole body. Your sensuality is a gift. Your voluptuous sweetness is all your own.

When complete, close your container and bring your hands to your heart and your beautiful belly, massage them with light circular motion, connecting your whole body. Take three long slow breaths, inhale, feeling your hands rise and fall as the breath fills you, and then exhale, letting go. Thank yourself for moving in this fabulous way just for yourself. With your hand still connected to your skin, tell yourself, *I love you.*

Movement Suggestions for Sensual Freedom

- Move sensually and joyfully.
- Let your body move however it wants.
- Let the pelvis and hips awaken.
- Let the music lead you.
- Have a playful conversation with your body.
- Move smoothly like liquid, pulse, and undulate.
- Stretch, elongate, contract, and relax.
- Have a conversation with your sensuality and ask for its guidance.
- Let your body tap into what it needs as you dance.
- Dance for the sheer pleasure of moving and feeling your own sensations.
- Close your eyes during your private dance, feel into your body.
- Replenish your energy.
- Move like honey, warm oil, thick liquid.
- Feel every cell bathed in golden light.

Sensual Freedom Personal Practice Journaling

- Are you comfortable being sensual in your body?
- Do you feel expressive, sexier, and freer?
- Did shame or judgment arise? If so, go to Mystical Inquiry: A Visualization to Free Yourself from Judgment, which follows.
- Can you make a connection between feeling good and manifestation? Are you buzzing even more positively from the last chapter?

Mystical Inquiry: A Visualization to Free Yourself from Judgment

If you felt uncomfortable or heard judgmental and shameful inner voices arise while you were dancing this quality, I have a psychodramatic remedy for you. If you want to bring more sensual freedom into your body and into your relationships, if you were taught that you shouldn't enjoy sex and/or that you should feel bad about your desires, or that you should feel uncomfortable with your body, consider this an opportunity to reclaim your sensual self without shame or judgment.

This exercise was developed by somatic therapist and JourneyDance facilitator, Jenna Abernathy, and can be used to help free yourself from internalized judgment of your inherent sensuality and your body, whatever shape, size, age, color it may be. This process is similar to the psychodramatic splits we did in the Alchemy Transformation quality. Here you will embody two distinct parts of you: the Sensual Self and the Inner Judge.

In the practice, we take on the Inner Judge, the part of you that judges your sensual and sexual expression, and moderates how you look, move, and behave. The Inner Judge's thoughts might come from societal or familial conditioning, or even from partners, friends, or childhood experiences that resulted in lingering pain and hurt. Some of us are so accustomed to thinking negatively about ourselves that we don't even notice it's there, chatting to us in the background, creating shame, shutting us down, or leading to rebelliousness.

First, answer the following questions as they prompt explorations into your sensual, uninhibited self. Let's look at your judgments. This is a moment for you to take back your power and own the judge as part of you and make peace with it. You can ask the judge a few questions:

- Do I judge myself harshly, and if so, why?
- Am I rebellious with my sexuality?
- Whose judgments are these anyway, and where might they come from?
- If I knew my judge was just trying to protect me, what would the message mean?
- Am I judgmental of others' sensuality or sexuality? (Sometimes the way we judge others gives us clues as to how we may be judging ourselves, aka, projection.)
- How loving am I with others? (Similarly, the way you give love to others often represents how you want to receive love and what you want more of in your life.)
- How can I love myself better?

Now it's time to move. Start the Transformative Ritual: My Sensual Soul Heals the Inner Judge playlist.

Create a circle on the floor. Let's call it My Judgment-Free Zone. Walk around it, setting up your container, and use your hand to physically draw the circle. Inside this circle you are in your safe space for the Sensual Self, where you will dance freely and sensually without judgment. Step into the circle and let yourself move exactly as you wish, just like we did in the Sensual Freedom movement practice. Enjoy everything about your body and your movements. If you are struggling, use an "act as if" mindset and listen to the lyrics as you move, remembering that no one is watching. Dance for the sheer pleasure of moving and feeling your own sensations.

After a couple of minutes, step outside your circle. On the outside you will embody your role as the Inner Judge. Now, walk around this established circle, feel how the Inner Judge moves and walks. Look at yourself from the voyeur's perspective, as if you are in the center, dancing with sensual freedom, and listen to how you judge your own body and your expression. See how you treat yourself unconsciously. Hear all the internalized self-judgments that come up. Walk around the circle, pointing to yourself in the center, and say the words that are appearing in your judging mind. We must acknowledge these thoughts in order to make peace with them, so we *externalize our beliefs in order to transform this tension we are carrying.*

After no more than ninety seconds, step back inside the circle and become the Sensual Self again. Take back your role, embody yourself, and dance freely.

Let the music continue as you move to the song, "I Put a Spell on You," by "Screamin' Jay" Hawkins, covered by Annie Lennox. From inside the circle, dance and sing the lyrics directly to the Inner Judge. Use the lyrics as part of the ritual, but change their meaning so that the "*You*" in the song is your Inner Judge. When you hear the words "because you're mine," see if you can own that the Inner Judge is actually a part of you: a belief structure that you have internalized. With this acknowledgment, you can create a new relationship with the Inner Judge. You can show the Inner Judge that you are so empowered in your beautiful, sensual dancing body that you no longer need their comments and confusion. Say aloud, "I choose to dismantle this old belief structure right now."

Staying in your Sensual Self, allowing your feelings of confidence to build, see if you can invite the Inner Judge to dance with you inside the circle. Gently move with the Inner Judge, staying in your role as Sensual Self. See if you can hold the Inner Judge in your arms. In your mind or aloud, tell the Inner Judge, *Thank you for protecting me, thank you for keeping me safe. I know you meant well. Your words are not actually my judgments of myself. I forgive you. Now I reclaim and reconnect with my body, with my sensuality with my sexuality, without shame.*

By the end of the song, merge back into oneness, knowing that you have energetically and emotionally healed the Inner Judge with your forgiveness. Pull the healed energy back into you. Dance freely again. Feel your power build, fully embodied in your Sensual Self. Celebrate your work with the third song, choosing either "Wonder Woman" by Lion Babe, "Video" by India Arie, or "Move Your Body" by Sia.

Close the dance with a slow, deep breath, and thank this moment with your hands on your heart.

Transformative Ritual: My Sensual Soul Heals the Inner Judge Playlist

- "You Look Like Rain" by Morphine
- "I Put A Spell On You by Annie Lennox"
- and more . . .

Messages to Strengthen Your Sensual Freedom

After your dance, say the following out loud:

I am sensual.

I am sexual.

I am luscious.

I delight in my body.

I delight in my senses.

I love my life.

Close the Sensual Freedom Practice with a *Prayer*

Dear Goddess, Mother, Gaia,

I know that I come from you, my natural mother.

I am part of Nature, like my mother, and her mother before her, and all my ancestors.

Thank you for bestowing upon me this natural beauty.

I deeply love and appreciate my body.

More and more, day by day, I love my body exactly as it is.

I accept the changes and shifts my body makes as I travel the path of life.

I deeply and truly forgive my body for any ways I may have felt betrayed by it.

I deeply and truly forgive myself for any ways I have hurt my body consciously or unconsciously.

My body allows me the pleasure of being alive.

Allow me to connect to my senses.

Let me revel in my living experience.

Show me how to enjoy being in a body, to taste the sweetness, to smell the fragrance, to touch the softness, to hear the symphony.

Open me to pleasure and the vastness of my senses that I may find a new gratitude for all the little things in which I find delight.

May I create beauty, walk in beauty, and feel the beauty of my own inner being.

May pleasure be mine.

May I take my joy into all that I do, being so completely in the moment, that my pleasure gives others pleasure too.

I love you, my body. I love my blood, my skin, my bones, my muscles, my organs down to my very cellular core.

From this moment forward, I see myself and love my body fully and completely.

And so it is. 

CHAPTER ELEVEN

Open Heart

The heart is a true mystery, an unfolding vast and endless source of love, something the mind cannot begin to grasp or truly understand. Yet we can experience it, embody it, learn how to feel its love, with all the wisdom it may bring to us. The heart represents our most vulnerable, sensitive nature, sitting at the center of the soul. I'm speaking of the heart as an energetic space, a nexus of feeling, not the blood-pumping organ. The center of our physical body is considered the lower abdomen, the space just underneath your belly button. As a dancer, I was taught to pull up and pull in from this space because it is the center power point of movement. In our energy body, the heart is at the center of the system. The heavens are the highest point, and the earth is the lowest. And the heart is the communication center between the two. The heart is the most powerful space between our mind and our body, our adult self and our inner child. It's the love that we are, the love that we long for, the love we long to become.

After taking the courageous risk of identifying our thoughts, expressing and processing our emotions, transmuting our patterns, and claiming our bodies, we arrive here with an open heart. At this point we might feel a tinge of tenderness, a sweetness that feels like a loving embrace that may bring tears to our eyes. This is not the melancholy of brokenness; it is the awakening of love within our very souls. The Open Heart space often appears when we are ready to see ourselves anew and feel more voluminously, when we are forgiving, empathic, compassionate, and loving.

We open the heart by giving it attention and quieting our minds to listen. Your heart is one of your most important guides, yet it doesn't always carry the loudest voice. Sometimes it is drowned out by the old, tired mental repetitive voices that you know so well. We want to overwrite those messages with compassion and attune to your heart's voice.

Opening our hearts can feel scary, like entering unknown territory, especially when we've been hurt before. We so rarely share our hearts, usually doing so only in our most intimate relationships and not much more. We forget that we are interconnected, and an open heart feels it all. Yet allowing the flow is like medicine that changes us at our core so we can become sages, wise ones, who can process and forgive. I remember a moment when I saw a heart open while leading a JourneyDance workshop. A burly, muscular man took a huge risk with his heart. He was so opened up by the dance that he cried in front of a circle of participants. He was so overcome with emotion that he had to sit down, so I invited him to lean into me, and he cried in my arms. This cry allowed him to tap into the feelings he had been storing about his relationship with his father, with whom he'd never been able to be his authentic self. I saw him years later when he was featured in a magazine, and he had left his career in sales and was singing professionally, opening other people's hearts with his music—and expressing his divine purpose.

The quality of Open Heart is here for you now. Moving and being with your heart can allow you to connect with this mystical, undefinable, unfathomable, enigmatic energy. In this quality, you learn to listen to your heart, hold space for yourself, and connect with this most innocent part of you that wants to be seen, heard, and held. This is where you can become empathic, compassionate, and forgiving to yourself, and extend that gift to others.

THE HEART RELEASES ANGER

As I've said earlier, I fully acknowledge that there are some experiences, hurts, traumas, and events that are simply unforgiveable. In my own life I strive to reach a state where forgiveness can become possible. I have learned the hard way that holding on to anger and rage only hurts myself. Many spiritual teachers have synthesized the Buddha's writings on anger in this way: "Holding on to anger is like grasping a hot coal with the intent of throwing it at someone; you are the one who gets burned."

The reason why we forgive is to mend ourselves. I love the way author and futurist Erwin Raphael McManus speaks about forgiveness: "To understand forgiveness as a strength is one of the most powerful mind shifts you will ever make. Forgiveness is not an emotion. Forgiveness is an art form. It is the most elegant expression of love. Forgiveness requires a level of mastery that very few ever attain. It is the highest level of thinking when it comes to human relationships and the health of your soul. And it is the only way to keep your negative experiences from writing the story of who you become."

Most of us, including myself, have to process all our emotions—the anger, the pain, the grief—to reach the possibility of forgiveness. It's an undulating ride, but when we can digest all these emotions, and offer authentic forgiveness, we can experience

an incredible state of freedom for the body, the mind, and the heart. A new wave of energy becomes available to us.

Grief Is Love with No Place to Go

Pain is a part of life and it's a part of us. The heart can feel pain, but this pain is grief caused by a lost connection with love. The heart pours its love out to another and is vibrationally returned on an energetic level. But when there is no one to receive that love, it pours into an emptiness, and we experience grief. When we can hold our own pain and hold our own hearts, we gain the capacity to hold others in their pain and become a giver of love and healing.

More than one of our JourneyDance facilitators and participants has experienced the deep grief of losing a beloved, and the deepest grief of losing a child, whether by suicide or school shooting, accidental overdose, all tragedies. They have shared their stories of how this dance has given them the space to process their grief, connect with their beloveds on the dance floor, and move with their painful processes. Now they share this gift of becoming whole again with others.

If you are experiencing grief, I invite you to walk tenderly through the Open Heart quality. Allow yourself to move in whatever ways are available for you. You might ask your body, *What story do I need to grieve?*

Holding back the grief takes much more energy than slowly letting go. When I say letting go, I don't mean letting go of or forgetting the person or the situation; I just mean letting the emotions *move through* you. Some of our grieving dancers have shared that they dance with their loss, and in some cases, more love is available to them than they ever thought possible.

The music of this quality can support your process like it's a good friend. You may need to let your body pause to cry and release. You can have a conversation with your heart and your beloved, and fill yourself with love. You can listen to the whispers of your grief, remembering that there is nothing wrong with you; you are simply feeling and healing.

As we allow grief to be felt, it will transform, as all emotions do. If you can find some release, you will find some relief, and the tenderized heart can become a great strength and comfort.

A Prayerful Inspiration for Grieving Hearts

Dear Indwelling Spirit, My Soul, and that part of me that lives in universal consciousness,

May I awaken to the fullness of my being.

May I allow my grief to become a gift.

May that grief be felt and not feared, be embraced and not stuffed.

May my grief be moved and transmuted into love and compassion.

May I find the deepest gratitude that I can even feel such grief, because feeling means that I am alive, and feeling grief and sadness means that I can love. I can deeply love.

May I now bless my experiences on this journey of life, my hardships and my celebrations, that I may rejoice in my ability to love.

With this grief, I expand my love wider.

May each one of us be held in a circle of support, a divine circle of other women, men, beings, and souls, past and future.

Spirit guides and protective ancestors, hold us as we feel and heal.

Thank you for your support on this journey.

And so it is.

I Open My Heart

I used to think of the heart as a door that could be opened or closed, locked, and armored, but the more I learned about love, the more I see it now as a wave, because there is always love moving through you. Our love can range from the small consistent ripples lapping the beach to the larger waves in which ride and play in the sea to a tsunami's extreme magnitude and consequence. Whether we are talking about the consistent waves of love from a parent to a child, or the wild, tumultuous waves of a passionate relationship, it takes great courage to give, receive, and experience love. It takes a willingness, a vulnerability. Some loves will open us and require us to bear extreme waves of risk-taking, and others will gift us with the small, constant waves we can count on to support us. Our commitment is to keep the heart open so that the waves can continue flowing. If we try to suppress the waves, we risk numbness and isolation.

Oh, the woes of the heart! And to think of how many thousands of books, songs, and movies have been made to express, grieve, and inspire all that love fails and all that love brings. I have written my fair share of breakup songs.

I have also experienced true love in many different forms. Having my children, the love I felt was like the Grinch when he returns the stolen goods and hears the people singing, "My heart grew three sizes that day." In matters of romantic love, I've had many relationships and often regretted my mistakes, hurting others, giving my heart away, staying too long, getting too close, staying too distant. I could write another book about my own epic loves, marriages and divorce, new loves and old loves. For now, I continue to tell my stories to the dance floor, to move and heal my heart so I can stay open and keep flowing. Dancing with my embodied heart, whether I'm hurting from my past, or my inner child needs to be held and danced, or hurting from empathy for the world of war and violence, I have to take time to express on the dance floor all I feel and mend my heart with tenderness. The heart has a voice, and when we take the time to hear, feel, and dance with it, we can get to our deepest needs and wants.

Many years ago, during a heartbreaking moment, I had to come to terms with the complexity of my heart. Not that I had taken love for granted, but I was not in the right relation to my heart and sought many different forms of idealized love. In a state of pain and grief around an unrequited love, I wrote a song based on Kahlil Gibran's teaching, *On Joy and Sorrow*, and how their natures are completely intertwined. The chorus went something like this . . . and yes, I know I was a bit of a romantic.

> They say the guitar must be hollowed out to make its beautiful sound,
>
> They say that the clay must be burned by the fire to hold the healing wine.
>
> I wonder what happens to me . . .
>
> After this hollowing fire?
>
> I wonder what happens to me . . .
>
> Will I? Will I shine brighter?

In this song, I was questioning if love is worth feeling and asking the universe, If I let myself feel, will I become more loving? Can I keep my heart open even in the face of pain,

whatever it may be? Does more love deepen my experience of life? I have to believe that the answer is yes, it does.

The Open-Heart Experience

On the physical level, we dance in waves, waltzes, with momentum and suspension. We let our hands and our hearts lead us, traveling in shapes and slow movement. We connect to our heart energy and express what is calling.

On the emotional level, we feel, we flow, and we allow ourselves to be touched. We connect with the melodies and lyrics and focus on embracing our heart, love, and possibly, forgiveness. If tears come, we let them. We hold nothing too tightly, and we hold nothing back.

On the mental level, we are listening deeply, we are in an inquiry, we may ask questions, we may listen for the *inner whispers* of our heart, and we are witnessing our own inner dialogue. We may give ourselves messages we need to hear.

On the spiritual level, we connect inward to locate ourselves inside love. We may experience insights, open any blocks that keep us from loving freely, and allow our compassionate heart to express itself.

Music: Explore the Open Heart with Me

The music of Open Heart is touching, evocative, deep, orchestral, piano, voice, message lyrics, classical, light, airy, free, strings. The playlist has a variety of tones. Not all saddening and melancholic; though there will be some of that, there will also be some uplifting, cinematic, magnificent pieces. Even some joyful lighter pieces. My intention is for you to feel, flow, and viscerally experience your openhearted nature.

Remember, this is the beginning of the playlist:

- "Follow Me" by Toni Bergins
- "We Move Lightly" by Dustin O'Halloran
- "Whole Heart" by Ruby Amanfu
- "Unfolding" by Luca Fogale
- "All We Want Is Love" by Ane Brun
- "Bring Me Back" by The Majestic Ones
- "Sirenita Bobinsana" by Orka
- "Folding" by Abimaro
- "Dance for Me Wallis" by Abel Korzeniowski
- "Like Water" by The Brothers Koren
- "You Can't Rush Your Healing" by Trevor Hall

Find the full playlist in the *Embody* portal.

A Song I Wrote for You

To deepen your practice, take a moment to listen, or read the lyrics out loud:

FOLLOW ME

Your heart is in the center
In the center of the labyrinth
Hidden behind the walls
waiting for you

Grandmother of all
Told me my secrets
She said, "You are the maze
And I am the key"

Your heart is breaking open
I know it's feeling hard
But you can do it my love
Just let down your guard

And follow me
Follow me
Follow me
Follow me

You hid all the pain deep in the
doorway's twists and turns
You hid it to protect your fragile
mind
But your heart is strong and your
power runs deep
What they've sown, they so will
Reap

All these memories flooding

Over the into the sea
Just put down your weapon and
Follow me
Follow me
Follow me
'cause the mother will hold you and
she will heal you, she will
hold you and she will heal you

Wait for the light to come through
the trees
where the wind dances with the
leaves
The pink sunrise with the bursting
green
will heal your nightmares and your
sweetest dreams

So many others have come before
you now
We walk in beauty and we walk in
strength
Take every twist and turn on your
maze
And pick up your broken pieces
from the ground
Follow me
Follow me
Follow me
'Cause the mother will hold you and
she will heal you, she will
hold you and she will heal you

Your heart is in the center
In the center of the labyrinth
Hidden behind the walls
waiting for you

Open-Heart Invocation

Dearest Heart,

I'm sorry if I haven't been listening.

I'm sorry if I missed what you needed.

I'm sorry if I've been careless with your tender sweetness.

I'm sorry if I hurt you.

I know you have needs and feel deep longings.

Do you think you could share them with me?

I open my heart to feel. I open my heart to love.

Allow me to be fearless in feeling what I truly need to feel that I may deeply heal and move forward with grace, joy, beauty, and connection.

Soften me with my own tears. Allow my rivers to open to oceans to vast horizons of new expanding love. Let me be a part of the greater healing.

My heart, I do love you and I'm here now.

The Open-Heart Movement Practice

The Open-Heart movement practice invites you to hold yourself, your heart, and your inner child, and embody being

there, present with yourself. The movements and music allow you to be vulnerable, intimate, and undefended. The dance for this quality invites you to connect with your heart and follow its impulses, feelings, passions, explorations, deep dives, and soaring flights. This is a time for deep listening, energetic rejuvenation, and an intentional conversation with your heart. Your heart is always sharing information with you; sometimes you just have to talk to it first and create a relationship with it.

The heart dance is slow and expansive. We bring back our scarves as a psychodramatic representation or *projective object* (meaning you will project what you need onto it), to represent your heart or inner child and dance with it. We might even open our voices and sing out.

Dr. Steph says the heightened state generated by the preceding stages allows the prefrontal cortex to stay actively aware, creating the ability to witness our own deep emotional processing without becoming washed away by our emotions. The nervous system is in a state of parasympathetic resolution and arousal is waning into relaxation.

Enter your container, have a scarf in your area, and turn on your music. Choose your favorite songs from the playlist and dance with your heart.

Begin by just listening to the sounds as they enter your space. Bring your hands to your heart and let them make contact with the body's energy and emotion. Notice what you are feeling. Let your body begin to move slowly and simply. Move with your heart, slowly rocking side to side.

Continue listening to your heart and make shapes that express where you are in this moment. Explore moving your arms up over your head in an overhand curve, or down, in an under curve. Follow them with your whole body, moving side to side. You might swing and spiral, float upward, or sink downward. Remember, every time you come to this music you may feel differently, so be just where you are and know that this is authentic and real for you.

Take all the time you need for this dance. Feel each movement as you make it, totally embodied and present. Allow your hands to lead you as you travel through your space. Listen to the energy of your heart. Allow yourself to be led by your heart, your chest, and express your emotions and your passion. Your feet may want to lead in slow waltzing steps or flying leaps; you have your own individual relationship with your heart.

When you feel ready, locate your scarf. Lift it slowly off the floor, move with the scarf floating in the air. Explore how it dances and travels or wrap it around your shoulders, for a sensory experience. Take a moment of pause and hold it in your arms. Look at it as if it was your heart or your little one inside. Ask it, "How are you, my darling?" Hold and move with it as you listen for its whispers.

Holding the scarf in your hands, ask it, "What do I really need for healing?" Let your heart tell you a story. Follow your scarf through the room, feeling the music, and notice if it's got a sense of joy, a sense of melancholy, a sense of expansion, a sense of depth. Let the music inspire you to express with waves and spirals, circles, or expansion and contraction.

Let yourself talk to your heart some more. "Do you want to stay close?" If so, follow its call and press it into your body and hold your heart. Talk to your heart softly and tell it that it matters and that you love it.

Sometimes, our hearts want to travel, fly, be close, wrap around us like wings. Allow your heart conversation to

become a dance and move freely at your own pace. Ask, "Do you want to open up and fly?" If so, you can gently unfold the scarf, add momentum to your dance, and let your heart scarf dance on the wind of your movement.

Practice listening. Ask your heart a question you have been pondering to which only your heart would know the answer. Let your mind hold the question gently. Move and listen and wait. If emotions arise, let them come. Tears, sounds, full-on release—whatever comes, hold it gently.

Only you will know when you feel complete in this dance. At that time, you can release your scarf by gently placing it back on the floor. With a gesture, pull your energy from the scarf and bring it back into your heart. Keep your hands on your heart as long as you like, just breathing and listening.

To close your container, come to stillness with your hands on your heart, and tell yourself, *I love you.*

Movement Suggestions for Open Heart

- Use a scarf to represent your heart, or just use your hands.
- Move with your heart, slowly rocking side to side.
- Ask your heart, "How are you, my darling?"
- Let your heart scarf travel through your space.
- Have a conversation with your heart: does it want to play, does it want to be heavy, light, close to you?
- Tap into what it needs as you dance with it.
- Add spirals, circles, waving in the wind to your dance.
- Ask your heart what it longs for and listen to the whispers.
- Tell your heart it matters. Give your heart attention.

Open-Heart Personal Practice Journaling

- What makes your heart sing loudest? What makes your heart feel most alive?
- If you could share your greatest heart's knowing, what would you tell your inner child?
- How have you shifted your relationship to love?
- Can you listen to the whispers of your heart?
- Are there voices that block this secret inner voice, or is it easy for you to hear?
- Can you feel an opening or expansion of love as you dance?

Mystical Inquiry: The Art of Letter Writing

After dancing, we are in an altered state from the movement, the music, and your intention. We are in a more open place of communion with our hearts so we can delve deeper into transformation. This exercise will help you tap into a new sense of tenderness, forgiveness, and kindness. At the end of this exercise, you might feel more love than ever.

What would you do differently if you listened to your heart? Our hearts know what we want and need. Initially, we might consult our minds about our desires, but now it's time to listen to our hearts and our bodies. When we live from our hearts and ask ourselves, *What would my heart do?*, we might receive a completely different answer than what our mind would dictate.

If you were to replace the question, "What should I do with my life?" with "What does my heart desire?" Or "What does my heart long for?," you can shift your patterns and affect your future choices and direction. You might realize, "You know what? My heart really wants to be held. My heart really craves connection. It wants to be known deeply and to know others deeply. It might yearn to sing, or dance, or to create art, whatever it may be."

Let's begin a letter-writing process, both to and from our heart. Let your heart tell you a story as you write. Try to just listen and let your pen move on the paper as if you were dancing. Please answer the prompts with your heart, not your mind. Let's begin by sitting in a quiet space and play the Open-Heart playlist.

A Love Letter to Your Heart

Write your own heart a love letter, telling yourself all that your heart needs to hear at this time.

> My Dearest Heart,
>
> I see you, I hear you, I love you.
>
> I know you need healing on ________, I am here for you now.
>
> With love, Me

A Love Letter from Your Heart

Wonderful! Now let's reverse the process and ask your heart to write a letter to YOU! Start with one of the following prompts:

> Dearest [your name here],
>
> My message to you comes from the deepest place within . . .
>
> I'm here, in the center of your labyrinth, hidden behind the walls, waiting for you . . .
>
> With love, My Heart

A Love Letter from Your Heart to Another

Whom do you love so much that just thinking about them opens your heart? Who desperately needs your love and maybe even your forgiveness? Who does your heart need to express your deepest truth to? Who needs your apology?

These are powerful acts. If you feel you can give that forgiveness, share your truth, express your love, make an apology, then write these letters for yourself. You never have to send them; just the act of writing them can change your relationship to this person, clear out resentments, open you up to more love, and put you back in right relation. Write a letter expressing your love and care, forgiveness, or truth.

After completing this process, give yourself some time to just *feel*, sitting in meditation or contemplation. Allow your feelings to come up and to clear. You may want to dance another Open-Heart dance. Take care of yourself—you are healing on deep levels.

Messages Your Heart Needs To Hear

Say the following out loud:

I am lovable.

I am valuable.

I am adorable.

I am open to love.

I am open-hearted.

I love me.

Close the Open-Heart Quality Practice with a *Prayer*

Spirit of Love, Source Energy, Divine Connection,

Please allow my heart to be held and let me feel the peace that comes from that.

Let me trust that more and more my heart knows I am listening to it and loving it.

Show me how to heal a little more each day, so that my heart can love freely, giving and receiving love in equal exchange.

Let me trust that my heart can open and allow more love to enter my life.

Thank you, heart, for loving me and prioritizing me as worthy, valuable, and adorable.

Let me know that I am lovable, and that it's safe for me to love.

Teach me how to hold my tenderness as my power.

I am love itself.

Thank you, love, for your guidance today and every day.

CHAPTER 12

Prayer and Bliss

Prayer isn't thought, it's feeling. It's actively seeking the beloved within, reaching out for spirit, longing for source connection. The greatest writers of all time have expressed prayer in many ways. Poet Kahlil Gibran has written, "Faith is an oasis in the heart which will never be reached by the caravan of thinking." The celebrated Sufi poet from ancient Persia, Rumi, has said that prayer is seeking *the beloved*: "Lose yourself, Lose yourself in this love. When you lose yourself in this love, you will find everything."

When I talk about prayer, I'm not speaking religiously; I'm speaking metaphorically, in a similar vein to Rumi's inner longing to meet "the beloved," which is God, Source, Cosmic Universe. I think of prayer as the *communion* with spirit, the *connection* with source energy, with the divine.

And I believe that each of us *is* a prayer, a soul. You are not just a body. You are not just a mind. You are not just emotions. You are so much more than this body, yet you are *in* this body.

You are the prayer itself. Your breath, your body, your emotions, and your thoughts. Your movement and your stillness, your full awareness, your unique expression. The energy of you is so much larger than the body. *You are a divine spark.* Your divine spark is your inner energy, the essence of you. The core or, shall I say, the *soul* of you. This energy is your knowing, eternal consciousness. No matter what has happened to you in this life, there is this part, completely untouched, unharmed, and purely and uniquely *you.* When you are connected to your divine spark, you know you're essential. It brings a deep sense of self-trust, where you can be a happy, creative being, a vibrant soul, a wholehearted person.

When I am in Prayer, I can feel layers of energy all around me and I can touch it, feel it, move it, and follow it. I am in my senses so completely and so in the moment that nothing else exists: pure timelessness. My mind is quiet, free, clear, and positive, my emotions are clean and open, my body is flowing and expressive. The smallest shape I make feels like I'm expanding a thousand miles. My consciousness expands from a pinpoint focus to the galaxy. All the while I am IN my body, so connected to the *beloved* that I feel my feet and my head and my energy simultaneously. I feel in communion with something so large, so vast, that it is beyond my comprehension; yet my energy is palpable, it's right there in my hands as I move with it. My hands buzz with sensation, like I'm holding a million sparkles of light.

Some of us can easily sit in meditation and find this sensation of connectedness, and some of us need movement to experience the same level of perception of the cosmic flow. In meditation, many of us struggle and find ourselves in loud, internal thought. When we add music and movement, all that mental chatter can cease. In the Prayer quality dance, I can rapidly connect to that beautiful source energy, because of all the work we have done prior. The body and energy are primed for this profound moment for ourselves to experience.

The Prayer quality is the time for reemergence, out of our cocoons of deep feeling and processing, and into the energy of light and consciousness expansion, where we can access hope, gratitude, and inspiration. This is the end of your movement journey. Your mind is clear and your emotions are processed, the layers and filters we had been using as compensating strategies have been removed. Now you can stop looking at yourself and others through a lens of judgment and perfectionism. In this collective meta state, you embody your Prayer energy, where you find your divinity, and connect to spirit, universe, source, and every single person in the world.

My hope is that you may find yourself in your own movement Prayer and be able to say: *I am the Prayer, it is Me.* When you are in this state, you can feel love, compassion, and empathy. True self-love is realizing that you are a divine spark.

Then, I invite you to bathe in this divinity. Take moments of bliss as you surrender to the earth. You rejuvenate and become infused with the sensation of the divine source within. I've come to realize that this is the part of the journey that keeps people returning to the practice again and again. Yes, they are coming to find wild joy in Funky Connection; yes, they are coming for the emotional and creative expression and shaking off all their *glunk* in Evocative Emotion and Alchemy Transformation. But they're truly coming to find that divine source inside themselves because I believe that everyone longs for oneness with their divine spark.

Organized religion did not serve my divine connection, but this quality does. For me, religion was more cultural tradition than prayers and stories that did not inspire a personal

connection to Source energy. By dancing the Prayer into Bliss, we can connect viscerally to that sense of the divine. I invite you into the cosmos, into the energy of love itself.

Touching the Cosmos

When I was divorcing the father of my children in 2009, I was in a lot of emotional pain. I had two small children and a very toxic relationship that I needed to exit quickly. I was angry at my ex and myself, sad at the loss of the family dream, scared to be on my own, and carrying a mix of shame and guilt for failing.

Even though I was working out my emotions on the dance floor, I knew I needed something else to get me out of my victim mode and back into my power.

I started working with an extraordinary, intuitive coach, Linda "Rose" Levenberg, whom I met when I was teaching at the Esalen Institute. We spent hours on the phone as she midwifed me through all my mixed feelings. I had been working with her for a number of months and I was starting to feel a little more like myself, but not entirely there. Rose recommended that I come see her in person in California and do three days of intensive healing work.

At first, I was conflicted about her suggestion. I had to get comfortable with the idea of being even more vulnerable than I had been with her on the phone, but I was also excited because I really trusted her. I knew that to have three days to drop into healing work was going to be intense. It was going to be a big shift as I was usually the healer for others, always taking care of everyone in my life, and I had to make sure all the details for my sons were attended to while I was away. So nervously but hopefully, I made the arrangements and went to California.

The moment I saw Rose's face, I knew I had made the right decision. She was so sage-like and vibrant, and I was profoundly grateful, and relieved, to have someone hold space just for me. The first thing we did was her very special matcha tea ritual.

Later in the day we got started with meditating and journaling. She set me up in her backyard with a blank journal book and a large sheet of paper. I wrote for hours. Her method was called the *spiral process.* She had me draw a wide spiral on the large paper. In the center of the spiral I put my birth, and then I was guided to fill in the spiral from the inside out, writing down as many events as I could remember and at what ages, under a set amount of time. I didn't have time for every memory, just the most significant memories and events, and kept going until the time ran out, all the way to the present.

The next day, Rose prepared me to go on a hypnotic journey. I thought we were going to be talking and processing my spiral, but she had something else planned. I really didn't know if I was going to be able to be hypnotized. I never thought it could happen because I'm always in control of my faculties and I don't let go of my mind easily (except on the dance floor!). I wasn't really sure it would have an effect, if I'd go anywhere or see anything. I remember telling her not to be disappointed if she couldn't hypnotize me. Rose didn't seem fazed. She laughed as always and said, "Let's just try, honey. It's not classic hypnosis, it's more like your JourneyDance, so just relax."

Then she had me lay down on her couch and talked me into a gentle, hypnotic state. I slowly relaxed into this feeling of floating in stasis. I left my body completely, and I went right along with her on a guided journey as she read my memories to me, along my spiral, going back in time, scanning the stories of my life. And this is all without psychedelics, by the way. The only thing I had was matcha!

We looked at all the events in my life's spiral in order to unhook me from my relationship patterns. I revisited many of my life's moments that stood out as significant, some very painful formative experiences, and some joyful, wonderful experiences.

I traveled back, and back, and back in time, similar to a regression. I went all the way back to my pre-birth (yes, I know it sounds strange but stay with me). By this point I felt like I was floating in a beautiful cosmic sea of light and particles. I felt it, could sense it, and saw what it was like being inside the Milky Way. But it wasn't the "me" of reality: I was just energy. It was like there was a dissolving of me into the particle substance of energy. This is when things got even more interesting.

I heard Rose's voice, beckoning me to come back. She said, "Toni, it's almost time to come back. I want you to ask the cosmos, 'Why did I come for this lifetime? Why am I here? Who called me back into a body?,'" Then she asked me to speak what I was seeing.

Boom, in my mind's eye, I saw myself as an energetic being in a fetal posture, bowing. It was like I was in a sci-fi movie. I was just particles. The energy me was bowing deeply and praying at the feet of two enormous figures. One was masculine and one was feminine.

Are you ready for this? Their energy was swirling within me. The masculine one gave me a blue spiral and thrust it into my body. The feminine one gave me a pink lightning bolt and dropped it into my body. They were energy illuminated, and I saw the blue and the pink mixing into me; it was so surprising that the blue was a soft spiral and that the pink was a powerful bolt, unlike what I expected for these energies.

Then I asked, *Why am I here?* I got my response in two seconds, and it was a crystal-clear vision. I heard, "You were called by your mother and your sisters who have known you many times before." (They are the closest people in my entire life.)

Rose whispered, "What are the gifts? What are you bringing forth?"

I heard, "You're here to awaken and activate personal transformation in others."

In the background I could hear Rose's voice, whispering again, "It's time to come back." But I didn't want to leave the energy. I was completely in being, in a state of peace, bliss, and joy, and I really wanted to stay there. Slowly, I had the sensation of being compressed, and thought, *Okay, I'm going back into the body now. Back into the body. Now I'm in the body again. Now I'm back in this solid form.* It was so intense. Little did I know it had been four hours that I had been in a cosmic state of euphoric floating.

Upon reentering, coming slowly back into this reality, I gushed with tears, I wept endlessly. I felt both energized and exhausted. I went outside and sat under what Rose called her "grandmother tree." I grounded myself and stretched; I wrote in my journal, sitting under that tree, in deep contemplation. That was when I had my realization of what I know to be the *first blessing* and the *first grief.* The first blessing is to be alive in a body, the first grief is the *illusion* of separation from the divine source.

I could suddenly understand why babies cry at their first breath. All my energy was so compressed into my body, and yet felt disconnected from that source. The massive energy of the entire universe is compressed, squished, and compacted into each of us. I felt the pain of separation from Divine love, the source, cosmic flow, and I knew that that pain was an illusion because human pain is part of the human incarnation. I knew that inside this pain was a searing joy that was also a blessing, a blessing of life only felt by the living.

When I came back home, my teaching was next level. I was committed like I'd never been committed in my whole life. I was able to let go of the myopic consciousness and went into the open expanse, where I can see everyone as beautiful, and at the same time feel the beauty of the collective. I could see every person's divine spark on the dance floor. I was in the energy, and by releasing my mind I was able to feel complete and total love. Now, every time I come to the dance floor I tap into that sensation and connect to divine love.

I created the Prayer and Bliss qualities to give you a palpable, embodied experience of that energy. By dancing the Prayer, I invite you into the sensation that I experienced because it was life-changing for me. It was like meeting God without religion. Every time I do the Prayer dance I am instantly back there. Honestly, that's why I keep dancing. All the other qualities are here to get us to this cosmic connection of Prayer and Bliss.

I have since had many similar experiences during deep meditation and shamanic journeying, and through plant medicine journeys. I have developed a strong visual sense, but before I met Rose, I never saw anything. Now when I go on shamanic journeys, I can see what the shaman is telling me to see. I can see the waterfall of light. I can see the guide; I can follow the details of the journey. This is a faculty that developed for me over time, and if you don't see anything or experience anything the first time, there's no need to judge. Just relax, feel, and imagine, and allow your visualization power to awaken.

The Prayer and Bliss Experience

On a physical level, we move with intention, slow and focused. We are one with our breath, we sense an expanded energy, we extend our awareness to every part of the body. We follow the energy of the body into shapes that feel like prayer. We feel the palpable energy as substance. We move into the earth, we stretch and prepare our bodies to lay on the ground in deep rest, total stillness.

On an emotional level, we feel so present, our senses are acute. We may feel the blessing and the grief, the longing for a Divine connection. We may feel a deep gratitude, empathy and compassion, a sense of love, inspired hope or ease.

On a mental level, our thoughts are quieted, and we can enter a deep state of peace, prayer, *no-thing-ness*. We can be mindful and sense the expansion of our energy and our conscious awareness.

On a spiritual level, we may have an insight or feel a sense of oneness, unity, or an open, heightened awareness. We can sense our own consciousness, rising up to the divine and sinking down into the earth simultaneously. We may journey, visualizing with the mind's eye.

Music: Enter Prayer and Bliss Music with Me!

The Prayer and Bliss music is especially beautiful. It is slow-paced, sparse and thin, or harmonic and orchestral. The sounds are deep, with cello and chants, or light and spacious with ambient sounds and voices, tender and inspiring. This selection is relaxing, has no constant rhythm, and feels wide, expansive, grounding, soothing, and divine.

For Prayer (this is the beginning of the playlist):

- "Lay Your Head" by Toni Bergins
- "Reflections" by Sona Jobarteh
- "Prayer 2" by Jami Sieber

- "Lost Song" by Ólafur Arnalds
- "An Ending, a Beginning" by Dustin O'Halloran
- "Hold Yourself" by Jai Chand + Grayson
- "Illuminar" by Poranguí
- "Viento de Atacama" by Ayla Schafer
- "Healer Might" by Ben Noble

For Bliss (this is the beginning of the playlist):

- "The Magic Star" by Essie Jain
- "Initiation" by Peter Kater and R. Carlos Nakai
- "Earthwatching" by Bob Holroyd
- "First Light" by Harold Budd and Brian Eno
- "Devorzhum" by Dead Can Dance
- "Lokah" by Carrie Grossman
- "I Am Light" by India Arie

Find the full playlists in the *Embody* portal.

A Song I Wrote for You

To deepen your practice, listen to my song from the playlist, or read the following out loud:

LAY YOUR HEAD

Hey little girl, why you crying,
They never meant to cause you
such pain
You're out on your own,
You're so far from home,
been alone for too long . . .

Lay your head on my shoulder
Lay your head on me
Lay your head on my shoulder
'Cause you're safe right here with
me . . .

Hey little boy, why are you so mad
they told you not to cry when you're
sad
But what if they were wrong
and it's your tears that make you
strong,
I know you didn't learn that from
your dad

Lay your head on my shoulder
Lay your head on me
Lay your head on my shoulder
'Cause you're safe right here with
me . . .

All the people we are trying
To fight what's been pulling us down
But just look around till you have
found,
You're not alone in your fear
(And I'll always be here)

Lay your head on my shoulder
Lay your head on me
Lay your head on my shoulder
'Cause you're safe right here with
me . . .
you're safe right here with me . . .
you're safe right here with me . . .

Prayer and Bliss Invocation

Read aloud:

Please show me the way to know that I am the prayer in every cell of my body.

May I move through the world with a gentle knowing of the divine that pervades my being.

May I stop questioning my value and own that I am enough, worthy of the divine abundance of this world; this beautiful world in which I am a blessed being.

May I honor my being, that inner part of me who knows the beauty of my existence.

Please allow me to instill this message into the depths of my soul, so that I remember daily.

I am the prayer, my body, my breath, my thoughts, my feelings, my energy, my essence.

I am good, I am enough. I am a divine spark!

I now carry this knowledge across all time, space, and mind, past, present, and future.

And so it is.

Prayer and Bliss Movement Practice

The Prayer quality can be best described as a slow, moving meditation. We begin by feeling the heat from our hearts and solar plexus. We slowly allow our hands to float outward, aware of this palpable energy, as we send our roots into the ground. Then, we let the body move authentically and organically, following the energy. Our movements come spontaneously as we whisper to ourselves, "I *am* the prayer." We can visualize ourselves grounded to the earth through our feet and connected to the sky in our hands and our spirits.

We embody the prayer with our intention. We merge with the music. We open to receiving mode, allowing this energy to fill us. We open ourselves to giving mode, and may even feel inspired to send a prayer or sing out to Source or to ourselves or the world.

A divine realization and deep source connection is possible for us at this point in the dance. A moment may come to you when you feel completely connected to *all that is*, to the universe itself, to the energy of life. We may create our very own personal prayer ritual—which may take the form of moving with our spirit guides, angelic presences, or beloveds, or we may find an exalted state of peace, feeling the vibrational, expanding energy that we are.

Finally, we bring this energy back into the earth, into the body, and integrate into stillness, in what I call *Bliss*. We rest and relax, becoming revitalized and renewed. We visualize resting on the earth in the arms of the mountain and the grass, we breathe, we naturally expand our energetic awareness. We invite the body to release into gravity, giving our weight to the earth. We deepen our physical release, letting go completely. This is a time to integrate all we have experienced.

Dr. Steph says that these qualities activate and strengthen mirror neurons and insular activity, which may indicate increased emotional processing, self-awareness, or empathetic response in the brain. The activity of expressing gratitude and witnessing the self, others, in a pair or group, inspires both the ability to be more self-aware and also more empathetic toward others. Resolution, relaxation, and parasympathetic dominance, the part of the nervous system that brings us into a state of calmness and reduces the body's response to stress, combined with a gentle reawakening of the body, allows us to stay with our experience and become fully alert to the world so that we can reintegrate back into our daily lives.

Let's begin our Prayer practice and enter your container.

Stand tall. Start by placing your hands on your heart and your solar plexus/upper belly. With a light to medium pressure, rub and make circles until you feel some heat and friction. Then take your hands slowly away, bringing them about 3 to 6 inches away from your body. Can you feel a taffy-like sensation of pulling energy between your hands and your body? You can make the energetic sensation stronger by rubbing your hands together for a bit or singing aloud. You can visualize it as a ball of light if you like.

Now, face your hands toward each other. Feel your energy grow between your hands. Notice how your hands are connected at the center of your palms. It could be like taffy, or cottony and fluffy, or you may feel heat, buzzing, or tingling; it's different for everyone.

Get a palpable sense of your energy. Pull your hands apart wider, and press them back in closer. Sing a light *aahhh, om,* or *hu* sound to the energy and let it expand. Pull it, press it, move it. Play with the energy between your hands as if it was a Slinky or water you could pour back and forth between two glasses.

Now you can begin moving the energy. Carry the energy up over your head, lifting your arms to the sky, connecting your energy to the sun, the stars, the moon, the heavens. You can open your arms as if you were a golden chalice and receive light and energy. Fill yourself up. Notice the music lifting you up and breathe. Slowly and gently pull the energy down and cover yourself with your own field. Cascade it over your body. Give yourself an energy bath, moving your hands from your head to your face, to your throat and chest, your heart and lungs, down to your belly and pelvis, and down your legs to your toes.

Trust your body, slow dance with it, making your own shapes of prayer, whatever that means to you in this moment. You can expand and open up into wide shapes; you could come close in and hug yourself. You can explore different planes of movement, standing tall, bending down to midlevel, or coming low to the floor, just keep listening, merging with the music, and following the energy. The prayer dances that come out of us are the most beautiful things I've ever seen.

After a while, you may enter an altered state, where you're feeling the energy of life. As you are slowly moving and feeling, implant your consciousness with beautiful messages. You can choose to work with the prayer I whisper while dancing with my essential essence: "I am the prayer." Breathe every word, in and out. "I am the prayer. My breath is the prayer." Inhale and exhale deeply, and say, "My body is the prayer." Move tenderly and lovingly, thanking your body. "My laughter is the prayer. My tears are the prayer." Let all your emotions be embraced. "Everything about me is the prayer. I am moving prayer. I am the prayer itself."

Send roots through your feet into the floor. Notice if you can sense your energetic consciousness expanding into space. Open your arms wide overhead as if you are a golden

chalice. Feel your energy fill your arms. Keep listening and follow the palpable energy in your body.

We are now primed to become a *blesser* and gain wisdom from our Highest Self in a soft loving way. What does it mean to you to bless yourself? If you feel called, continue to move, dance, and shape, and say what needs to be said, exactly what you need to hear at this moment. No one knows you better than you: you know exactly what you need to hear; you know what touches your heart and soul. What if you could give that to yourself right now, and remember it on a cellular level? Memory is made with emotion, so let's create a new memory for you in this deeply peaceful, loving state. Offer yourself a closing hug, touch your face or heart, wherever you need your touch.

When you begin feeling complete, allow your body to feel the earth below and surrender to gravity. Bring yourself down slowly with reverence. You may pause in child's pose, connecting with the earth. You may stretch and cool your body down, or come straight to stillness, laying down for Bliss. Get comfortable with a blanket or cushion. Feeling your connection to your breath, the energy of beingness, bring it all back into the earth, into the body, and integrate into stillness. Lie on your back in the yoga posture called *Savasana*, or resting pose, with your palms facing up and your feet slightly apart. Let the mind sink into the floor, let your head sink into the floor, and let every muscle relax and exhale. We're going to go deep down into the earth to be held and feel surrender. Let your chest sink with an exhale, then your stomach and pelvis. Let it all release; each breath sinks you deeper. Notice your exhales. Let your legs and feet go, sinking and relaxing. Let your arms go, then your hands. Feel as if your back is resting into the earth itself. Imagine roots going down into the earth.

Feel your body relaxing heavily into the earth while your energy expands into the sky.

Once in this surrendered place, you can choose if you want to go deeper into a journey or just rest. You can continue to let go completely into the earth and just breathe, rest, peacefully rejuvenating the body with the music. Let yourself feel the light energy of Bliss cover your body, enter your body, fill your body with light, color, sparkles, or fluffy thickness.

As you are blissing out, you might see a sky full of stars come into view. You might see a bird in flight, soaring on the wind. Or you might see a golden energy or iridescent light, coming down through your whole body, washing over you.

Allow your consciousness to expand and your energy to soar up, spreading beyond the confines of your room, going miles in every direction. Notice the light you can see inside your mind's eye. Rest deeply, nothing to do, nothing to fix; allow the earth and sky to nourish you and fill you with light.

After five or ten minutes, I invite you to notice your hands again. Awaken your palms by gently pumping your hands. Feel that buzzy, tingly, fuzzy, thick energy in the center of your palms. That is *you*. Bend at the elbows and lift your hands, raise them so slowly upward toward the sky, allow them to slowly descend, and become aware of your fields of energy. Gently place your hands on your heart and belly or anywhere you'd like to bless yourself. Take a few breaths, connecting to your body. Then, draw your knees up and bring your feet onto the ground. Gently roll your body to one side, coming up very slowly into a meditation seat or whatever is comfortable for you. Take your time coming back into presence. Slowly open your eyes, and see your hands. Bring your hands to your heart with gratitude. You can bow inwardly or nod with reverence to yourself, honoring your courage and beauty, and with that same reverence, kiss your hands, kiss your shoulders, and complete the practice. Offer a *mwah* to the universe by slowly lifting your hands up to the sky and say, *mmmmmwwwwaaaaahhhhh!*

Movement Suggestions for Prayer and Bliss

- Place your hands on heart and belly.
- Feel the energy moving in and out; sing to your energy.
- Following the energy of you, make shapes of prayer.
- Fill yourself like a golden chalice.
- Whisper to yourself: "I am the prayer—my breath, my body, my movement, my stillness, my feelings, my thoughts are the prayer."
- Find your way slowly to the earth.
- Become comfortable, feeling each breath melting you deeper.
- Notice your expanded state of awareness.
- Inhale sky, exhale earth; you are the connection between.
- Feel your body relaxing heavily into the earth and your energy expanding into the sky.
- With eyes closed, notice the light inside.

Mystical Inquiry: The Rose Meditation

It's said that the rose is the highest vibrational frequency of all of the flowers and fragrances. The rose is associated with the Divine Mother. If you want to bring this visualization to life to open your heart, anoint yourself with rose essential oil.

Start the Rose Meditation playlist. Take a deep breath, and sink into the earth just as we did in the Bliss practice. Begin to visualize roots coming from the back of your head, letting all the thoughts travel down, little tendrils of spring green. Let the roots come down the back of your shoulders gently, tiny squiggles of green energy, slowly coming down through the low back, through the legs and the bottoms of your feet, rooting into the earth and allowing all these vibrant spring green tendrils to absorb earth energy. Allow that energy to come up the roots and into your body.

As you face the sky, allow yourself to feel the beautiful cosmic sun, the Milky Way, moonbeams, whatever light source you visualize. Let the rays shine down upon you and allow them to come in through the top of the head and shine down over your face. Smile to receive this light energy. Let the rays pour down over your whole body. Slowly, you are filling up with shining light, all the way to your feet.

Imagine in your heart center there is a little bud, a rosebud, just slowly forming. See its color tightly wrapped in petals. Focus your energy in your heart and invite the bud to bloom and become larger. Visualize the petals expanding with nutrients from the earth and sun and allow the bud to turn into a beautiful bloom. Rest in that blossoming energy of the heavens, the heavenly shining light coming down to the earth, and the energy coming up through the roots. You are becoming this highest vibrational rose of love. Breathe and bathe in this light. Imagine the fragrance of the rose bathing you in this light of the divine. See the petals open and share their color with you.

When you feel complete, gently bring your hands to your heart. Keep the rose in your heart in whatever form you want. Keep it as a bud or a full bloom. Gently pull up your tendrils from the earth and come back to your breath. Lift your hands slowly upward toward the sky, and allow them to slowly descend onto your belly, or anywhere you'd like to bless yourself. Take a few more deep breaths.

Then, draw your knees up and bring your feet onto the ground. Gently roll your body to one side, coming up very slowly into a meditation seat or whatever is comfortable for you. Bring your hands to your heart with gratitude. You may say to yourself, *I walk in beauty as the rose,* and take this high-vibe version of you into your life. You can bow or nod inwardly, with reverence to yourself, honoring your courage and beauty, and in that reverence, kiss your hands and your shoulders and complete the practice.

Rose Meditation Playlist

- "Beginnings" by James Heather
- "How I Love You" by Chloë Goodchild
- "Still" by Ola Gjeilo and Voces8, arranged by Lawson
- "Rose" by Ayla Schafer

Prayer and Bliss Personal Practice Journaling

- What energy state comes over you as you dance your prayer?
- Can you feel a connection with Source energy or spirit, or that which you call Divine?
- What is Prayer to you?
- Do you find it easy to relax deeply?
- What do you notice in your body and energy during deep relaxation?
- Do you see colors? Images? Or do you feel sensations?

Messages to Connect to Source

Say aloud in a loving voice:

I am a divine spark.

I am an expansive being.

My body is my home.

I am at home in my body.

I am the Prayer.

It is me.

Dance the Question

Jeffrey A. Kottler, Jon Carlson, and Bradford Keeney shared this ancient story in their book *American Shaman: The Odyssey of Global Healing Traditions.*

A famous rabbi arrived at a village, and, after the initial welcome, he was taken into a large room where people had gathered, expectantly waiting to ask their questions. There was tremendous anticipation and excitement all around.

The rabbi walked silently around the room, he didn't say a word or ask for questions. Instead, he began to hum a melodic tune. Before long, everyone started humming along with his soft voice. As people became comfortable with his song, the rabbi started to dance. He danced everywhere in the room, and, one by one, every person danced with him. Soon everyone in the whole community was dancing wildly together. Each person's soul was healed by the dance, and everyone experienced a personal transformation.

Later in the night, the rabbi gradually slowed the dance and eventually brought it to a stop. He looked into everyone's eyes and said gently, "I trust that I have answered all of your questions."

Close the Prayer and Bliss Practice with a *Prayer*

Infinite Spirit, Divine Mystery, You that cannot be named,
God, Source, Universe, Holy Mother/Father, Beloved One,

Open the way for my highest good and for the highest good of all.

May I be the Prayer in my thoughts, intentions, and actions.

Each day may I open myself to holding my highest vibration.

May I bathe and nurture myself in my divine energetic presence.

May I see all beings as part of the divine matrix of life.

I commit to myself to cultivate my relationship with Source energy and wield this energy for my highest healing, my highest potential, and for the highest good of all.

May I remember the sheer beauty of being alive, and that I am soul, I am spirit in a body.

I commit to embody the highest version of me!

And so it is.

PART THREE

Move into a New Story

CHAPTER 13

Dancing into Self-Mastery

Once you are embodied, you'll begin to notice significant changes in how you show up in your life. Through the combination of movement, dance, and psychology, you have touched not only your conscious mind but the subconscious, creating new ways to process and digest your life experiences. Through the dance, we created new memories infused with joy, freedom, and love. Now we are called to raise our awareness of the mind's role in our continued transformation.

When we deeply know ourselves, respect and honor our emotions, embrace all our parts, be as present and compassionate as possible, pursue our passion and our dreams, we can live an authentic and fulfilled life. That doesn't mean that you won't ever have to deal with pain or uncomfortable emotions again. The goal of personal growth and inquiry isn't to create a life free of suffering; it's to work toward *self-mastery.*

Self-mastery is *not* about becoming perfect; it's about honoring who you are, your gifts, your talents, your story, your challenges, your lineage. It's understanding and intuiting your reactions, your responses to life's situations, so you can stay in your centered power when challenges arise. It's expanding your bandwidth and finding the courage to take risks to grow. It's harvesting all the lessons of this practice and using your personal medicine for good. If we strive for self-mastery, we can navigate life as it happens.

For me, gaining self-mastery is my North Star, my arrow in the air, my true aim to know myself. I've been working steadily on attaining this level of mastery for most of my life. It has not been simple or easy—I'm still a work in progress. I have practiced and applied many different ways of processing my emotions and shifting my state of mind, from breathwork to ceremony to somatics to psychodrama, on and off the dance floor. In this final section, I want to offer a few powerful tools for your mind that will keep you moving with confidence on your path to self-mastery.

I invite you to get even more curious as we delve into this layered process of being human. These exercises are meant to overlay positive, empowering thoughts where negative ones live. With a better connection to your body and a clearer mind, you can begin to chart what's next—to see life from a fresh perspective.

Staying on this path takes fortitude, and I know you have that. Wherever you are in your life and whatever you are going through, your body can be a wise teacher, your emotions can be your "internal guidance system" (a concept from spirit channel Abraham Hicks), and your mind can become your greatest asset. Unlike your conscience, which mentally evaluates right versus wrong, your internal guidance system, your bodily awareness, can steer you toward more joyful experiences. Having both an embodied and emotional awareness is a huge step on the path to self-mastery, so that no matter what you face, you'll have the bandwidth to cope, the practices to process, and the desire to fully engage in life.

BODY TIME VERSUS MENTAL TIME

Change takes time, so give *yourself* the gift of time.

Matt Kahn, a spiritual teacher and author, once explained a concept I have never forgotten in one of his many online talks. Someone once asked him, "Why do people often say, 'Get over it already' when it comes to getting past hurts?"

He explained that the body is only as old as you are, but the mind and your consciousness are eternal and incalculable. Each of our bodies is new to this planet and new to this life, and experiences everything in real time. That's why we have to be gentler and forgiving with our body, our feelings and emotions, and understand that change takes time. We cannot be mad at ourselves for holding onto an old story, pain, loss, or grief because the body processes at body time, which is like Earth speed; it's not like the lightning-fast processor of our mind that thinks we should be "over it already!"

With our high expectations of ourselves, we think we should be able to let go of pain quickly and so rapidly be done. Yet, we have to give our body and our mind time to process. There's nothing wrong with you. You are learning to navigate your own healing. We're all on the same learning and growing path. And we have to evolve. The way we evolve is through embodied awareness, consciousness, and the desire and willingness to change. This is the practice. We can apologize to the body for rushing ourselves, saying kindly, "I'm so sorry. I know you are healing on your own timeline."

MindBusting Techniques

The mind is a powerful judge, an evaluator, a cynic, a believer, a logician, and a researcher. It's a fabulous magician that can compartmentalize, hide, and bury. It's an inventor, engineer, creator, and designer and can imagine amazing things. It's also the record keeper. Please don't judge it; it's doing its best. If you can learn to take the reins of this powerful part of you, you can begin to aim it wherever you want it to go.

Some of our stories are hard, difficult, awful, and can leave us feeling wounded and raw. Some of our stories are beautiful, loving, and joyful. We all need to process our stories in safe containers because emotion is energy, and when your energy is locked up in your old story, you feel stuck. When your old story runs your life, you stay stuck. When we keep repeating our story just to prove our limiting beliefs are right, we can't soar to new heights. Join me in shaking up the old patterns and limitations and get the energy unstuck. When your energy is flowing, you feel alive! Let's get living our fullest expression and change our minds so that we can move into a new story!

When I was twenty-five years old, at my very first meeting with Ariana Shelton, I was telling her my story, full of negativity and self-criticism. She asked, "What would you prefer to think?" and that question changed how I work with the mind forever.

So, I ask you with her permission, what would you prefer to think? The truth is, you *can* change your thoughts (or at least not believe the mean ones). Every once in a while, even when I'm feeling very embodied, negative thoughts creep up, sabotaging my progress. Not to worry; I have some tools to share with you if you struggle with them also.

Everyone has moments when negative story loops and self-doubt rush in. But if those negative tapes are running constantly, they can prevent us from living a full life, from feeling good, and from doing the things that we love. The negative inner voice can create a bodily sensation of low energy, tension, or what might feel like depression. What we need to work toward is noticing and recognizing that *not everything we say to ourselves is true.*

As Byron Katie, spiritual teacher, author, and creator of The Work: An Inquiry of Thought and Truth, says, "A thought is harmless unless we believe it. It's not our thoughts, but our attachment to our thoughts, that causes suffering. Attaching to a thought means believing that it's true, without inquiring. A belief is a thought that we've been attaching to, often for years."

Byron Katie believes that most of what we think of as our darkest, most painful thoughts and judgments are actually untrue, and we loop these thoughts to stay in an emotion we have found comfort or identity in. When we can see our thoughts from a different perspective, we can gain insight and enlighten the mind.

I remember a time when I was raging with negative thoughts and masking my emotions with food, deprivation, or bingeing. I would often think, *You're so fat, why did you eat that today?* As soon as I heard this thought I could fall down that rabbit hole and write a list of all the foods I had eaten that day, count their calories, become obsessed and then depressed. Deep down I knew that this thought was not true, but it was telling me something. It was one of my trigger thoughts that, over time, I learned meant, "You are sad and you need to feel it, you need to cry." My mind found its perfect mental loop to keep me protected from my feelings. Once I realized it was just a repetitive thought that held no truth, I learned to hear it as my cry for help, which I listened to. And once I knew what the false thought really meant, the loop stopped, and I didn't hear it anymore.

If you're stuck in a negativity loop, it's a sign that there are feelings needing to be felt, or that you're overriding your body with your mind. When negative thoughts come up, ask yourself, as Byron Katie instructs in her book *The Four Questions, Is this thought true? And am I certain that this is true? How do I react—what happens—when I believe that thought? Who would I be without the thought?*

Many people believe that your thoughts are you; some meditation traditions explain that thoughts come from the collective field and that we pick up on certain ones and we can put them down. One of my clients used to say, "Oh, I'm so stupid" without taking a breath, just going on and telling me her story. I asked her if she noticed that she said, "I'm so stupid" five or six times while we were talking. She didn't even notice that she said it. She told me her mother used to say that phrase all the time out loud to herself. So, you can imagine how easy it was to pick up this statement and just store it and use it as if it were normal. Meanwhile, she was diminishing herself many times a day. Another woman with whom I've worked used to say, "Sorry" every other sentence. Same story but significantly different. She told me that when she was growing up, the children had to say, "Sorry" often to get out of harm's way or avoid confrontation with their parents.

My MindBusting techniques are ways to separate your core self from your negative thoughts and stop a thought in its tracks before it becomes a feeling. It offers a chance to go to the subconscious level and overlay old beliefs with new possibilities. Self-mastery is cultivating the presence to choose your thoughts and avoid having life be one long ride on the emotional roller coaster. With this process, we can choose: 1) not to hook into the negative thought or allow it to become a feeling, and; 2) not feel bad about having them anymore. MindBusting is my playful way of saying, like in the *Ghostbusters* movies, "Who you gonna call? MindBusters!"

I remember teaching in the late nineties and discussing the concept of choosing our thoughts. A woman approached me after class, tears in her eyes. We talked for a while, and she broke down and confided that she had never heard such an idea before. She explained that she had always believed every thought she had and struggled with intense negativity due to her strict upbringing and cultural expectations. Learning that she could choose her thoughts brought her a sense of freedom. Years later, I encountered her again, and she hugged me, expressing her gratitude for the transformative insight that had stayed with her. The power to choose her thoughts had changed her life forever.

As you learn to use the following exercises to work with your critical, negative thoughts, it will become easier to sniff them out, and you will notice their subtlety versus their obvious nature. You may have to work harder to uncover the quieter, negative thoughts because we have established many defense mechanisms to keep our patterns in place. When we go into a negative feeling loop, we tell a story about ourselves. And every time we tell the story, we imprint the feeling a little bit deeper.

For example, in the past, I'd be driving my car behind somebody who was a slow driver and I'd become so angry. My mind would be running through a ton of judgmental thoughts: "What an asshole, what a stupid jerk, can this person drive any slower?" I would get myself all angst ridden about it. I later realized that every time I judged someone, I was actually protecting myself from another emotion that I didn't want to feel, and specifically from having bad feelings about myself. The truth was usually that I was running late, and getting to where I needed to go was my responsibility. So, to protect me from shameful feelings, my mind played this game and blamed the other person for my lateness. This was not an inherently bad strategy: I unconsciously set this pattern up to keep me safe from my feelings. Yet when my mind created safety, it also created an avalanche of negative patterning that needed to be freed and released.

Let's get off the hamster wheel! After practicing my MindBusting techniques, you will become unencumbered to the point where you can even have periods without criticizing thoughts. Can you imagine that? I don't mean you'll stop thinking, I mean you'll make space for new thoughts, where creativity begins to flow. I remember when I first started this mental journey of clearing and choosing. When I reached periods of virtually no thought, I would wake up at 4:00 AM with brilliant downloads of information needed for my work! It was a special time. I made a request to the universe after a few nights of this: "Can we please have these amazing conversations during the day?"

Through these practices, you'll be able to slowly walk yourself away from negative thoughts and recognize defense mechanisms that keep your old patterns in place. After practicing for weeks, months, or years, you will notice that you speak to yourself in a whole new way, loving and respecting yourself. Your whole world might even notice.

100 MONKEYS CAN'T BE WRONG

When we change our thoughts, we impact the collective consciousness, and we might just change the world! It's like the Hundreth Monkey Principle, an intriguing concept stemming from an observation of Japanese macaques on the island of Kojima in the 1950s. Researchers noticed that one female macaque started washing sweet potatoes before eating them.

Over time, this behavior caught on with other monkeys on the island. When the hundredth monkey adopted this habit, suddenly monkeys on neighboring islands began washing their sweet potatoes too, even though they had no direct contact with the original group. This principle suggests that there's a tipping point where a critical mass of individuals adopting a behavior, idea, or thought can trigger widespread acceptance or adoption, even across great distances. While not yet scientifically proven, it's a compelling theory. We can see it being used today in algorithms of social media, so let's spread *new uplifting and highest healing thoughts*, starting with ourselves. (It can't hurt!)

Option #1: The Mental Fast

Let's begin with a powerful mental experiment: How many negative thoughts do you think you have each day? How many judgments do you make about other people? How many judgments do you make about your body, your actions, and your emotions? The fastest way to see your degree of self-acceptance is to notice how judgmental you are.

I was bombarded with negative thoughts daily and really wanted to change. With Ariana Shelton's guidance, I put myself on a mental fast. We think of fasting as going without food, but you can do a fast on anything. If you decided that you weren't going to eat sugar for a week, that would be a sugar fast. In a mental fast, we focus our attention on our thoughts and assess what's happening in our mind. Our fast is intended to help us to give up routine, negative thoughts.

On your mental fast, you need to choose a number of days you can commit to assessing your thoughts. Three days is wonderful, three weeks is difficult; I recommend something in between. For this exercise, all you'll need is a blank journal. You'll be writing down *every* negative thought for a while, so make sure you have plenty of paper and some time. If you are a very busy person, you can make a list as the day goes on and do the process later.

Use a full left and right spread; make sure to skip a page between each day so that nothing is written on the backs of any pages. You'll need to be able to remove the left pages with your lists of negative thought patterns and keep your right pages for the process work. Label the top of the left-hand pages the I Release You pages (or the Vomit pages if you prefer). Label the right-hand pages the Yes to Life! pages.

On the left-hand side of your notebook, write down all your thoughts from each day that stand out as *negative, self-abusive,* and *not preferred.* On the right-hand page, write an opposite thought—what you would prefer to think. When we do this, we realize that we don't have to accept the old thought.

It was very intense to write out all my negative thoughts because it exposed my blind spots: It was both a rude awakening and a great awareness. I clearly saw my negative mind right there on the pages, and I felt compassion for myself when I saw how hard I was on myself. There were so many awful thoughts I internalized and kept alive from my family, my life experiences, and outer judgments. At that point I made the commitment to change, and purposefully choose thought patterns as best as I could.

If you don't like what you just heard in your head (or saw on the page), you can say to yourself, *Hey wait a minute! I prefer to think something different.* Ask yourself, *Will I allow this thought to claim me or will I reject it and move forward?* Then you can start to replace the not preferred thoughts with something better, more accurate, and less damaging. Let's say you had the thought, *I hate myself.* When that thought comes in, if you choose to accept it, you create more of that in your body. Not only is this thought destructive, it affects your emotions and your body. You might clench and tighten or crumple and sink, you might hide your head and bend in an effort to become smaller. These physical changes create another emotion, which can then make you feel even worse.

However, if you can say to yourself, *I don't accept that thought, I reject it as untrue,* then you have the freedom to ask, *What would I prefer to think?*—and give yourself some love.

Most people say, "I hate myself" when they think they've done something wrong. What if you could catch that thought and replace it with: *I'm feeling sad or angry with myself right now.* Can you hear how that's a much better thought because it's an identification, not a judgment? It's telling a truth instead of being critical. When we judge ourselves, we create more of the same blame.

Remember, it's a process to go from the demeaning, negative thoughts of *I hate myself* to positive thoughts of *I love myself.* We have to take baby steps in order to fully reframe. First, we can try saying, "Wouldn't it be nice if I didn't hate myself?" Yes, that would be nice. This simple shift of saying "Wouldn't it be nice if . . ." (thank you again, Abraham Hicks) feels so much better in the body. The next time, you can try, "Wouldn't it be nice if I learned to love myself ? I'm feeling more ready each day to love myself fully." See what I mean? You take these little journeying steps from one thought to the other as you build a bridge to rewiring your thought patterns and internal messages.

We want our new thoughts to live on and become better beliefs. Use the following transforming statement in your journal:

In the name and power of I am or *In the name and power of* ______ (insert any higher being that matches your beliefs), *I now disallow this thought in my consciousness, and I now choose this new and loving thought.*

For example:

LEFT PAGE: I Release You pages. RIGHT PAGE: Yes to Life! pages

I hate myself. In the name and power of I Am, *I now disallow this thought in my consciousness, and I now choose this new and loving thought*: each day I choose to love myself more and more.

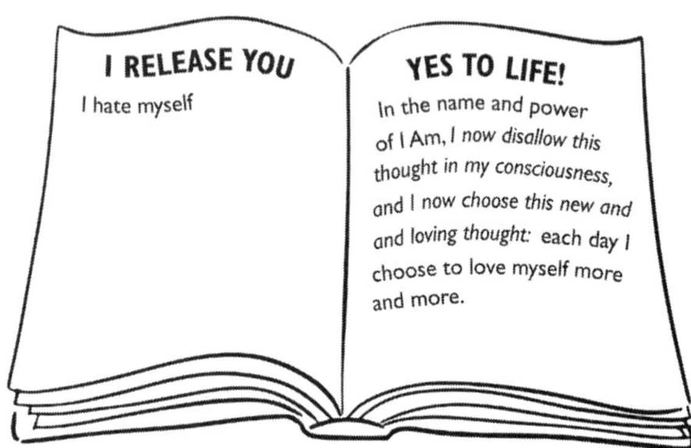

When you complete three days of listening to your mind, you'll learn a lot about yourself. It may not be easy, but it will be revealing. If you become overwhelmed with your thoughts, *dance* and *move*: go back to Evocative Emotion and Alchemy Transformation. If you feel

saddened, give Funky Connection a try, and turn on your body joy. You might even choose to do the entire *Embody* process by dancing all the qualities you have experienced. This efficiently clears the mind and gets you back into your body, and allows you to release stuck energy and get flowing.

If you don't have many negative thoughts, acknowledge with gratitude that you are well on your way to self-love and self- acceptance, and share that love with others. If you have 300 or more, you are perfectly normal; remember, the mind is a lightning-fast processor, recorder, and keeper of data! So be kind and don't judge yourself; just commit to the healing.

When you have completed the days of your mental fast, take the left pages and burn them in your own private ceremony or ritual. Let go of the I Release You pages so you can make space in your mind for the new. Leave your preferred thoughts from the Yes to Life! pages in your journal and read them nightly for a week. Read as many as you can. If you have 300, you don't have to read them all, just remind yourself that you have made a new choice for your thoughts, and that it's possible in every moment to say Yes to Life!

Option #2: MindBusting Boxes

Here is a physical and creative tool to keep you on track with your self-mastery. Repetition is the creator of experts, so if you can keep up your MindBusting and change those thoughts, you'll get better at it. The more I keep busting my own beliefs with creativity and love, the more I enjoy my growth.

I invite you to find two boxes: shoeboxes work well. You can decorate them exactly as you wish, keeping them simple or wildly and beautifully adorned. Next to each box, have

some small pieces of paper and a pen. Separate the boxes far enough away from each other that you have to take a short walk from one to the other.

- Label the first box: My Compost Box or I Release You Box, and if you want to be cute about it, call it the Dump All My Shitty Thoughts Box.
- Label the second box: My Dream Box, My Manifestation Box, or Wouldn't It Be Nice If Box.

Whenever a thought you don't prefer comes up, go to the I Release You Box. Write down the thought, crumple it, and throw it in the first box. Then, the essential step is to head over to the Wouldn't It Be Nice If Box, and write down your new, improved, preferred thought. Fold it, give it a kiss, and place it in the second box.

If you're dreaming up your future, having lots of positive thoughts, you can go to your Wouldn't It Be Nice If Box and grow that feeling by writing it down. You can go to the Wouldn't It Be Nice If Box as many times as you want, but every time you go to the I Release You Box, remember to complete the thought-transformation process.

Option #3: Toni's Embodied MindBusting Shortcut

Ariana's Mental Fast and Yes to Life! processes have taught me so much about thought transformation. I developed an embodied, physical component to use as a shortcut anytime I need instant help with my negative thoughts, particularly when I need to lighten up when I'm being hard on myself.

This MindBusting technique is supposed to be a little bit funny and lighten your mood. You can create a gesture or movement to shift your negative thoughts instantly. Being able to act in a split second when you hear the thought and you *decide* to think something else, is your key to freedom! Choosing is not nearly as powerful as deciding:

My shamanic teacher taught me that a decision is transformative because it cuts off all other options. *I decide.*

Okay, before we go, one caveat: you're going to want to do this process in private!

Notice where your negative thoughts come into your mind. Does it feel like they appear on the right or left side? Above or below your eyes? Once you locate their position, you can gently flick the thought away as if swatting a bug and see if it leaves with just one flick. If it leaves, just say thank you and move forward.

If the thought persists, you can try a little air punch, just notifying it that you mean business. If it continues coming in, you can give it a swift kick, and I mean stand up and kick it! I know it sounds funny, but interrupting negative patterns requires keeping a sense of humor! You can even imagine you have some green goop and spray it at your thoughts, à la *Ghostbusters.* Let's not do this in the supermarket!

If a thought becomes unbearable, remember all the work you've done so far. You might want to get back on the dance floor and step back into your feelings. Have a deeper conversation with yourself and ask, *What is this negative thought protecting me from feeling?* Ask your heart, *How can I embrace and feel what I need to feel?*

Once you have done the flick, punch, or kick, if needed, replace the thought in your mind or out loud.

Option #4: Collective/Meta MindBusting Exercise

At this critical time in history, unpacking our programmed beliefs is essential to disempowering systems of oppression, ending racism, and advocating for equity and diversity across gender, sexual orientation, size, religion, age, and ability. We can use the same MindBusting techniques and find what truth lies under our cultural conditioning and make new choices.

What, if any, were the negative messages you received as a child, either from parents, friends, school, teachers, social media, or religious structures? You might have to dig a bit because these messages are deeply rooted and drilled into us from societal structures and systemic oppression. These imprinted thoughts could drive your life on a path that was never meant for you—a path that doesn't include your heart, your desires, and your beautiful being. Rarely did anyone say, "Just be YOU!"

Now, use any of the MindBusting techniques and correct these beliefs with an overlay of what you know *is* true.

Get the Message

Now that you have MindBusting down for how to navigate your negative mindset, it's time to fill up with positive, life-affirming thoughts. This is another important step toward self-mastery. When you take ownership of your mindset, you can release yourself from victimhood and become empowered. You won't tolerate unacceptable behavior because you are no longer treating yourself poorly. We teach others how to treat us, so if we learn to treat ourselves with love, care, respect, and honor, the people around us can learn to treat us that same way, even if it takes them time to adjust. As you feel more empowered, you'll know how to respond to situations and your embodied intuition will guide you. Most importantly, when you feel positive and energized, your vibrancy and presence can lift up all your relationships.

Throughout the book I've shared many affirmations for you to read aloud. Yet I believe that *hearing* something important is different from saying it yourself. The following messages are positive thoughts I want you to *hear*. Some are so simple but may come as a surprise, especially if your parents didn't give you positive core messaging.

Choose the ones that resonate with you or read them all. Listen with your whole self. Be present.

- You matter.
- You are enough.
- You are beautiful.
- It's okay to be seen.
- It's brave to be seen.
- It's brave to feel.
- You are courageous.
- Your past does not define you.
- Your pain does not define you.
- You are resilient.
- You need to be heard.
- You deserve love.
- You are wise.
- You're so amazing.
- You are the Prayer.
- You are powerful.
- You are adorable, lovable, and valuable.
- You are sensual.
- You are creative.
- You are divine.
- You are loved.
- Your voice is beautiful.
- You are needed.
- Be love and you will be loved.

For more messages, go to my blog on JourneyDance.com, and look for The Ten Gifts.

The Embodied Lifestyle

You are a sparkling diamond being compressed and shaped under massive pressure, a shining soul getting brighter as you move through your experiences of life. Everything about you is going to be different now that you are embodied. It's going to change how you nourish and take care of yourself, how you process your emotions, and how you are more fully present every day. Here are a few of my favorite tips for tapping into embodiment even when you're not on the dance floor.

Don't be afraid to ask your body for what it needs. Let's say you're exhausted, so you might instinctively reach for a second cup of coffee. Being embodied, you might recognize that your body actually needs a nap and some rest or change of environment, like going outside or putting on some music. When it comes to nourishment, listen to what your body needs, not just what your mind is craving. Many of us eat on autopilot without tuning in to how we feel when we eat. Being embodied allows us to turn off autopilot and puts us in touch with the foods we really need.

Cherish the uniqueness that is you. We're not supposed to be the same, to think the same, to look the same. We're all beautiful in our own way, and worthy of being seen and honored. Each of us has a special contribution and gift to bring to our world, whatever it may be.

Ask for help whenever you need it. I'm sure you've heard the expression "It takes a village." I once did a funny skit at one of my teacher trainings about how I had my psychotherapist, my psycho-dramatist, my psychic, my soul counselor, and my shaman, all on speed dial. It was a joke, and I was making fun of myself, but the truth is I needed different kinds of support from all those people over the years. Each person that I worked with gave me insights and healing that I couldn't have come to on my own.

It takes a village to build a person. Now that you're embodied, you may feel more than you've felt before. Spend some time unraveling the messages of your parenting, schooling, or society to uncover the truth of who you are and what you came here for. You may discover that there are particular wounds or patterns that need more of your attention to heal. You can do this work whenever you want, telling your stories and clearing your energy. And you might find that you need the help of others. Do you have support? If you need, like I did, a psychotherapist, psycho-dramatist, psychic, soul counselor, or shaman to hold space for you, know that it's okay to ask for help.

THE FOUR HEALING SALVES

"In many shamanic societies, if you came to a shaman or medicine person complaining of being disheartened, dispirited, or depressed, they would ask one of four questions. When did you stop dancing? When did you stop singing? When did you stop being enchanted by stories? When did you stop finding comfort in the sweet territory of silence? Where we have stopped dancing, singing, being enchanted by stories, or finding comfort in silence is where we have experienced the loss of soul. Dancing, singing, storytelling, and silence are the four universal healing salves."

—Angeles Arrien in the foreword to
Maps to Ecstasy: The Healing Power of Movement by Gabrielle Roth

One Last Story: Eat the Cookie

Many years ago, my grandfather needed transportation to move from his New York City apartment into a nursing home near my parents' home. My father couldn't accompany him, and since I lived in the city, he entrusted me with the task. Despite being family, I had never spent one-on-one time with my grandfather before. We'd only connected at family gatherings. This was a man who infrequently left his neighborhood because he didn't drive, so this experience was quite a big deal for us both.

As I was driving him away from his longtime home to his new place, I asked him about his life. To my surprise, he confided in me about one of his unrealized dreams—he had attended Juilliard to study music as a baritone singer. However, he gave up his beloved aspiration to marry a woman whose father promised him a stable job as a pharmacist, and at that time, that's what people did, period, end of story. As we drove, I learned much more about him than I'd never known because he was never willing to reveal his heart to me or to any of us. He even shared some grief and sadness he carried about his lifelong marriage. "She was a lovely woman," he said, but he didn't share much about his love for her, as I mentioned it was an arranged marriage of sorts. I felt the preciousness of this moment.

Later that day, after settling him into his new room, I gave him a batch of cookies I had baked for him. At this time, I was in my midtwenties and was nearing the end of my dysfunction around body image and disordered eating, but I hadn't planned to eat with him. We sat for bit, and he took out a cookie and was very excited as he ate it. In a very childlike voice, he said it was delicious. He kept looking at me and nodding for me to take one.

Then, with his mouth full in his grumpy-sounding deep voice, he asked, "Why are you not having a cookie?"

I sheepishly said, "Oh, no, I'm not eating those, they are for you."

He looked me in the eyes with his powerful, old, glassy eyes, and said loudly, "Eat the cookie, Toni . . . Eat . . . The . . . Cookie."

For reasons I was yet to know, his words resonated deep in my soul. He was telling me to really live this life, dream my dreams, take the risks that he wasn't able to take.

Take the risk to feel, be heard, be vulnerable, be resilient, be caring. Take the risk to get out of your own box, to move into a new story, turn your angst into art, and dance this life, and of course, eat the cookie.

Come Dance with Me!

So here we are, ready to open our hearts and live our lives in our fullest expression! I hope you have gained significant self-awareness as you've danced, moved, and felt, and have become empowered to discover your *Self*, with a capital S. You now have all new skills and processes, and anytime you need to go back and lean on them, they are here for you. Every time I come to the dance floor, I still get super curious: What's going to come up today? What's going to be available for me to look at, investigate, feel into, move with, and learn more about?

You might need more experiences to honor yourself, embrace your parts that have been hurt, the parts that have been wounded, even the parts that hurt others. Maybe you have to forgive yourself. There are so many opportunities to heal and find joy. You can have the full JourneyDance experience now, in the final playlists in your Embody book portal: the JourneyDance Flow, where you can dance all the qualities in one flow, transitioning from one to the next as the music changes.

Or come dance with me, or my team online, or check out my schedule of events, workshops, and trainings. All my programs and workshops are guided on the principles of embodied healing, emotional process work, shifting mindset, being seen and heard, being witnessed, all through the creative processes of dance, movement, writing, theater, music, singing and songwriting, expressive art, collage making, and process painting. I can't wait to meet you!

Closing Prayer
Thank You

Dear Reader, Mover, Dancer,

Thank you.

I'm grateful that you are here.

I hope you have found comfort in your own body, in your own heart, and in your own mind.

I hope you have loved the music and the movement and that you have expanded your emotional bandwidth.

I hope you have experienced joy, self-love, and a deep appreciation of who you are.

May you heal your relationships from the smallest to the largest, from the personal to the collective, from your partner to your parents, sisters, and brothers, to your ancestral lineage.

Let's imagine that we could all forgive together . . . just for a moment. Take a breath. Feel that.

I truly believe that we will change the world.

Sending massive LOVE your way.

Mwaaaahh,

Toni

Acknowledgments

To my badass spiritual counselor and mentor Ariana Shelton, who has expertly, lovingly, and intensely guided and taught me for thirty years, and shared wisdom I continue to impart to others. To my intuitive coach Linda "Rose" Levenberg, who has enlightened me during crucial journeys in my relationships and helped me uncover more of who I am. To my shamanic teachers Cristhian Cadenas and Christopher Beaver, I am eternally grateful.

I want to thank Kripalu Center for Yoga & Health for supporting the healing of hundreds of thousands of people. Thank you to every employee—staff member, teacher, healing-arts service provider, programmer, maintenance person, campus security, and CEO—who makes it a spiritual home to so many.

Thank you to all my amazing teachers, and especially Dan Levin, founder of Soma Soul and Shake Your Soul, Megha Nancy Buttenheim, founder of Let Your Yoga Dance, and Ken Scott Nateshvar, the maverick inventor of the once-famous Danskinetics, now called Kripalu YogaDance. Thank you, Peggy Schjeldahl, who asked me to teach my first Saturday class in 1995. I'm also grateful to Rasmani Deborah Orth, EdD, who trusted my work and invited me to lead my first workshop at Kripalu in 2001, and for the opportunity to create, grow, and serve through movement for the last twenty-seven years.

I'm beyond grateful to my JourneyDance (JD) Team: Joan White-Hansen, trainer, collaborator, and artist, who has been by my side for fifteen-plus years, supporting all our trainees and teachers with her lightness and depth of presence. Joy Lynn Okoye, trainer and co-creator of The Remedy, a JourneyDance and writing process, whose commitment to healing through creativity brings us hope, inspiration, laughter, song, and poetry. Rodrigo Gonzales Zazoya, trainer in the United States and Mexico, who blesses us with his professional dance background, gestalt therapy, and trauma training, enriching every program. And Frankie Mueller, director of JD Operations and CFO (if I had one), who has been my constant support in the company, teaching me and our entire teacher community how to get our shared vision for this healing work out into the world. To the JourneyDance teacher community, whose constant faith in me and this work brings tears to my eyes and buckets of gratitude. To each and every one of you, I'm proud and honored to know you—game-changers, every single one! To the JEDI JourneyDance Equity & Diversity Team: Michelle Brass, Joanna Hollis, Sarah Henteges, and Liza Pitsirilos—for your countless hours teaching and growing with us. To the JD Trauma Awareness team, Amie Koontz, Rodrigo Gonzales Zazoya, Lorena Norwood, and Alyson Quinn for helping our entire company, trainers, and teachers become trauma aware and hold better space for our dancers, movers, and participants.

I have a massive thank you to my dear longtime friend, from

contact partner to DJ and collaborator, Rueben Cuthbertson, aka DJ Root, for the many years of dancing with me and his integral role in the creation and qualities of JourneyDance. Thank you for the music, for throwing curve balls, and for picking up the gems we dropped on the dance floor.

Thank you to Dr. Stephanie Shelburne for your friendship and beautiful study of this work, your articles, and your essential contribution of the science for all our students and in this book! I am beyond grateful.

My dear friend and mentor Aviva Gold, founder of Painting from the Source, was a key supporter on my path, with whom I painted and danced at Kripalu, the Esalen Institute, and elsewhere. I want to thank more of my teachers: Lani Nahale (Lisa Schmidt) for helping me get into my body in many ways, teaching me to trust with contact improvisation and body-mind centering technique. And to my contact teachers, including the founder, the late Nancy Stark Smith, and my teacher Shakti Andrea Smith. Thank you, Earthdance, for being my first home for many years of learning, trainings, and teaching. Thank you, Vinn Marti, founder of Soul Motion, with whom I got to dance just for me. You have no idea how important you are to me and what an inspiration to be my authentic self that you continue to be.

I want to thank The Brothers Koren; I wish they were my real brothers, but in some ways they are. Making music and songwriting with them brought me a new sense of confidence to allow my voice to be heard; that translates right into this experience of writing my first book.

Thank you to movement pioneer Gabrielle Roth for opening the gates for healing dance to thrive. To Mark Metz,

for our many wonderful conversations about "conscious dance" and for bringing so much great work to the world in your magazine and website. I want to thank all my brave and inspirational colleagues in the conscious dance and ecstatic dance world, who keep bringing the music! The movement! The sweat, tears, and laughter! I can't name you all; that would take all day and that's a *gooooood* thing!

Thanks to all my coaches, therapists, shamanic practitioners, Family Constellation leaders, ShadowWork teachers, and Playback Theatre teachers. Thank you to the amazing founding members of DramaWorks and director Dr. Erik Muten. Thank you to Tim Van Ness, my first teacher of Playback Theatre and voicework, for supporting me in launching JourneyDance in 1997.

Thank you to the Omega Institute who invited me to teach in 2007, and who have supported the JourneyDance teachers to lead classes in their mind-body program.

Thank you to Gareth Esersky and all our conversations that led you to say yes and be my agent. I know how you love dance! Thank you for believing I had a book in me. Thank you, Christine Belleris, editorial director at publisher Health Communications, Inc., for saying yes and for all the support and trust. To Larissa Henoch for the design and images! To Sam Laiz, my nephew, tattoo artist, and illustrator of the dancing shapes in this book.

Thank you to the amazing Pam Liflander, whose incredible mind and incredible patience helped me weave my work of movement into words. Thank you for being always supportive, even when I found things difficult. I seriously cannot thank you enough for your brilliance, your capacity and skill, and constant sense of humor. I mean that; I looked up all the ways you could say thank you, but none of them cut it.

To my good friends and warriors, dancers, and healers Cristi Christensen and Sierra Bender. Carrie Grossman, John de Kadt, Wah!, and so many collaborators—thank you for all the inspiration we co-created.

Finally, to my children, Angel Xicohtencatl and Texoloc, who are the loves of my life.

To my sister Jana, author and my closest friend, who got me on the spiritual path! Thank you for taking me to my very first spiritual seminar that got me on the path of transformation, and for inspiring my move to the Berkshires, where I found Kripalu, my other home. And for being my constant support and inspiration with your writing. To my sister Pam, for keeping me laughing and addicted to chocolate, and for showing me how to live life as an adventurer. To Mom, who taught me empathy, listening, and true caretaking. And to my genius dad, my role model for critical thinking, social justice, and forgiveness, who lovingly supports me in living my dreams.

About the Author

Toni Bergins, M.Ed., is an embodiment trailblazer who has taught at premier holistic healing centers. She is on faculty at the Kripalu Center for Yoga & Health, and has worked there as a movement artist, dance educator, expressive arts workshop leader, and expert in creating transformational workshops. She has led JourneyDance® programs at the renowned Esalen Institute, Omega Institute, 1440 Multiversity, The New York Open Center, Pure Yoga, Blue Spirit, Wanderlust Festival, Expressive Therapy Summit, and countless others.

Toni is also the co-founder of The Remedy Retreats, a workshop to turn your angst into art to be seen and heard. She has been teaching this powerful creative healing process with her team member, Joy Okoye, since 2020.

Toni graduated summa cum laude with a master's degree in education from New York University. She received her bachelor's degree in both Psychology and English at Binghamton University and is a member of Phi Beta Kappa. Toni has also studied a wide variety of healing, movement and theatre forms ranging from Playback Theatre, ShadowWork®, psychodramatic processes, modern dance, contact improvisation, Emotional Freedom Technique (EFT), breathwork, comedy improv, stand up, vocal training, guitar, piano, to song writing. She is the mother of two sons, and resides in the Berkshires of Western Massachusetts.

Move with Toni! Scan this code or visit journeydance.com to join a beautiful community for those on the path to joy, healing, and embodiment. Every week is a transformative experience of the complete Embody flow.